Danny's lucky. You're a good mom, Toni," Clark said.

She stopped so suddenly he nearly ran into her. "Toni?" He touched her shoulder lightly. She lifted her hand to her mouth, and as he turned her around, he saw that tears were streaming down her face.

"Want to talk about it?" he asked quietly.

"I'm sorry for getting so emotional…"

"It's okay, Toni. You don't need to apologize to me."

He wanted to kiss her, but something told him if he did, he wouldn't be able to stop. Kisses weren't what she needed right now. A listening ear was.

"What's been hardest for you in all this?" he asked.

Toni didn't hesitate. "Knowing it's my fault. Knowing the choices I made in the past are still affecting Danny's present—and *my* present. Knowing the consequences will never go away."

"That must really hurt."

She nodded. "I'm trying to let it go," she said, her voice cracking. "But it's hard."

Clark pulled her into his arms. "You're doing it, Toni," he murmured into her hair. "You're doing what's best for him even though it's hard for you. You're a wonderful mom."

He gently turned her face toward his. *Now* was the time to kiss her.

But she placed a hand on his chest and pushed away. "Clark—I don't know…"

Palisades.
Pure Romance.

FICTION THAT FEATURES CREDIBLE CHARACTERS AND

ENTERTAINING PLOT LINES, WHILE CONTINUING TO UPHOLD

STRONG CHRISTIAN VALUES. FROM HIGH ADVENTURE

TO TENDER STORIES OF THE HEART, EACH PALISADES

ROMANCE IS AN UNDILUTED STORY OF LOVE,

FROM BEGINNING TO END!

A PALISADES CONTEMPORARY ROMANCE

SNOW SWAN

BARBARA JEAN HICKS

PALISADES

SNOW SWAN
published by Palisades
a part of the Questar publishing family

© 1997 by Barbara Jean Hicks

International Standard Book Number: 1-57673-107-3

Cover illustration by Corbert Gauthier
Cover design by Mona Weir-Daly
Edited by Diane Eble

The Holy Bible, New International Version (NIV) © 1973, 1984 by
International Bible Society, used by permission
of Zondervan Publishing House.

Printed in the United States of America

For information:
QUESTAR PUBLISHERS, INC.
POST OFFICE BOX 1720
SISTERS, OREGON 97759

Library of Congress Cataloging-in-Publication Data
Hicks, Barbara Jean.
   Snow swan/by Barbara Jean Hicks. p.cm.ISBN 1-57673-107-3 (alk. paper)
   I. Title
   PS3558.I22976S5   1997   97-968
   813'.54—dc21   CIP

97 98 99 00 01 02 03 04 — 10 9 8 7 6 5 4 3 2 1

To the courageous men and women

for whom active recovery is a way of life,

and

to the friends who contributed to the content and spirit

of this story: Janice Byram, Michael Cobb,

Eric Huelshoff, Vickie Pierson, and Stan Thornburg.

Thank you for sharing your lives.

❧

Wash me, and I will be whiter than snow.

PSALM 51:7B (NIV)

D anny?" Toni Ferrier called through the screen door to the backyard as she fished for the car keys in her purse.

There was no response from her son, but the Irish setter standing guard at the base of the apple tree yelped, chased her tail for a turn or two, then galloped toward the door, careening away just before she would have plowed through the screen.

Crazy dog! Toni thought, shaking her head. Even for an Irish setter, Brannigan was bonkers.

"Danny!" she called again.

A mop-haired boy poked his head through the window of the tree house Pop had built in the crook of the old tree. "In the fort, Wart!" he hollered over Brannigan's barking.

"Name's not Wart, Sport!" Toni returned. "You and Brannigan ready to go?"

"Yeah!" he shouted, swinging through the doorway of the wooden structure and clambering down the rope ladder.

Toni shook her head in amusement as the boy and his dog raced twice around the tree and then across the backyard toward the kitchen door. "Car's in the driveway," she said. "Hop in the backseat and buckle up. Be right there."

"See you soon, Moon!"

"Name's not Moon, Goon," she said to his back as he disappeared around the corner of the house.

Eight-year-old Danny had picked up the rhyming routine from a family friend who was a terrible tease. Calling his wife "Katie Milady" wasn't so bad. Kind of cute, in fact. But "Danny Bananny"? And worse, "Toni O-zoney"!

"Only because you're so clearly *not* an airhead, you know," Keith had reassured her.

"Keith, I've done some pretty empty-headed things in my time. Do you have to remind me?"

"Maybe you're right. How about Toni Baloney?"

"*So* much better," she'd laughed.

At any rate, Danny loved to rhyme, and she'd turned it into a kind of game that was almost second nature now.

Closing up the house, she joined Danny in the car. "Come here," she said, digging in her shoulder bag for a comb. "You're a mess! How about we get your grandpa to cut your hair tonight?"

He put an arm out and dodged her when she tried to run the comb through his curly hair. "We're just goin' to the park," he protested.

She sighed. "Okay, okay. *Look* like a little ragamuffin." She ran the comb through her own hair instead, still a bit damp from the shower. The brush-and-go style her hairdresser had given her last week was perfect for a working single mom. Her days seemed more and more hectic; anything to buy time.

"I have two stops before we get to the park, Danny," she told him as she backed out of the driveway. "Two minutes each, tops. You and Brannigan need to stay in the car, you hear?"

"Are we going to see Aunt Ruthie?" he asked eagerly.

"*I* am going to pick up my paycheck from Aunt Ruthie. *You* are going to wait in the car."

Five minutes later she pulled the old Plymouth Valiant up to the curb in front of a weathered brick building in the Beaumont district. *Paper Chase Social Stationery,* the gilt letters on the window spelled out. She turned off the engine and opened her door. "Be right back."

Brannigan barked and wagged her tail as Toni got out, slamming the car door behind her.

She pushed up the sleeves of her oversized sweatshirt. *Warm for a May afternoon,* she thought. It was a perfect day for a boy and a dog to splash in the fountain at Grant Park alongside the whimsical bronze statues of Henry Huggins, Ramona Quimby, and Ribsy. It had been too long since she and Danny had done something fun together. Who had time?

Ruth was on the phone at the front counter when Toni entered, jangling the bell on the shop door. Otherwise, the store was empty.

A petite, fine-featured woman in her early fifties, Ruth Denton radiated warmth and energy. Her streaked, strawberry-blonde hair was pulled back in a classic twist at the nape of her neck. She smiled and nodded at Toni as she finished up her conversation. "Three o'clock tomorrow, then—yes, that's fine. I'll be expecting you."

She set the receiver back in its cradle. "Local printing company with a new line of wedding stationery," she explained. "I thought you and I could look it over tomorrow."

"Don't forget I have that appointment with Danny's teacher tomorrow afternoon…"

"Oh, that's right! Fiddlesticks! Well, maybe the rep will leave a sample book. You have such a good feel for the wedding market. I don't want to decide without your input."

Toni glowed. "Thanks, Ruth! You don't know how good that makes me feel!"

"You *should* feel good! You're my star, you know. We've

13

doubled our wedding business in the last year since you took over the department." She straightened the display rack on the counter. "You've definitely got the retail knack."

"That or a good teacher," Toni said. She glanced out the door to check on Danny. He had his window rolled down, and both his and Brannigan's chins were resting on the door. She lifted her hand in a wave and turned back to her boss. "Not that I wouldn't love to visit, Ruthie, but Danny's in the car with his dog. Paychecks ready?"

Ruth was already heading for the office. "Um-hmm. Let me—"

The phone on the counter interrupted her. Toni reached for it. "You get the check; I'll get the phone."

"Thanks!"

"Paper Chase," Toni said pleasantly into the receiver. "May I help you?" She heard the shop bell jangle behind her as Ruth disappeared behind the curtain separating the retail floor from the small storage space and office in the back corner.

"Eleven to six Monday through Saturday, noon to five Sundays," she answered the query on the other end of the line. Then, "You're welcome. Thanks for calling Paper Chase." Resetting the receiver, she glanced over her shoulder with a greeting on the tip of her tongue.

She gasped.

The door was swinging shut behind Danny, who was hanging on to Brannigan's collar with one hand, barely able to hold the dog back as she danced toward Toni.

"Danny!" Toni shrieked.

The big red dog barked joyously and broke away from the boy.

Crash! Down came a card rack. *Bang!* A table suffered a whack from Brannigan's tail and dumped its display of boxed stationery every which way. *Boom!* Toni herself was on the floor,

14

knocked off her feet. Her arms and legs flailed as the exuberant dog tried to lick her face.

"What in the world!" Ruth came running from the back of the store.

Toni grabbed hold of Brannigan's collar and pulled her into her arms, trying to calm her down. She narrowed her eyes at her son. "*Daniel—Terence—Ferrier!*" she said between her teeth. "Didn't I tell you to stay in the car? *Didn't* I? You disobeyed me! Just *look* at this mess!"

Danny stared at the floor and mumbled something unintelligible.

"*What* did you say?"

He looked up, his chin set defiantly. "You're *mean!* I just wanted to see Aunt Ruthie!"

Toni was trembling with anger. If she hadn't felt Ruth's gentling hand on her shoulder, she was sure she would have lost it.

"It's nice you wanted to see me, Danny," Ruth said, her quiet voice cutting through the tension between the boy and his mother. "Easy does it," she soothed Toni as she helped her up, still holding Brannigan's collar. "Nothing here that can't be fixed. Be glad it's not a china shop!"

She brushed at the dust on Toni's leggings. "First thing to do is get that dog out the door before she does more damage…"

Toni fled the store with Brannigan, not daring even to look at Danny. He'd been testing her a lot lately, but she didn't remember ever being so angry with him.

After she got the dog settled in the car, she walked rapidly around the block, her anger slowly dissipating with the exercise. Back in front of the store, she sat down on the curb and cradled her head in her hands, her eyes closed, breathing deeply.

When she'd come back home, almost a year and a half ago now, Danny had been a dream child—sweet, affectionate, eager to please. Over the last few months he'd become a different boy—constantly testing her, perfecting that defiant tilt to his chin, almost daring her to keep him in line. Sometimes she wondered if he even *liked* her anymore.

Hugging her arms across her chest, feeling chilled despite her sweatshirt and the warm spring sunshine, Toni glanced over her shoulder through the window.

Danny was happily helping Ruth set the store to rights, as if he'd had nothing at all to do with its disorder.

Clark McConaughey felt a surge of excitement as he approached the Interstate Bridge from Vancouver, Washington. *Columbia River,* the green sign unnecessarily informed him. *Welcome to Oregon,* another sign greeted him as he reached the apex of the long steel bridge. Through the girders to the east Mount Hood rose in an almost perfect cone, snow-capped and shining in the afternoon sun.

Home again! Not just for a whirlwind business trip, swooping into town for a day or two to schmooze with prospective clients or present a training seminar before he zoomed off again; home to *live.* Home to Aunt Ruthie and Uncle Jack, unrelated by blood but more like parents than Royce and Molly had ever been. For thirty-one of his thirty-six years, Portland had been home. It felt right to be here again.

Ten minutes later he exited the freeway toward downtown across the Morrison Bridge. The company owned a third-floor condo at RiverPlace on the Willamette River, which divided the city into east and west. Until Clark was settled into permanent office space and found a house, the apartment overlooking the river would serve as both workplace and living quarters.

By six o'clock, his clothes and personal belongings were

moved in, and the guest room had been transformed into a temporary office. Whistling cheerfully, he let himself out onto the deck outside the living room and leaned against the wooden railing, gazing over the crowded marina below. He liked the view, the straight masts and slack lines of the sailboats silhouetted against the pale blue of evening sky reflected in the river. A family of mallards and a gaggle of Canada geese fought for position next to the dock where a young boy threw bread crumbs into the water.

Across the marina, two sternwheelers floated alongside the dock. "The *Snow Swan!*" Clark said aloud as one of them pulled slowly away. Jack Denton's boat. A longtime dream for the retired policeman, the sternwheeler had belonged to Uncle Jack for six months now. Clark was looking forward to checking her out.

He stretched and groaned. The drive from Seattle and the dozens of trips back and forth between his car in the underground parking garage and the third-floor apartment had taken their toll. After a quick, hot shower, he'd give Ruth and Jack a call. Maybe they hadn't had dinner.

Clean and refreshed, he picked up the portable phone in the bedroom ten minutes later and dialed the Dentons' number. When no one answered, he hung up without leaving a message. It would be more fun to pop in on them tomorrow, anyway, he thought. He could see the sternwheeler, then hop on over to Ruth's store, only fifteen minutes away. Ruth would be as excited as a kid on Christmas morning to know he was back to stay.

No one had ever made him feel so loved and so welcome as Aunt Ruthie always did. "Sure you don't want to adopt me?" he'd teased her over the last twenty years. Her daughter Sonja—Sunny, as her family and friends had called her—had always protested. "You can't be my brother!"

"Why not?" he'd ask, knowing what her answer would be.

"Cuz I'm gonna marry you," she'd say confidently, grabbing hold of his arm with both hands. The eighteen-year difference in their ages didn't matter to Sunny; she'd been planning to marry him since she was three.

"That works," Ruthie would say, playing along. "Then I'd be Clark's mother-in-law."

Sunny would smile happily. "I like that better."

Dropping his eyes to the phone in his hand, Clark hesitated, then punched out another number and listened to the ring at the other end. Two rings, and then an answering machine clicked on. He sighed in relief, then had to ask himself why he'd bothered to call Will when he obviously didn't want to talk to him.

"Because he's still my brother," he muttered aloud. "No matter what. Because he hasn't had the chances I've had." Because you feel guilty for not liking him, a voice inside him added.

He shook his head, unwilling to explore the idea further, and hung up before Will's recording finished. If his half brother was still waiting tables, he was probably working tonight. There was no telling where; Will changed jobs as often as some people change their socks.

Years ago, Will was the reason Clark had returned to Portland the first time, after finishing his MBA at the University of Washington in Seattle. It had been difficult to turn down the prestigious offer from Seafirst Bank, but Will, a teenager by then and living with their mother and her third husband, was sorely in need of a big brother. Clark had felt an odd sort of responsibility for him back then.

Funny, now that he was coming back a second time, seeing Will was one of the things he dreaded most…

Suddenly restless, he decided to eat out alone. There were half a dozen restaurants within walking distance, and after dinner he could spend the evening reacquainting himself with the RiverPlace shops and galleries and Waterfront Park.

It was dark by the time he reached Salmon Springs on his after-dinner stroll. He stopped to enjoy the lights on the fountain, then took a seat on a wooden bench, sharing the night with half a dozen other souls. It was peaceful, he mused, sitting there in the darkness, listening to the traffic and the splashing of the water.

Through the cascade of the fountain Clark watched the distorted figures of a man and a young girl walking toward him. He wasn't sure why they'd caught his attention until they stopped for a moment to watch the water at play. The girl, a stocky blonde dressed in a gauzy skirt and blouse, clasped her hands in front of her chest, obviously enraptured. "Shall we sit, Princess Ivy?" the man asked her. He bowed and gestured dramatically toward an empty bench near Clark.

Ivy turned in his direction, giggling like a much younger child, grabbing hold of the man's hand and swinging it high. "You're funny, Dad!" she said.

Clark's heart jumped. Even in the dim glow from the streetlamps and the colored spotlights on the fountain, he recognized the awkward gait, the short, broad forehead and flat face, and, as the girl approached, the slanted eyes behind her glasses. The classic signs of Down's syndrome. Sunny's syndrome.

Sonja Denton had been Ruth and Jack's only child, and despite her handicaps, a blessing by any definition. Neither she nor her parents had ever let her limitations get in the way of living life to the fullest. She skied, she sailed, she roller-skated. She danced and sang. "Sunny" was a nickname that aptly described her spirit—ever cheerful, always smiling, delighted and delighting.

Until a drunk driver had wiped the smile off her face forever—off the faces of everyone who'd loved her. Ruth and Jack. Clark. Will.

Clark felt the anger rise inside him. How, after losing Sunny that way, could Will possibly abuse alcohol the way he did? Even drive while he was drunk? Sunny had been only eight years old when she died. Even after ten years, it was hard to accept.

Toni sat up in bed with a jolt, her heart thumping. She made a quick survey of the dimly lit room. Moonlight filtered through the swaying lilac branches outside her window, casting strange shadows that moved back and forth across the walls in a hypnotic dance. The red glow of the digital clock on her nightstand read 3:45.

What had startled her awake?

"Pop?" she called softly. "Danny?"

No one answered.

She felt bruised, as if someone had been shaking her, yanking at her arms, knocking her around. A dream, a nightmare... She grasped at the images, but they were gone. Nothing left but the rush of adrenaline and an ebbing tide of unpleasant feelings. She tried unsuccessfully to name them: Fear? Anger? Despair?

In the eerie light, her bedroom furniture mutated into a horde of misshapen monsters closing in on her from all sides, pointing crooked fingers, silently accusing her of nameless sins.

No, she told herself. She clutched the blankets to her chest and forced herself to look around the room more carefully. This time the shadows were only patterns of dark and light, the threatening forms only a dresser, an armchair, a vanity laden with bottles of perfume, a hall tree hung with scarves and hats.

A band of yellow light arced through the window as a car swung around the corner, its noisy, popping engine interrupting the predawn stillness of Dearborn Street. Throwing back the covers, Toni crawled out of bed and reached for the white terry-cloth robe draped over her vanity chair. She slipped her arms into the sleeves and padded down the hall to Danny's room.

The door was ajar. When she pushed it wider, the dog curled up on the foot of the bed opened one eye, raised her head, and yawned. *I should* think *you'd be worn out*, Toni thought as she glared at Brannigan from across the room. The big red dog dropped her chin to her paws and closed her eyes without so much as a whine.

The lamp on the nightstand was switched on; Danny was afraid of the dark, even with Brannigan lying at his feet for protection. He'd kicked the blankets off in his sleep. Toni tiptoed across the room to tuck them around him again. She held her breath as he moved restlessly, but he burrowed into his pillow without waking. Sitting carefully on the edge of the bed to avoid disturbing him, she smoothed a stray curl back from his forehead and studied his face.

He looked so heartbreakingly innocent lying there, so fragile and vulnerable. His body made only a small mound on the bed. The lamplight pooled on his pillow like a halo around his dark curls, making his pale skin seem almost translucent. His dark lashes quivered as his sleeping eyes moved beneath their lids.

Inexplicably, Toni's eyes filmed over with tears. Standing abruptly, she stumbled toward the door. She didn't want to wake him. She didn't want him to see her cry.

Back in her own room, she dropped to the bed and curled into a ball on her side, weeping silently, feeling as if her heart might break, not knowing why. Unwilling, for now, even to explore the possibilities.

She drifted in and out of sleep and heard Pop get up, turn on the water in the bathroom, rummage around in the kitchen. Later still, the sound of the truck starting up in the driveway woke her. As dawn began to creep through the lace at the windows, she rolled tiredly off the bed and made her way to the kitchen. Her head was throbbing.

Pop, typically thoughtful, had brewed her a pot of strong coffee before leaving for his weekly breakfast meeting with Keith. She missed having coffee with him on the mornings he discipled Keith Castle, but she knew their time together pleased them both immensely. Pop had known Keith since he was a little boy; there had always been a special bond between them.

If Keith and his wife, Katie, hadn't been such good friends to her as well, she might have been jealous of their relationship with her father. For more than a dozen years, from the time Toni was two until she was a sophomore in high school, they'd been important in Pop's life when she hadn't even known who he was. Her father had deserted them, Mina made a point of telling her. She wondered how different her life might have been if only...

Not going down that path, she told herself firmly. Pouring herself a cup of coffee, she gulped it down black, standing there at the counter, welcoming the burning in her throat. Embracing the sensation so she wouldn't have to think about her mother.

Refilling the cup, she carried it with her to the bathroom. Twenty minutes remained before she had to get Danny up for school. Maybe the combination of strong black coffee and a hot shower would derail the freight train running through her head.

Shrugging and rolling her shoulders beneath the stream of hot water, she felt the tension in her muscles begin to ease. She let her head drop forward and backed into the spray so that it beat down on her neck. She couldn't afford to be tired and tense today. Her schedule was full: morning appointments with two brides to proof wedding invitations, lunch with Katie to talk about the camping trip her church Growth Group was planning, window displays to change at the store, the meeting with Danny's teacher after school, Pop's retirement dinner at the college…

She took her time washing her hair, massaging the shampoo into her scalp with her fingertips, but the headache wouldn't go away. She needed more coffee. Probably the entire pot.

With her wet hair wrapped in a towel and the terry robe cinched at her waist, she raised her fist to rap at Danny's door. Odd that it was closed; she'd left it partially open earlier.

Before she had a chance to knock, she heard a loud *whap*, and then Danny's voice: "Stupid, stupid, stupid!"

"Danny? What's—phew!" She wrinkled her nose as she swung the door wide. Danny was beating his pillow against the wall in frustration, his pajamas clinging wetly to his legs. The blankets were thrown back over the foot of his bed, and a yellow stain spread across the bottom sheet.

"Oh no!" she groaned. "Not today!"

He threw down the pillow and started to jerk the sheets off his bed, not looking at her.

"Stupid!" he said again. "Stupid *babies* wet the bed."

Toni took a deep breath. This was the third time in two weeks. Pop said that before now he hadn't wet the bed since he was three. What was going on with him?

"You're not stupid, Danny. Even big boys have accidents," she said. "Don't worry about the sheets. I'll get them. You go hop in the tub, okay?"

He trudged off to the bathroom. Sighing, Toni bent to gather the wet bedclothes. It was going to be one of those days.

The *Snow Swan* was a beauty, Clark reflected later that afternoon as he made his way from downtown to Beaumont, where Ruth had her card-and-stationery store. He hoped Jack would be able to make a go of the business.

The older man had always had a boat of some kind, but owning a sternwheeler had been a dream for years. "Ever since I read *Huck Finn,* if you want to know the truth," he had told Clark. "Got pretty excited as a kid when I found out we'd had paddle wheelers right here in our own little corner." A hundred years earlier, before the network of roads and railroads linked the isolated communities of the Oregon Territory, riverboats had been the primary form of travel up and down the Willamette and Columbia Rivers.

Clark had spent the morning shopping for groceries and office supplies, then surprised Jack with sandwiches and deli potato salad for lunch aboard the *Snow Swan.* "After you've given me a tour, of course," he had told his friend.

They'd had a good time reconnecting. "Ruth was talking about you just this morning," Jack had told him. "She'll be happy as a hog in mud to know you're home to stay."

A sense of community permeated the Eastside neighborhoods, Clark mused as he made his way between the rows of older homes after exiting the freeway. Though he'd grown up in the more affluent West Hills, he'd always liked this part of town. The porches on the houses were meant to be sat on; walks with well-behaved dogs were meant to be taken on the tree-lined sidewalks; small family businesses in the commercial districts were meant to prosper. In fact, Paper Chase was part of the thriving commercial center of the Beaumont neighborhood.

School buses idled in front of Beaumont Middle School, across the street from Ruth's shop, where a crowd of adolescents hopped and jostled like Mexican jumping beans. Clark made his way through the intersection carefully. Since Sunny's accident, he'd always taken special care in school zones. Turning off Fremont, he found a parking spot on a side street and parked the car.

The late afternoon sun reflected off the west-facing windows of Paper Chase as he crossed the street at an angle. As he stepped up on the sidewalk, the sun dipped behind a cloud, and the window was transparent again.

Clark stopped suddenly, so off-balance that he almost lost his footing on the curb. A woman in a softly draped dress the color of midnight, cut to accentuate her height and slenderness, stood in profile in the window of the store, not six feet in front of him. She seemed to be posed, her back arched and her arms stretched gracefully over her head. Something about the way her long white neck rose from the scooped neckline of her dress, something about the curve of her shoulder and the soft line of her profiled jaw, made him think of a swan, all grace and beauty.

He realized as her upper body swung toward him that her arms had been raised to attach a length of fabric to one corner of the window frame. He watched in fascination as she moved along the length of the glass wall, oblivious to her audience of one, lifting and lowering her slender arms in a graceful sort of dance as she swagged the gauzy white fabric over and around a rod above the window.

When she reached the end of the long window, she flipped the fabric over the rod one last time and let it fall along the sash, then bent to arrange the folds. When she stepped back, she raised her slender arms again, this time to thread her fingers through her short dark hair as she surveyed her work. She nodded, as if satisfied with what she saw, and smiled a smile that

26

almost made Clark forget to breathe. Dropping her hands, she turned away from the window in a fluid pirouette, the flared skirt of her indigo dress swishing around her legs as she disappeared around a rack of cards.

He released his breath in a long sigh, as if coming out of a trance, and walked slowly to the corner. It seemed appropriate that soft music from an oldies station greeted him as he pushed open the door: "Girl of my dreams…"

Behind the counter now, she glanced up at the sound of the shop bell, looking straight at him with a direct and steady gaze. Her eyes were extraordinary, more almond than round, the color of night falling—dusky, blue violet eyes, framed by thick black lashes and perfectly shaped brows. Her flawless ivory skin, in startling contrast to hair so black it shone blue under the light, stretched over well-defined cheekbones and an aquiline nose.

"May I help you?" The tiny frown forming between her brows reminded him he'd been staring unabashedly.

Before he could answer, Ruth swished through the curtain from the back room, a pair of half-glasses perched on her nose and a long adding-machine tape in her hand. "Toni, do you know—"

She stopped when she saw him, her face lighting with pleasure. "Clark, honey!" she shouted, slurring the words together as she always did, as if "Clarkunny" were his name. He laughed in genuine delight and held his arms wide.

Ruth rushed around the counter with her arms open. He swept her up in a bear hug, then danced her around the floor for a moment, in time to the music playing in the background, before letting her go. "Clark, honey!" she said again. "You look good enough to eat! What are you *doing* here?"

"Couldn't stay away another minute, Ruthie! Hadn't seen you and Jack since Thanksgiving."

"Does Jack know you're here?"

"Just came from the boat. I'm staying at the RiverPlace condo."

"And how long you here for this time?"

He glanced again at the clerk behind the counter, then wished he hadn't; he didn't want to tear his eyes away. "The duration, believe it or not," he said, his eyes dropping to her hands on the counter. He watched in fascination as the woman's long, slender fingers began an agitated dance against the display case.

"I'll believe it when you join the Chamber of Commerce and buy yourself a house," Ruth teased. When Clark didn't respond, she added in an amused tone, "It looks to me as if I need to make an introduction here."

He felt heat wash over his face. *You are making a rather obvious fool of yourself,* some part of him noted, as if far away and detached entirely from this other part of him that couldn't take his eyes off the woman.

Suddenly he realized her right thumb was nervously rotating a narrow gold band on her left hand. She was married!

Surprisingly, the feeling that flashed through him felt more like relief than disappointment. He lifted his eyes to meet hers again, but now *she* seemed to be studying her hands.

"Toni, you've heard me mention Clark McConaughey? This is him, in the flesh. Clark, my star performer, Toni Ferrier. Antonia."

Toni finally looked at him again, her lips curving into a dazzling smile, a smile that seemed almost to cast light across the counter, like a beacon in the night.

"Toni will do just fine. And it's *Clark,* is it?" she asked innocently. "Not Clarkunny?"

He laughed, her playful response to Ruth's introduction breaking the spell he'd seemed unable to break on his own.

Raising one eyebrow, he teased back, "You can call me Clarkunny anytime you like." He held out his hand. "I'm pleased to meet you, Toni."

"Thanks. Nice to meet you, too." She reached for his outstretched hand, but a jolt of static electricity made them both jerk back from the brief contact. "Quite the electric personality, I see," Toni said dryly, shaking her fingers. "Ruth must be right about you."

"Meaning?"

She crossed her arms and cocked her head to one side. "A direct quote: 'I've seen Clark bring a dead deal back to life with a single handshake,'" she said. "You carry one of those joy buzzers around with you, or what?"

He laughed. "I was about to ask the same of you."

"You're Ruth's hero, you know," Toni said.

The older woman rolled her eyes. "Enough out of you, girl! You'll give away all my secrets!" She looked over the top of her glasses with a severe expression. "Don't you have to be somewhere?"

"On my way, Boss!" Toni reached under the counter and pulled out a large handbag, draping it diagonally across her shoulder. "It was nice meeting you, Clark." That direct blue violet gaze again. He could wander around in those eyes for a week and not know he was lost.

The radio was playing an old Anne Murray song: "Could I Have This Dance?" He felt alive with energy; he wanted to grab her as she walked past and waltz her around the store as he'd done with Ruth.

He crossed his arms over his chest instead. "Perhaps we'll meet again," he said, watching her walk across the floor.

She was undoubtedly the most beautiful woman he'd ever seen. Scary, how beautiful she was. Thank goodness she was taken.

3

He's dangerous, Toni told herself as she flipped on her turn signal and pulled from her parking space into the street.

Ruth thinks he's wonderful, she argued with herself.

No one who generates that kind of excitement could possibly be good for me.

She smiled sardonically. *So what am I waiting for? Someone to bore me to death?*

Stopping for a red light, both hands resting at the top of the steering wheel, she absently rubbed the gold band on her ring finger and contemplated the undeniable exchange of energy she'd felt between herself and Clark McConaughey. *Good, clean energy,* she told herself.

Maybe he hadn't noticed the wedding band...

She'd worn the ring for a year now—paid thirty-five dollars for it, placed it on the ring finger of her left hand, and hadn't taken it off since. "Protection from unwanted attention," she'd told Ruth and Pop. They accepted her explanation at face value. It was a given that Toni's looks attracted attention. A handy thing when she'd been making her living as a model. But in real life, she'd decided, more trouble than she cared to deal with.

The wedding ring and her repertoire of stories about her son usually discouraged advances. The kind of man who didn't so easily give up was the kind she tried to stay away from. She didn't trust men.

More to the point, she didn't trust herself. Not with her history of attraction to dangerous men. Not with her genes.

Her mother had always had to have a man. There'd been so many, Toni couldn't even remember all their names. She'd already proved herself her mother's daughter in too many ways she wasn't proud of. No sense in pushing her luck.

She pulled into the parking lot of Carver Elementary School, her tires crunching over the gravel, and found a slot near the front entrance. Before getting out, she rested her forehead on the steering wheel for just a moment, suddenly despondent. She knew the life that she was living was the life she really wanted, that the choices she was making were healthy choices, honoring herself and honoring God.

But she also knew her weaknesses.

Sometimes when she was lonely and afraid, she remembered how powerful a man could make her feel when he wanted her, how loved when he took her in his arms. Those memories came easily; she had to struggle to remember how empty she'd felt when he'd used her up and moved on. Lonelier than ever. More afraid...

Wearing the wedding band just made things easier.

She lifted her head to gaze at the school building, her despondency replaced by apprehension about the meeting with the counselor at Danny's school. Mr. Gibbons had called several weeks earlier to request permission to do some "informal observations" on Danny.

"Is there a problem?" she'd asked.

"His teacher and the reading specialist have expressed some concerns about his progress and behavior," Mr. Gibbons had answered. "We just want to be sure we're doing everything we can to encourage his strengths..."

It hadn't seemed like a big deal at the time, but when Danny's teacher, Ellen Shaw, had called to set up an appointment, Toni had started to wonder.

Maybe Danny is acting out at school the way he is at home, she thought, as she walked slowly toward the entrance to the building—defying his teacher. Or maybe he was having problems getting along with the other kids. Pop had told her he'd thrown some punches once, while she'd been away.

His report cards hadn't been glowing, but then, hers had never been either. He'd been slow to pick up reading—he'd been meeting with the reading specialist every week since the beginning of second grade—but he was getting better. At least he tried to sound out words on his own.

She checked in at the office. "I'll let Mrs. Shaw know you're here, Mrs. Ferrier," the secretary told her. She buzzed the classroom and left a message, then offered Toni a cup of coffee, which she gratefully accepted.

Mrs. Ferrier, she thought. Both her own and Pop's names were listed on Danny's school records as his guardians. Since they had the same last name and lived at the same address, the secretary assumed they were husband and wife rather than father and daughter. There was no reason Toni should disabuse the secretary; her personal life wasn't anybody's business but her own.

The door to the office opened, and Ellen Shaw entered, a warm smile on her face, a coffee mug in her hand. "Hello, Ms. Ferrier! Good, you've found coffee." The spry, gray-haired woman, a veteran of almost thirty years in the classroom, extended her hand and shook Toni's vigorously. "I need a cup myself," she said, gesturing toward an open doorway. "Like a warm-up before we get started?"

"Good idea. Thanks." Toni rose and followed her into the

teacher's lounge behind the office. After a slow start in first grade last year, Danny had been specially placed in Mrs. Shaw's room for second grade. "She's kind of old, like Grumpy, and she's *real* nice, Mom," he'd told her after his first day. Toni had laughed. "Old and wise, I'll bet. Listen well, Danny. You'll be so smart by year's end I won't know what to do with you!"

"We'll be meeting in my classroom down the hall," Mrs. Shaw said, setting her mug down and reaching for Toni's Styrofoam cup to refill it. "I'm glad you could make it today. It's difficult to get all the specialists together at a time that works for the parent, too, but somehow we managed it."

Specialists? Toni wondered, her heartbeat quickening in anxiety. She knew Mr. Gibbons would be there, but what was this about specialists? She was afraid to ask.

Mrs. Shaw was still chattering away as she opened the door to her classroom. Toni's stomach lurched. A group of men and women sat around a low table in child-sized chairs. A couple of them glanced up as Toni entered the room, but the others continued conversations among themselves. She felt intimidated by their casual camaraderie, an outsider to the education and social standing they held in common.

Their size relative to the furniture in the second-grade room made them seem larger than life. In contrast, Toni felt herself shrinking more and more as they introduced themselves: Mr. Gibbons and the reading specialist, both of whom she'd met before; the speech-and-language pathologist; the school psychologist; the learning specialist. Why did she feel as if these strangers held her son's fate in their hands?

"We invited your caseworker from CSD to our meeting today," Mr. Gibbons added, "but he wasn't able to make it this afternoon. He did fill out a questionnaire and send it back."

Toni stared at him, her heart in her stomach as she sank into a chair. She'd probably signed something sometime giving the school access to Danny's records with the Children's Services Division—or maybe Pop had—but the idea that all these strangers knew about her history with the state agency that handled child-abuse and child-neglect cases made her feel even smaller in their eyes. No one in this group would make the mistake of calling her "*Mrs.* Ferrier."

"The Student Study Team meets once a week to talk about kids who've been referred for one reason or another by their classroom teacher," the counselor explained. "As we discussed on the phone, after Mrs. Shaw and Miss Jennings expressed some concern about your son's behavior and progress, I met with Danny, and several of us did informal observations of him in various settings. The purpose of this meeting is to discuss those observations with you and talk about what might be an appropriate next step."

Every eye in the room was on Toni. She nodded, afraid to open her mouth, and tried to listen as each person at the table pulled out their checklists and notes and talked about her son as if he were an insect pinned beneath a microscope.

"*Behind grade level in reading and math...unresponsive... doesn't finish work...tends to play alone...mood swings...outbursts of anger...periods of hyperactive behavior...problems staying focused...*"

They said some positive things as well, that Danny's oral language and motor skills were good, that he was very creative, that there were times he could be sweet and helpful. But Toni couldn't seem to help but focus on the negatives.

The meeting went on and on. After all the group members had shared their comments, the probing began: What's he like at home? How does he respond to you? to his grandfather? to strangers? Any recent changes in his behavior? Any regressive behavior—baby talk, thumb sucking, bed-wetting?

And more. Questions about Danny's medical and family

history. If they had the CSD report, they must have known the answers already. Why did they keep picking at her?

Feeling smaller and smaller, Toni answered the questions automatically, hardly knowing what she said. It was clear by now that the "learning specialist" was a special-education teacher. Was this meeting about putting Danny in special ed? They obviously didn't think he was just going through a stage; they thought something was *wrong* with him…

In the end she signed the papers placed in front of her to authorize the recommended testing for a full case study. *This is the right thing to do,* she told herself desperately as she signed the consent forms. *I'm being a good mom to see that my son gets the help he needs.*

A good mom? another part of her snorted contemptuously. *If you'd been a good mom, Danny wouldn't be* having *these problems. If you'd been a good mom, he'd be fine!*

She felt the way she'd felt when she awoke this morning from her unremembered dream: bruised, worked over. The men and women around the table were like the monsters in her room, pointing their fingers, but this time naming her sins aloud…

Or was *she* the monster?

Ruth gossiped with Clark between customers for an hour, updating him on the store—Toni's work had apparently had quite an impact—and news at Tomahawk Community Church, where he'd been a member for a number of years before his last Seattle hiatus.

"Jack and I have joined a Growth Group that meets at Beau and Emily Bradley's every week," she said. "Remember Emily? Chappie and Mary Lewis's daughter? They have a little girl now. Chappie and Mary come, too, with all the younger kids."

Chappie Lewis was Clark's favorite minister on staff, with a practical, down-to-earth approach to life that both nurtured spirituality and made sense for one's day-to-day routines. "What's a growth group?" he asked curiously.

"A place to nurture relationships with God and with each other. We have a potluck, and then the teenagers watch the kids so the grown-ups can just be together—talk, laugh, cry sometimes. It's a place we can feel safe being real with each other, especially when we're dealing with 'stuff' in our lives."

"Stuff?"

"Yeah. Like Jack's mixed feelings about retirement. Or the feelings I go through every year on the anniversary of Sunny's death."

"Doesn't sound safe to me!"

Ruth laughed. "Spoken like a man who reaches for the Pepto-Bismol when he's feeling an emotion!"

"Aw, come on, Ruthie," Clark protested. "You know I'm not a macho man. I feel stuff."

Ruth raised her eyebrows. "A little testy, are we?"

He grinned. "See? You already caught me feeling something!" He leaned back on the counter, crossing his arms over his chest. "Anybody else I know in this 'touchy-feely' group?"

She ignored Clark's lightly mocking tone. "You might remember Katie, the little redhead who used to sing in church—still does, on occasion. She and her husband Keith come. And Toni, with her dad and son."

"Not her husband?" Clark couldn't resist asking.

"Her husband?" Ruth looked puzzled. "Oh! You must have noticed the ring. She only wears it to keep predators at bay. No husband."

He bit his lip to keep from asking more about Toni. He'd never hear the end of it if Ruth thought he was interested. *Am I?* he asked himself. *After a five-minute encounter?*

Ruth interrupted his musings with a question of her own. "What about Will, Clark? I don't know why, but he's been on my mind. Have you talked to him?"

Clark shook his head. "Not for months. He never calls you, either?"

"It's been more like years. You know how he was after Sunny died. He stopped coming around and never started up again. I still pray for him."

"You do?" Clark didn't know why he should be surprised; he knew Ruth had a long list of people she prayed for on a regular basis, including himself. But Will was so obviously uninterested...

He left Paper Chase armed with an invitation to join Ruth and Jack for breakfast in the morning. "I'll have you over for dinner one of these nights, but tonight Toni's invited us to her dad's retirement dinner at Columbia River College. You'll have to meet Doc—he's absolutely delightful."

"A professor?"

"Head of maintenance—for years. He will be sorely missed on campus. One of those guys who can fix anything—even broken hearts, I hear! Everybody loves Doc."

Clark found as he made his way home through the afternoon traffic that he was having as much difficulty keeping his mind off Toni as he'd had keeping his eyes off her in the store. It wasn't just her physical beauty that had so captured his imagination; there was a certain zing about her, a flash of fire in her blue violet eyes, an energy that seemed to rise to meet his own.

He remembered now that Ruth had mentioned her before, perhaps more than once over the last year or so. With admiration, if memory served him, and with a bit of maternal worry. He tried to recall the stories. She'd had a hard life—he was sure Ruth had told him that, though he couldn't remember any details.

38

Somehow it was difficult to believe a woman as beautiful as Antonia Ferrier could have had a hard life. Even if she had the personality of a peanut—which she certainly did not—a woman like that would have men jumping at the opportunity to take care of her, to love and protect her.

Then he remembered Ruth's explanation of the gold band she wore on her ring finger. *To keep predators at bay.*

So she'd had experience with men who'd had things other than love and protection on their minds. The thought made him unaccountably angry. *Why?* he wondered.

He thought about Ruth's teasing: *Spoken like a man who reaches for the Pepto-Bismol when he's feeling an emotion.* It was true that Clark was in the dark sometimes when it came to his own emotions. What man wasn't? Still, he was definitely "feeling stuff" about Toni—had been from the first moment he'd laid eyes on her. But what, exactly?

Incomplete.

The word flashed through his mind, as if out of nowhere, startling him.

I'm feeling incomplete.

He let out his breath in a long sigh. It was true. And it was completely outside his experience. Nowhere in his past could he remember the mere glimpse of a woman's face making him feel incomplete.

"A lonely childhood," Jack had once observed in one of his philosophical moods, "is an excellent training ground for self-reliance." Clark had practiced self-reliance for a very long time now—most of his thirty-six years. He knew how to take care of himself, to see that his needs were met. He even admitted to being a little arrogant about it.

He was self-contained to such a degree, in fact, that Ruth had wondered aloud if he'd ever fall in love. Ever let himself. Ever let a woman love him.

He'd wondered himself. He'd had plenty of girlfriends over the years, but no one had ever captured his heart.

Why now should this woman make him feel as if it needed capturing?

There was little in Clark's experience to recommend romance. Ruth and Jack were the exception: two strong, healthy souls who met each other as equals on the playing field of love, challenging each other as well as cheering each other on. In every other marriage he'd been close to, one partner took, the other gave. One needed everything; the other needed nothing. Like Molly and Royce. How had his parents ever hooked up in the first place?

Clark shook his head. He had no desire to be with a woman who needed everything. Demanded everything. A woman like his mother, never satisfied.

Nor could he imagine himself needing someone in the way that marriage suggested—needing a woman to be part of his life, to be there every day, to promise to be with him forever.

Until now.

Antonia Ferrier's exotic eyes seemed to Clark to hold the secrets of eternity, secrets he suddenly longed to know. The curve of her cheek seemed the very curve of time: past, present, and future all in one. The energy that pulsated beneath her translucent skin seemed the energy of the universe—ancient but ever changing, ever new. She was utter mystery, yet as familiar as a recurring dream. Disturbing. Compelling.

The part of himself he didn't know.

4

"Isn't it time to go yet, Grumpy?" Danny asked impatiently. "Where's Mom, anyway?"

Doc Ferrier looked at his watch and then out the window of his living room for what seemed like the hundredth time. "Her meetin' must a been longer'n she thought, Danny Boy," he said. Toni had hoped she'd make it home in time to drive to the retirement dinner with them. "She said if she's late to go on ahead, she'd meet us there. I know you're gettin' fidgety, but I figger we can wait another ten minutes or so. Be nice we all go together, eh?"

"I guess."

Doc glanced at his grandson squirming on the edge of the sofa, looking as uncomfortable as Doc felt in a dress shirt and tie. Since Doc was one of the six retirees from the college being honored tonight, he figured he'd best look halfway dressed up for the doings. "Sure you don't want t' take off that tie?" he asked for the third time.

Danny shook his head with vigor. "I wanna look just like you, Grumpy," he said solemnly.

Doc stroked his close-cropped beard. "Might not be so easy

as you think," he said, his eyes twinkling. He patted his tummy, which had grown even rounder in the last year and a half since Toni had been doing the cooking. "More like I'm the Santa and you's the elf. Whoever thunk t' see Santa and his elf in shirt an' tie?"

Ten minutes later Toni still hadn't appeared. Doc made one last survey of the street through the living-room window. "Looks like your mama got tied up in traffic, Danny Boy," he finally said. "Let's go save 'er a spot."

Danny nodded, gazing solemnly at his grandpa with thick-lashed eyes the same blue violet as his mother's. Doc's heart turned over with tenderness.

Toni wasn't sure how she ended up at the tavern on the out-skirts of Gresham, the one that had once been her regular hangout. She couldn't remember the end of the meeting at Danny's school, saying good-bye, getting in her car, driving there. All she could remember was feeling as if she were clinging to the top of a speeding train, holding on for dear life, her arms straining in their sockets as the engine raced completely out of control toward the dark hole of a fast-approaching tunnel...

An open pack of smokes lay on the bar in front of her. She stared at the cigarette smoldering between her fingers. Where had it come from? She hadn't smoked for over a year. When the bartender set a bucket glass in front of her, a clear drink gar-nished with a lime, she automatically stubbed out the cigarette.

Toni didn't remember ordering a drink. But she *did* remem-ber how drinking used to help when life felt overwhelming and out of control. She didn't feel guilty when she drank; she didn't feel lonely or angry or hurt or afraid. She didn't feel anything at all.

She lifted the glass.

"Three-fifty," the bartender reminded her.

"Oh!" She set the drink back on the bar and reached to pull the wallet from her handbag, which was perched precariously on the stool next to her. The long strap caught a button on the sleeve of her dress, and suddenly the contents of the purse went flying through the air and bouncing over the floor.

A new rush of an old rage she'd almost forgotten about surged through her—an anger at the universe, a universe that clearly had it in for her. The schools, the police, the Children's Services Division. Her mother, her father, her son. God. They'd all betrayed her.

Muttering words she hadn't used in months, she slid off the stool and scrambled to gather her things as the bartender knelt to help her. A compact, a comb, a couple of tubes of lipstick, her keys...

Her wallet lay open on the floor. Danny's latest school portrait grinned up at her. Beneath it lay an envelope. "Toni and Danny," it read. The invitation to her father's retirement dinner. Tonight's dinner.

She glanced at her watch and gasped, her anger transformed into self-reproach in the space of a moment.

You're the betrayer, a voice inside accused her. *You betrayed your son. You betrayed yourself. And here you are in a bar, ready to do it again.*

Standing abruptly, she pulled a five-dollar bill out of the wallet and threw it toward the bar. Then she fled as if the hounds of hell were at her heels.

"Hey!" the bartender called.

She didn't stop.

Thank you God thank you God thank you God, she silently repeated over and over as she jumped in the car and peeled out of the parking lot. *Thank you for smacking me to my senses!*

~ ~ ~ ~ ~

Danny tugged at the sleeve of his grandfather's shirt. "Grumpy, how come Mom's not here?" His voice was anxious.

Doc enclosed his grandson's small hand in his large one. "Like I said, her meetin' musta gone longer'n she thought," he said, trying to sound calm. "An' traffic's prob'ly all snarled up somewhere 'tween there an' here. Don't worry, Danny Boy."

Still, Doc knew that Danny couldn't have helped but notice his grandpa searching the main entry and glancing worriedly at his watch every few minutes since they'd arrived at Manderley Hall.

It was after seven-thirty now, and the servers were already starting to bring dessert platters to the tables. The program was scheduled to start in a few minutes. Doc would be horribly disappointed if his daughter missed it.

Doc was surrounded by loved ones: Danny sat at his side, and next to Toni's empty chair on his other side, Ruth Denton sat with Mary Lewis, while across from them their husbands discussed an idea for a Sunday school picnic aboard Jack's boat. Doc was especially happy to have Chappie here; the minister had been his friend since the first time Toni had come to live with him, eleven years ago. Few people knew as many pieces of Doc's story as Chappie Lewis did.

Keith and Katie Castle, who were like Doc's own children, sat directly across from him and Danny, laughing at Beau and Emily Bradley's tales of life with seventeen-month-old Elizabeth. Other friends and colleagues from his many years at Tomahawk Community Church and as head of the maintenance department at Columbia River College were scattered up and down the table.

But Toni was his daughter, his only blood child, and the fact that Toni was even alive and in his life seemed a miracle. He couldn't bear it if something had happened to her.

So it was with great relief that he saw her sneaking up behind her son, a finger lifted to her mouth as a signal for Doc not to give her away. Danny was scraping the sides of his pudding bowl when Toni wrapped her arms around his neck and kissed the top of his head. "Hi, baby!" she said brightly. "Nice haircut—where'd you get it?"

Danny wriggled out of her grasp and wouldn't look at her, or even say hello. Doc had never seen him so sullen, nor did he remember ever seeing on his daughter's face anything like the look of pain that flashed across her features now.

She didn't push Danny, leaving him to finish his dessert as she slid into the chair between Doc and Ruth. She linked her arm in her father's and murmured an apology. "Pop, I'm so sorry I'm late. The meeting went longer than I expected…" He didn't even listen to the rest of her explanation. It didn't matter. She was his daughter, he loved her, and she was safe.

Toni was home and in bed by ten o'clock, but she was too wired to sleep. She tossed and turned and changed positions, kicking the blankets to one side and pulling them back again.

Too wired and too scared to sleep.

She knew what had happened today: It was the old cycle beginning to kick in. The old, familiar pattern. She'd be feeling bad—guilty or lonely or afraid. She wanted a fix. *Needed* a fix to feel better. Not to feel *good*, just to feel okay for a few hours. Later, she'd be filled with guilt and self-loathing for her weakness, her lack of willpower. A fix was the only way to feel better. And on and on.

Spilling her purse seemed now like the intervention of Providence, stopping the cycle before she'd completely climbed on. *Thank you, God,* her heart cried once again. *Thank you for protecting me.*

She rolled over on her side, clutching her pillow. How could she have even *considered* taking a drink? *Life in recovery is too good to blow it now,* she thought. She couldn't lose her life again. Lose everything she loved.

Maybe you don't have a choice, a voice inside her said. Her heart beat faster. Maybe she didn't. Maybe long-term recovery wasn't possible after all. Maybe her life was slipping away, and there wasn't a thing she could do about it.

You do have a choice, another voice inside her argued. *And you're not alone. One day at a time, God gives you the strength to choose sobriety. You've done it every day for almost two years. You can do it again today. And the next day. And the next. God is with you.*

Her counselor at Red Rock Ranch had warned her this would happen, but in the glow of her first months of sobriety Toni hadn't remembered.

"It's natural to have a honeymoon period for a while," she'd said to Toni. "Expect it. You and your son, you and sobriety. Enjoy it! Have a wonderful time. But don't let down your guard."

She *had* let down her guard. Life had been good, and she hadn't wanted to hear it was going to change. She certainly hadn't wanted to believe the counselor's dispassionate assertion about her son: "Danny's going to be dealing with the effects of your alcoholism at every stage of his life—just as you are."

She had not been willing to look at the signs. She was not prepared for the honeymoon to be over.

Her mind drifted back to the first night she'd spent at the house on Dearborn Street after she'd come home from the clinic in Montana. Nothing had ever felt so sweet as the moment that morning when her son had tiptoed into her room and crawled into bed with her, cuddling close and shyly telling her his plans for the day.

"I have plans, too," she'd told him. "You're in every one of them."

"Forever?"

"Forever."

"Never go away again, Mama."

"Never," she'd vowed.

More than anything else—more even than her own sanity—Danny was her reason for sobriety. He needed her. It had always been as simple as that.

Now more than ever, she told herself.

She rolled back onto her stomach but couldn't sleep. Her mind was too uneasy, her body too restless. She'd never get to sleep.

Finally she gave up. She took a trip down the hall to check on Danny, who was sound asleep; eavesdropped for snores at Pop's bedroom door; then tiptoed to the kitchen, switched on the light, and closed the door.

She'd never phoned Georgine this late before, but her friend had made Toni promise she would call if she ever needed her. Well, she needed her. No one would understand like George would, not even Ruthie. George would know what to say.

A woman answered the phone with a groggy hello, and for a moment Toni regretted the impulse to call her. "George, I'm sorry to call so late—"

"Toni! What's wrong? Are you all right?" Instant alertness; no grumbling about how late it was, no hesitation, just immediate concern.

Toni had managed, just barely, to keep her emotions in check through the meeting at school, through her realization she'd ended up in a bar without knowing how she'd gotten there, through the discovery she'd forgotten her father's retirement dinner, even through Danny's sullen silence. But against George's tenderness she had no defense. She burst into tears.

They talked for almost an hour. Or at least Toni talked, pouring out her heart to her friend. "My life is *good*, George. I have a wonderful family and church and job. I have real *friends*, not just people who want to use me. Things have finally been making sense for me—until this afternoon. I don't know what kept me from taking that drink. I *needed* it. I didn't see how I could live through another hour without a drink."

"But you did, Toni," Georgine reminded her. "You didn't have it. You said no."

"Only because I dumped my purse all over the floor."

"Ironic, isn't it?"

"What d'you mean?"

"You, who I always think of as poetry in motion, saved by an aberration of klutziness!"

Toni knew George was trying to cheer her up, but she couldn't even bring herself to smile. She wrapped the phone cord around her arm. "I'm really scared, George. I can't afford to relapse. I just can't!"

"You won't, Toni. God is bigger than your addiction. You're going to be okay."

"I want to believe that so badly!"

"Are you feeling better about the meeting at school?"

"How could I?" Toni started to cry again. "I know they're wrong, George. I can't let them stick Danny in a special ed classroom and label him forever! The last thing he needs is other kids calling him a retard."

"If it's a way for him to get the help he needs, it seems the thing to do," Georgine said mildly. "There's no shame in taking a little longer to catch on to things. We're *all* slow at something."

Toni continued as if she hadn't heard. "I'll just spend more time with him, help him more with his homework, love him more to make up for those first few years when I didn't know how to love him enough—"

"Toni…" Georgine interrupted.

Toni waited.

"I know you're feeling overwhelmed," her friend said. "How can you help it? For ten years you used drugs and alcohol so you wouldn't have to feel your feelings. Now, all of a sudden, your feelings are *bombarding* you. How can you help but feel overwhelmed?"

When Toni didn't answer, she added, "I know you've heard it before, but it's easy to forget when you're in pain: feeling your feelings is part of the process. Don't shut down, Toni. This, too, shall pass."

Toni closed her eyes and rubbed her forehead tiredly. "I know."

"I'm sorry you're hurting. I wish I could make it better."

"Yeah. Well."

"What about talking to your counselor?" Georgine asked. "D'you think you could get in to see her tomorrow?"

"I don't really have a counselor anymore," Toni said. "My HMO changed the rules about how many times you can see someone, and I ran out of sessions. I can't afford that kind of money out of my own pocket."

"But this is an emergency! Surely someone will see you."

"I'll call. But I haven't had much luck in the past." Her lips curled in a sardonic smile. "Dealing with insurance companies is enough to drive anyone to drink!"

Georgine laughed. "See there? You made a joke! Feeling better?"

"You always make me feel better. Thanks, George."

"Anytime. I'll be praying for you, Toni. I love you. Hang in there."

Toni could barely say good-bye around the lump in her throat. *George is right,* she thought as she hung up the phone. She had committed herself to healing, and healing didn't happen without pain. Feeling her feelings was part of the process. She just needed someone to hold her hand.

If she couldn't afford a counselor, maybe it was time to check out an AA meeting or two.

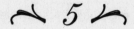

5

In the morning, Danny sat in sullen silence as Toni fried bacon and flipped pancakes for breakfast. He barely picked at his food. For a while Toni pretended not to notice, putting on her most cheerful face and chattering as if he were interested and responsive.

Finally she fell silent. Last night was the first time in over a year she hadn't kept a promise to him, hadn't been where she said she'd be when she said she'd be there. Would he ever trust her, or was this the way it was going to be for the rest of their lives?

"I'm sorry I was late last night, Danny," she finally said on the way to drop him off at school. "Maybe you and I can do something special tonight, just the two of us. Chuck E. Cheese's for dinner, maybe?" The pizza-parlor-cum-playground would be a zoo—it always was—but it was Danny's favorite.

He did look at her then, for a brief moment, and she could see the struggle in his eyes. "And a video afterward?" she coaxed. "You can pick." She knew she was shamelessly trying to buy back his favor.

Turning his head to gaze out the window, he mumbled, "If Grumpy comes."

"Sure! Okay. We'll make it the whole family."

She watched him trudge across the school yard a few minutes later, kicking at rocks, his backpack askew. Her heart felt heavy with sorrow.

Ruth had driven to Seattle on a buying trip for the day, but she'd left a note for Toni at Paper Chase inviting the three of them on Jack's sight-seeing "practice run" the following morning. His official summer tourist runs—the first since he'd bought the sternwheeler—would start over Memorial Day weekend, two weeks away, and he wanted to practice his spiel.

If tonight's enticements didn't work, a cruise on the *Snow Swan* should help get Danny back in her good graces. He liked boats almost as much as he liked Brannigan.

She kept herself busy at the store all day, between customers assigning herself projects that didn't give her time to think about her worries: restocking the card racks, arranging a display of garden tea party accessories, dusting the glass display shelves.

Doc and Danny met her at Paper Chase after work. By the time Danny had had his fill of play and pizza, he'd warmed up to Toni a little. On the way home she stopped at the video store and let him pick a movie, not complaining when he chose Disney's *Homeward Bound*, which he'd seen half a dozen times before. She let him stay up till ten and watched it with him even though *she'd* seen it half a dozen times before. His head against her shoulder as the credits rolled at the end of the movie made it all worthwhile.

The *Snow Swan* was scheduled to leave the dock at nine Saturday morning. At eight-thirty, Toni pulled the Valiant into the hillside parking lot off Front Street, overlooking RiverPlace. The day had dawned cool but clear. It was a beautiful morning for a boat ride.

"Okay, Danny, let's go try out your sea legs." Toni smiled over her shoulder at her son as he unbuckled his seat belt, pleased at the flash of excitement in his eyes. He'd been on the sternwheeler once before, just after Jack had closed escrow last fall, and had talked about it for weeks afterward.

Doc, next to Toni in the front passenger seat, unlocked the door of the old car and opened it. "Here's hopin' *my* sea legs hold out," he said as he pulled himself with difficulty out of the car. A couple of months ago he'd confessed to Toni that his rheumatism was bothering him "real bad," which was the major reason he'd decided to retire this year.

She knew the decision hadn't come easily. He was worried about finances; his Social Security and retirement pay might have been enough to take care of his own needs, but not those of a daughter and a grandson, too.

Toni hadn't said anything to Ruth yet, but she knew she was either going to have to figure out a way to start bringing in some extra cash, or find a different job. She made a higher hourly wage than the other clerks who worked at Paper Chase, quite a bit more than the going rate for retail work in the metro area, but it wasn't enough.

"Your work would be a bargain at twice what I'm paying you, Toni," her boss had told her at her last review. "I wish I could afford to pay you more, but I've been over and over the books, and I just can't."

Ruth had promised her extra hours now that Pop was going to be home with Danny, but she felt guilty asking him to baby-sit his grandson after the years he'd already put in. Of course he insisted that watching Danny wasn't work. *That might have been true once,* Toni thought, *but I'm not so sure anymore…*

"Look, Grumpy, Mom—there it is!" Danny tugged at her hand and pointed down the ramp to the dock where the *Snow Swan* floated on the Willamette River like a vision from the past. The boat stood out against the dark water, snowy white like the bird she was named after. The paddle wheel at the stern, the smokestacks, and the trim around the windows and deck railings were painted the lavender of swan-wing shadows or summer evenings, accented with a soft charcoal gray.

Both Ruth and Jack greeted the Ferriers as they climbed the gangplank onto the lower deck of the *Snow Swan* and crossed into the enclosed forward section. It was like stepping inside a beautiful piece of furniture, Toni thought, looking around to admire the polished brass and gleaming woodwork.

Jack, wearing white pants, a navy jacket with gold braid, and a captain's hat, shook hands with Doc. Then he bent down to extend his hand to Danny, who suddenly turned shy and looked at the floor.

Toni placed a reassuring hand on Danny's shoulder. "You're looking elegant," she told the captain, keeping her tone light.

"As are you," Jack said gallantly, raising her hand and kissing it lightly. He eyed her appreciatively. Dressed in a cranberry-colored brocade vest over a tucked-front white cotton blouse and a flowing tea-length skirt, she was ready for work when the sight-seeing cruise was over.

"So, Jack—smooth as ever with the ladies, I see," an amused male voice said from behind her.

Jack's weathered face broke into a grin. "Just part of the job, McConaughey. Glad you could make it."

Clark shook Jack's hand and pulled Ruth to his side for a hug. He smiled at Toni. "Nice to see you again, Toni." He dropped his arm from around Ruth's shoulder and extended his hand. His grip was warm and firm around her slender fingers.

"What, no sparks this morning?" she teased. "The way Ruth talks, I thought you were permanently charged!"

He opened his mouth as if to speak, then closed it again, apparently thinking better of it. But his mouth tilted in a mischievous grin, and his eyes crinkled in amusement as they met hers. There were sparks, and then there were sparks…

She watched him thoughtfully as he met her father and Danny. He might have been Ruth's son, with his reddish blonde close-cropped hair and his lightly freckled skin. He had a nice face, handsome in a "Dudley Do Right" sort of way, with a warm smile and an open expression that seemed eminently trustworthy. His direct blue gaze only added to the effect.

He was about Pop's height, a shade under six feet, and solidly built; he obviously took good care of his health. Dressed casually but neatly in cotton Dockers with a long-sleeved knit shirt open at the neck, he exuded self-confidence and goodwill. *Dangerous* seemed a ludicrous word to describe him now, despite the awareness of her attraction. Maybe her experience in the bar the other night had put "danger" in perspective.

"Danny," Jack said, "I thought you might like to steer the boat some after we get under way." He glanced around at the others. "Anybody object? Think he can do it without running us aground?"

Thank you, Jack! Toni said silently as Danny perked up. "I'd trust him with my life," she said with conviction.

"Same here," Doc agreed.

"Ditto," said Ruth, ruffling his hair.

Clark pretended not to be as easy a sell as the others had been. Propping an elbow in his hand and holding his chin, his head cocked to one side, he furrowed his brow and considered Danny for a moment. "Hmm…"

He leaned down, peered into Danny's ear, then stepped back to study him from a distance. Toni could see the glimmer of a smile twitching at her son's mouth.

Clark finally nodded. "I'd say he looks pretty steady. Quite possible he has the makings of a riverboat captain."

"Like to try it out, Danny?" Jack asked.

The boy looked at Doc for permission. Toni knew he didn't mean to hurt her by turning to his grandfather instead of to her. She knew that his response was involuntary. After all, Pop had been there for him for years when she hadn't. The knowledge didn't make it hurt less.

Doc nodded at Danny, his blue eyes twinkling. "I'd take 'im up on it if I was you, Danny Boy. I didn't get to steer a boat till I was near twenty. And it wasn't nothin' like this big ol' thing. Sure be somethin' to tell your friends about."

"D'you think I can do it?" Danny asked anxiously.

Doc waved his hand. *"Pfft!* Steerin' a boat's no different 'n steerin' a car! You been settin' on my lap doin' that since you was three or four."

"Okay. But you'll be there, Grumpy?"

"Right beside."

The men disappeared up the narrow stairway, Clark leading the way and Jack bringing up the rear. Toni started to follow, but Ruth restrained her with a touch on the arm. "Coffee?" she asked.

She poured a cup of the steaming beverage from the thermos on the bar and offered it to Toni before pouring herself a cup. Although he didn't run a restaurant on the sternwheeler as some of the other boats on the river did, Jack provided free coffee, sold soft drinks, and kept the bar stocked for private parties, which made up the bulk of his evening business.

"Thanks." Toni wrapped her long fingers around the insulated cup. "This is awfully nice of Jack, Ruth, letting us play tourist."

"He's a pretty nice guy, isn't he?" Ruth said with affection. "And we both thought you could use a break in your routine." She ran a finger around the top of her Styrofoam cup. "What's going on with you, Toni? You didn't seem yourself the other night."

Toni looked away from Ruth's concerned expression,

uncomfortable. "At Pop's dinner, you mean? It was just one of those days." When she glanced back at the older woman, Ruth's brow was still furrowed. "I'm okay, Ruthie."

"Really?"

"Really." Through the windows of the salon at the other end of the companionway, Toni caught sight of the huge paddle wheel at the stern of the boat as it began to move. "Oh, look," she said, to steer the conversation away from herself. "We're getting under way!"

Ruth sighed. "Okay, I get the message. But if you ever need to talk, come track me down, you hear?"

She led Toni down the narrow corridor past the tiny galley on the left and a pair of rest rooms on the right. "Sailors call 'em *heads*," Danny had informed his mother, quite proud of his newly acquired knowledge, after their first trip on the stern-wheeler.

They watched through the wide windows as the *Snow Swan* slowly pulled away from the dock. The water slapping against the paddle wheel and cascading off the rungs as the wheel rotated made a rhythmic, pleasantly hypnotic sound through the glass. The low ceilings and teak paneling created a sense of warmth and intimacy.

Several linen-covered tables were set at angles to the large windows, which ran the circumference of the salon. Toni glanced at the one occupied table, where a young family was enjoying a breakfast snack. Two boys, munching on bagels, sat contentedly on either side of their dad, who was pointing out the window and telling them how the sternwheeler worked. The fresh-faced teenage girl bounced a little one on her lap and chatted with her mom between bites as if they were best friends.

They look as if they might have stepped out of a Norman Rockwell painting, Toni thought with a quick stab of envy.

Growing up, she hadn't even known such families existed in real life.

Jack's voice over the speakers interrupted her musings: "Welcome to the *Snow Swan* for a unique view of a unique city…"

"Oh, let's go upstairs, Ruthie!" she said. "You can see so much better from the sundeck."

"Portland is built on the banks of the Willamette River where it empties into the Columbia," Ruth joined in with Jack as they climbed the stairs. "A river wide and deep enough that even huge ocean-going tankers can use the city as a port o' call. You won't find too many seaport cities a hundred miles from the ocean…"

"You have Jack's spiel *memorized*, Ruth?"

"I ought to. Helped him write it, then heard it over and over again for *months!* About drove me crazy."

Jack's spiel might have driven his wife crazy, but Toni, hearing it for the first time, enjoyed it thoroughly. It was lovely, too, just being out on the river on a beautiful spring morning, she told herself as they neared the end of the cruise fifty minutes later.

Clark came up beside her where she leaned against the railing. "A perfect way to see the city, isn't it?" he commented. "Jack's got a good thing going here."

Toni nodded. "How do you know Ruth and Jack so well?" she asked curiously. "Seems like you're almost family."

"I *do* consider them family. Even used to call them Aunt Ruthie and Uncle Jack." He leaned his arms against the railing next to her. "You know Jack's a retired police officer, right?"

"You're not going to tell me he arrested you one day?"

Clark grinned. "Nothing so exciting! When I was in junior high, Jack was in charge of a division in the police department that worked with the public schools to develop programs for at-risk kids, to provide ways for them to channel their energy constructively. Sort of an early gang-diversion unit."

"You were a *gang member!*"

This time he laughed out loud. "Hardly!" He looked at her sternly. "Now do you want to hear this story or not?"

Toni grinned mischievously. "Okay. I'll be good."

Clark explained that Jack and Clark's father, at the time a bank vice president actively involved in community service, had organized a program using volunteers from the business community to teach kids the basics of commercial enterprise. "They got a grant and loaned small amounts of capital to each kid to invest in a small business. They had to do market research and then manufacture and market a product of some kind. Anything they earned after the loan was paid off they got to keep."

"I remember a program like that when I was at Jefferson High," Toni said. "A great idea. Not that I thought so at the time, apparently, since I never got involved." *And believe me,* she added to herself, *I was a "high risk" kid.*

"Anyway," Clark continued, "when Ruth discovered my existence—a poor, lonely kid without a mother to speak of and with an obviously workaholic father—she took me under her wing. It was like having an instant family. I couldn't have resisted if I'd wanted to."

"I know what you mean. Ruth and Jack have that family thing down, don't they?" Toni swept her hair back from her face. "So you knew Sunny."

"Yeah." Clark stretched his arms out on the railing. "I've been thinking about Sunny a lot since I've been back. She was very special."

"Hey, Mom!" Danny interrupted. "Did y'know I was *steerin'* back there? And I didn't run into *nothin'!*"

"*Anything,*" Toni corrected automatically. She gave him a hug. "Good job, Captain!"

She glanced up to find Clark with his back to the rail, his arms crossed over his chest, studying her thoughtfully.

"What?" she asked.

He shook his head.

The sight-seeing tour had been a nice way to reorient himself to Portland, Clark thought as he climbed the stairs to his RiverPlace apartment after the river cruise. Seeing the city from the Willamette and hearing Jack's spiel about its history and commerce made him feel truly home again.

Funny how easily Toni Ferrier seemed to fit into that feeling. How could she be part of "home again" when he'd only met her two days ago? What did he even know about her? She worked for Ruth, she lived with her father and her son, she wasn't married even though she wore a wedding ring. She was drop-dead gorgeous.

And she was great fun to be around. When she'd come up to the sundeck from below, the crowd of sightseers had seemed to energize her, and she'd had the same effect on them. *Every gathering a party waiting to happen,* he'd thought as he watched her. Toni stepped in, and it was as if the party began. Her energy was wonderful.

It was clear from the easy affection between Ruth and Toni that the younger woman was much more to the elder than just an employee. Clark wondered if Ruth had taken Toni under her wing as a substitute daughter, had seen something in her that reminded her of Sunny in some way, or at least brought out her maternal instincts in the same way.

He'd wanted to ask Ruth some questions; but he'd held his tongue. He dearly loved Aunt Ruthie, but she had a penchant for meddling. And like many women who've found marriage to be a good thing for themselves, she was ever eager to promote it with her single friends.

"You might think you're happy on your own," she'd tell Clark when he tried gracefully to turn down her invitations to dinner parties to meet some woman or another "who would just be perfect" for him. "That's because you don't know what you're missing. Look at Jack. You don't think he thought he was happy before he married me?"

She'd turn to Jack, who tried with little success to keep out of these conversations, and ask, "And what's your opinion now, Jack?"

Jack would roll his eyes heavenward and lift his arms in a helpless gesture. "I admit, I didn't know what happiness was before I met Ruthie, Clark."

Ruth would ignore his teasing tone and tell Clark triumphantly, "See?"

No, he definitely didn't want to be giving Ruthie any ideas. Not before he'd figured out his own ideas, at least.

6

I hope you'll find a place in one of the church Growth Groups, Clark," Chappie said to Clark as he left church Sunday morning. "In fact, why don't you come visit ours tomorrow night? Don't worry about bringing anything—we always have plenty of food."

He knew the group Chappie was talking about was the same one Ruth and Jack attended. And Toni. Not that that would be his motivation for checking it out..

"Thanks," he said, shaking the minister's hand. "I look forward to it."

It was the time between now and then he wasn't looking forward to. He'd finally talked to Will, yesterday afternoon, and they'd agreed to meet for an early dinner at a downtown hotel close to the restaurant where Will was working. Their phone conversation had been brief but not unpleasant. Maybe his half brother would be different than he remembered; maybe he'd grown up some.

Twenty minutes past the time he had agreed to meet Clark, Will still wasn't there. Clark, seated in the waiting area, finally asked for a window table in view of the entrance, where he could have a soda while he watched for Will.

He liked being back at Tomahawk Community Church. He'd come to faith there as a teenager after several months of attending services with Ruth and Jack and Sunny. More than anything else, it was the sense of community that had drawn him to the church and kept him coming back.

Community had been in short supply in Clark's childhood. He'd been the prototypical latchkey kid, especially after his mother had left. His father worked long hours. He had no extended family living nearby, and there were few other children in his upscale Lake Oswego neighborhood.

It seemed odd to think about it now, since his livelihood depended on his abilities to meet people and develop relationships, but he hadn't been very good at making friends in school. He was too interested in studying and not interested enough in sports and girls to be considered "cool" at a time of life when "coolness" was everything.

The church family didn't seem to care if he was "cool" or not, especially when he eagerly volunteered to help out in any way he could: teaching children's Sunday school classes, leading singing for outreach programs, acting as an usher. He embraced the church in the same way he'd embraced the Denton family, extending all his energy and resources, grateful for a place to belong.

Clark glanced out the window and saw Will moseying down the sidewalk on the opposite side of the street with no indication in his unhurried pace that he was late for their appointment. Clark shook his head, annoyed. It was so like Will not to consider anyone's schedule but his own.

"One for lunch?" The hostess cocked her head and smiled flirtatiously at Will a few minutes later. He was good-looking, no question about that, with dark hair curling around his face and a reckless sort of gleam in his green eyes. He looked more fit than he had any right to look, considering the way he abused his body.

Will's eyes roved over the pretty girl hugging the menus in front of her. She flushed slightly as he touched her lightly on the arm and leaned in to answer her. Clark's stomach tightened in disgust. Will knew exactly how to use his charms. Clark couldn't believe how many women seemed to fall for his patently smooth approach. He was so obviously a womanizer.

"Two," he heard Will say. "Unless you'd be free to join us?"

She sighed. "I wish!"

I don't like my brother. The thought formed before Clark could check it.

Will caught his eye just at that moment. He raised an eyebrow and grinned rakishly, as if he knew what Clark was thinking. "Never mind, I see my brother's already here," he told the hostess.

"Well, Clark, you look as well-scrubbed as ever," Will said in lieu of a greeting as he pulled out the chair across from his half brother. It wasn't a compliment.

Clark felt his shoulder muscles tighten. *And you look as dissipated,* he thought. "Hello, Will. Did I get the time wrong?"

"Why, am I late?" He didn't bother to look at his watch. "Sorry." Obviously he wasn't. He met Clark's eyes straight on, challenging him to make an issue of it.

Let it go, Clark told himself. *Try to enjoy yourself.*

"Never mind. How are you?"

"Oh, just *spiffy.* And you?"

It took some work on Clark's part, but by the time their meals came, Will seemed to have put aside his sarcastic edge as they caught each other up on their lives, albeit on a superficial level. Clark made light of his work with Command Performance, Incorporated, not mentioning that he'd recently been asked to join the firm as a full partner. He suspected his half brother was jealous of his career success. There was no sense rubbing it in.

He was pleased to hear that Will had finished his computer-graphics program at a local business college, but he was disappointed when Will said he'd been fired from both jobs the school had placed him in. Neither job loss was his fault, of course.

"They never let me do what I was trained for, man. Had me sitting in front of a computer all day long, doing data input. I went to school for *this*? Drove me *nuts*. If they hadn't fired me, I'd have left inside a month."

Clark wondered if he'd shown up drunk at work or maybe not shown up at all. "You heard from Molly lately?" Clark asked, steering the conversation away from Will's employment woes.

"Mother dear? She called last week to say she and hubby number four just bought a house in La Jolla."

"La Jolla, California? San Diego?"

"That's the one."

Clark whistled. "Hubby number four must have some bucks."

"Not that *I'll* ever see any of it. He made her sign a prenup."

"Smart man," Clark said with a sardonic smile. "No one should marry Molly without a prenuptial agreement."

Will looked at him speculatively. "Can't figure out why *you're* not married, Superman. Haven't found your Lois Lane yet?"

Clark shifted uncomfortably. He knew Will's Clark Kent/Superman reference sprang from resentment and not admiration. He was mocking again. "Not yet," he answered in a neutral tone. "How about you? Thinking of settling down with anyone?"

Will laughed without amusement. "Do you really see me as the 'settling down' type, Bro? Look around you! So many women, so little time."

Clark couldn't stop his involuntary scowl. The phrase was,

unfortunately, a common one, though usually offered in jest. Not with Will. Will lived by it.

"I've been living with Peggy," Will continued, ignoring Clark's scowl. "But it's getting old. She's a jealous piece." He took a swig of beer and wiped his mouth with his hand. "Told her I'd run into an old girlfriend last week, a chick we both went to high school with, and she had a hissy fit. 'You so much as call that slut and it's over!'" he mimicked. "I've got half a mind to call her just because Peggy made such a big deal of it."

"So you're waiting tables again," Clark said, deciding the employment tack was preferable to this one.

Will frowned. "You make it sound like slumming."

Against his better judgment, Clark spoke his mind. "Will, you've got so much potential. When are you going to dry out and take advantage of your opportunities?"

"Opportunities?" Will said bitterly. "You're the one who had the opportunities, man. Blind luck you got the father with the money, and I got the one with the looks. Little good they did him." He held up his glass of beer. "You looking for alcohol problems, go look up my old dad. What opportunities did I ever have?"

"You don't have to be like him, Will," Clark said quietly. "Let me get you into a rehab program."

Will set his glass on the table, hard, his face angry. "Anyone ever tell you what a self-righteous jerk you are? Get outta my face, Superman. I can handle my life." He deliberately lifted his beer again, his green eyes narrowed, watching his brother's face. Then he drained the glass and wiped his mouth, not taking his eyes off Clark's.

"Nothin' wrong with me another drink won't fix," he said.

~~~~~

Toni didn't know why she was surprised that Clark showed up at Growth Group Monday night. She'd caught a glimpse of him at church the previous morning, and she knew Ruth and Jack probably would have invited him to join them. Except that Ruth and Jack looked as surprised to see him as Toni was.

As usual, the format for the evening was relaxed and relaxing. First the meal—good food and plenty of it—served and consumed with lots of noise and laughter. A mess of kids and teenagers, mostly Chappie's, made the house seem full to bursting. It was a good place for Danny to be.

After dinner the kids disappeared into the basement playroom with eighteen-year-old Owen Lewis and his girlfriend Julie, and things settled down considerably as the adults gathered in the spacious living room for coffee, tea, and sharing.

When Chappie introduced Clark, Toni realized the minister had been the one who'd invited him to join them. He was quieter than she'd seen him yet; she sensed that he was closely observing the dynamics of the group, taking in not only the words people said but also the ways they interacted.

Toni was subdued as well. She wasn't sure she liked Clark being there. Certainly his presence was one of the things that kept her from sharing her concerns about Danny. She knew the rest of the group would be interested, would want to know what was going on, but Clark was, after all, a stranger.

Somehow she and Clark ended up walking out the door at the same time when the group broke up. "What did you think?" she asked him.

"A nice group of people. Amazing how it quiets down after the kids leave, though." He smiled at her. "Even *you* were quiet."

She looked at him in surprise. "Meaning?"

"I've noticed excitement usually follows you around."

Toni laughed. "Should I feel flattered or offended?" she asked.

"Complimented. I like your energy."

Danny ran past them just then, chasing Chappie and Mary's youngest, Isabel, out to the cars. "That kid requires it," she said to cover her discomfort. Why were compliments so hard to take?

Her intuition told her that Clark was attracted to her, and she half-expected him to call her at the store or drop by sometime that week while she was working. But by late Friday afternoon, as she was counting out the cash receipts in the back room at Paper Chase, she hadn't seen or heard from him. Why did that feel so disappointing? After all, she'd been avoiding men for a year and a half.

The loud jangle of the shop bell cut through the silence of the store like the clamor of an alarm. Toni jumped, then sighed in resignation.

She should have known better than to post the books even ten minutes early, but the weather outside was miserable and she'd had only two customers in the last hour.

"Be right with you," she called.

Running her fingers through her short dark hair, Toni slipped her loafers onto her stockinged feet as she hurriedly scribbled down the amount of cash she'd already counted. She shoved the money tray and the record books into a drawer of the cluttered desk and locked it.

Drawing back the heavy curtain that hung between the office and the sales floor, she stepped out. A girl stood across the room, leaning against the doorjamb, dressed in baggy jeans and a T-shirt three sizes too big, with no jacket despite the rain outside. She had her arms crossed over her chest and a sullen expression on her face. Her hair was dyed an unnatural red,

One ear held a row of gold and diamond studs, and a gold ring jutted from her nostril. As if sensing she was being watched, she raised her head; her eyes, heavily made up, met Toni's with a glint of defiance.

Toni was sure she'd never seen her, but she felt an odd lurch of recognition.

She took a deep breath and walked down the aisle toward the girl, who might have been anywhere between the ages of twelve and twenty—closer to twelve, Toni suspected. The teenager deliberately looked away, her chin set stubbornly, but not before Toni felt another lurch of recognition. The dark eyes held something more than hostility. Longing. Vulnerability. Fear. Feelings Toni knew well.

"May I help you?" she asked.

The girl jerked her head toward the reception area Toni and Ruth had set up for wedding consultations: three folding chairs drawn up to a small lace-covered table stacked with sample books. Toni's eyes followed her silent directive. A woman sat at the table, her back to Toni, leafing through one of the note-books. Pale blonde hair flipped above the collar of a red leather jacket. Her slim, fitted jeans were tucked into high-heeled boots.

"You do weddings?" the woman asked without turning around, as if making eye contact with a shop girl were beneath her.

Toni stiffened at her haughty tone. "We meet all your stationery needs," she said shortly.

The woman looked over her shoulder then, her eyebrows raised. Her face was beautifully made up, though a bit over-done; she had a flair for the dramatic. Toni had learned to do on-camera makeup when she'd modeled, and she appreciated an expert hand. This woman's makeup couldn't, however, soften the hard lines around her mouth or warm the coldness in her eyes.

Another jolt of recognition.

"Are you Antonia Ferrier?"

Toni looked surprised. "Yes…"

"I'm getting married in three weeks. My hairdresser said you could put the wedding together for me."

Hairdresser. Probably Janna Blaine, from church.

"I want it elegant, intimate, and preferably outdoors," the woman continued.

"Elegant, intimate—did you say *three weeks?* You haven't done any planning yet, Miss—?"

"Suzanne DeJong." She ignored Toni's question. "My fiancé's got the money. Whatever it will take. Can you do it or not?" she asked impatiently.

"I—"

Toni stopped as her mind raced ahead of the question. She'd been assisting the wedding coordinator at Tomahawk Community Church for almost a year now; she knew what it took to put together a wedding. At this late date, it would be tough to find a bakery, a florist, or a photographer, let alone a facility to hold an "elegant, intimate, and preferably outdoors" event. June was not the month for a last-minute wedding.

But if she *could* pull it off…

"How many guests?"

"A hundred. I made up the list this afternoon."

Toni swallowed. A garden big enough to hold a hundred guests. A private garden—the public ones would have been reserved for months already. And then someplace for the reception. . .

It wouldn't be easy. On the other hand, maybe a project was what she needed right now. Something to occupy her time and energy. Something to take her mind off her troubles…

"Yes," she said suddenly, surprising herself. "Yes, I can do it," she repeated, feeling a sudden surge of adrenaline rushing through her veins. *Yes.* She *could* do it. She didn't know how yet, but she could. She *would.*

Once again the shop bell jangled. "Mom?" Danny called.

"Here, Danny," Toni called back. She lifted her chin and returned Suzanne DeJong's haughty look. Toni knew that the woman knew if Toni didn't do her wedding, she'd be getting married by a justice of the peace in three weeks, an option she apparently didn't want to pursue or she wouldn't be here.

"My son and my father are here. I'm closing the store, and we're going to dinner. Come back tomorrow morning, and we'll talk about your wedding." She extended a hand. "I'll meet you here at eleven."

The woman stared at her, frowning, then rose from her chair, ignoring Toni's hand. She was beautiful, in an Ice Queen sort of way, Toni thought—or would have been except for her furious expression. Suzanne DeJong wasn't used to being dismissed.

Toni leaned over to give Danny a hug, catching the eye of the teenager leaning against the doorjamb as she did so. Something passed between them—a sudden lift of excitement, a sense of triumph.

I understand, Toni said silently to the teenager. *I know what it's like to live with your mother. I lived with her, too.*

"Hi, Pop," she greeted her father. Straightening, she smiled at the girl. "What's your name?"

The girl pushed away from the wall. "Wynona," she said shyly, her soft voice a surprising contrast to her hard appearance. "Or Wyn. I like to be called Wyn."

Suzanne swept past Toni toward the door, not acknowledging the little boy or the bearded, white-haired man who stood hat in hand inside the entrance, and barely glancing at her own daughter as she reached for the door handle. "If I wanted you to be called Wyn, I wouldn't have named you Wynona," she said coldly.

"Wyn?" Toni said as the girl turned to follow her mother. Wynona glanced back over her shoulder. "Come back with your mom in the morning. You can watch Danny for me while she and I are talking over wedding plans. I'll pay you."

The girl smiled. Toni caught her breath at the transformation. She was beautiful.

7

When Toni arrived at the store the next morning, fifteen minutes before her appointment with Suzanne DeJong, Ruth was vacuuming. Toni had taken special care to dress professionally in a pale yellow suit with a fitted jacket over a white, lace-trimmed blouse and a straight, kick-pleated skirt.

Ruth looked up from her task in surprise as Toni let Danny and herself in the front door. "Toni!" She turned off the vacuum cleaner. "Did you forget you have the day off?"

"Nope." Toni smiled in excitement. "I have an appointment with a client this morning."

Ruth looked at her blankly. "Like I said, did you forget you have the day off?"

"Hang on." Toni pointed Danny to the sample-book table and handed him a tablet and a box of crayons. "How about drawing Aunt Ruthie a picture, Danny? Maybe Brannigan loose in the card store. So she'll remember."

Ruth rolled her eyes. "As if I'd ever forget! Now would you mind telling me what's going on?"

Toni pulled her fingers through her hair as Danny settled at the table, apparently happy with his assigned task. "This woman came in right before I closed last night, so I told her to come back today. I didn't have time to write you a note. She's getting married in three weeks."

"Three weeks! The invitations need to go out *today!* Did you tell her it'll take at least a week to get them from the printer after she's decided what she wants?"

"She doesn't have much choice if she wants engraved invitations. Although, since that new print shop wants our account, I thought I might be able to coax them into a quick turnaround on this order."

"Maybe." Ruth still looked perplexed. "But you don't have to come in on your day off, Toni. I can take care of her."

"It's not just the wedding stationery." Toni grinned at Ruth, barely able to contain her excitement. "She wants to hire me to plan her wedding!"

"What's going on out here?" a male voice interrupted.

Toni turned to see Clark poking his head through the curtain from the back room. "Hi, Clark! What are *you* doing here?"

"He's looking over the books for me," Ruth answered for him, then continued as if they hadn't been interrupted. "Let me get this straight. This woman is getting married in three weeks, she hasn't started to plan her wedding, and you think you can put it all together by then? Toni, it's the last week of May!"

"I can do it, Ruth, I know I can! I stayed up late last night figuring things out. Look at all the creative people at Tomahawk we know! Musicians, we've got plenty of. Karen's a fabulous cook; she's catered a couple of the church weddings I've done. And have you seen Marie's cakes? The woman's an artist!" Toni rattled off another three or four names of church members who might be happy to make some extra cash putting their talents to work.

Toni's enthusiasm was contagious. "I like it!" Ruth said. "You could get your own little business network going through

Tomahawk. It's a great idea, Toni."

Clark cleared his throat. "Anybody interested in a cup of coffee?" he asked.

"Oh, thanks, Clark, honey, but we don't have time!" Ruth exclaimed. "I've got a store to open, and Toni's got a wedding to plan!"

"Yeah," Toni said. "If I can find a place to hold a hundred guests."

Ruth smacked the heel of her hand against her forehead. "She hasn't even reserved a *location!* Who *is* this woman?"

"I don't know, but she says money's no object. I'm taking her word on that."

"No, no, don't take her word. You need a contract. And half the money up front."

Toni felt her confidence slip for the first time since she'd taken hold of the idea of doing this wedding. Maybe she didn't have the experience to pull it off after all. Her anxiety must have shown on her face because Ruth added, "Don't worry about it. I'll help you out with the business part of it. First you've got to get bids from the vendors…"

Toni laughed, her confidence returning. With Ruth on her side, she knew she could do it.

"I thought I'd take Suzanne down to the coffee shop and get a detailed idea of what she wants, then bring her back to Paper Chase to let her look through the sample books. Is that okay?"

Clark, who'd disappeared behind the curtain, reappeared with two steaming Styrofoam cups. "You need coffee," he said, grinning as Ruth reached for one without hesitation.

"Cream and sugar?" she asked.

"Of course. Toni, I left yours black. Anything I can get for you?"

"Black's fine, thanks." She cracked a smile at Ruth. "I thought we were too busy for coffee."

"We are! Clark, take the vacuum back to the office with you."

Toni and Clark exchanged amused glances over her head. Once in a while Ruth took this boss thing over the edge. "Yes, *ma'am!*" Clark said, pulling the plug from the outlet and winding the cord.

"This is what you want to do on your day off, Toni?" Ruth asked.

"To tell the truth," Toni admitted, "I haven't been this excited for a long time. I'm pumped! D'you think I'm crazy?"

"As a loon." Ruth grinned. "Crazy enough to pull it off."

Toni's smile was brilliant. She gave Ruth an impromptu hug. "Thanks for believing in me, Ruthie. You're the greatest!"

She glanced at the table where Danny sat. Clark McConaughey sat across from her son with a crayon in his hand. He looked up just then, his eyes meeting hers.

"We're coloring," he said unnecessarily, raising the crayon in a wave. "Danny says you like purple."

Toni wrinkled her brow in puzzlement. "Yes…"

He held up the paper he'd been working on. Purple flowers, a purple sun, and a big purple message: GOOD LUCK, TONI! BREAK A LEG!

By one o'clock that afternoon Suzanne had chosen her wedding stationery, and Toni had written several pages of notes. The invitations couldn't be ordered until she found a location for the wedding, but she could drop by the print shop that afternoon and see what she could negotiate for next week. She didn't know how, but she fully intended to have a wedding site by Monday morning.

Suzanne had also given her a list of wedding guests and addresses. If the bride wanted to pay to have someone address the invitations, that was fine with Toni. If she didn't have time to do them herself, she could contract the hand lettering out.

She shook her head in amazement. How did she even *know* this stuff? She'd had no idea the education she was getting working for Ruth Denton.

Wynona had taken Danny for a walk while Toni and Suzanne conferred. Suzanne was irritated her daughter wasn't back by the time she was ready to leave. "Send her to the bakery," she told Toni imperiously. "If I'm not there, she can check the market. I can't be waiting around."

"Wyn, thanks so much for watching Danny while your mom and I worked out the wedding plans," Toni told the teenager as she handed her a folded bill several minutes later. Wyn looked like a different person than the sullen brat she'd appeared last night, softer and sweeter despite the harsh make-up and gaudy jewelry.

"You're welcome," the girl responded shyly. Her eyes widened as she saw that Toni had given her a five-dollar bill. "Wow! Thanks, Toni!"

"If Danny was happy, you were worth every penny," Toni said. "How was your walk?"

"We had fun, didn't we, Danny?"

"Sure did, Squid!" Danny threw his arms out and twirled around on the sidewalk outside the store.

Wyn stopped and looked at Toni. "Did he just call me *Squid?*" she asked in surprise.

Toni rolled her eyes. "'Fraid so. It's a sort of game we play, and if Danny's let you in on it, it means you're one of the 'inner circle.' He doesn't let just *any*body play."

"What're the rules?"

"Danny starts it by calling you a name that rhymes with whatever else he's said, like just now: 'Sure did, Squid.' Your part is to say back, 'Name's not whatever-it-was-he-called-you,'

79

and then add another rhyming word."

"Like, name's not Squid, Kid! Right?"

"Right."

Wyn scrunched her face and shook her head. "Weird."

Toni grinned. "Very. We're a weird family. Would you like to baby-sit Danny again sometime?"

"I'd love to!" she said eagerly.

"What d'you think, Danny? Would you like that?"

Danny stopped twirling. "Yeah!" he shouted, thrusting his arms in the air. "Then she can see my fort and meet Brannigan. We saw lots of dogs on our walk," he informed his mother. "German shepherds and a black lab and a wiener dog. But no Irish setter. I wish we coulda had Brannigan."

Toni thought it best not to pursue that train of thought. Brannigan had been banned from car outings for a month, and Danny was none too happy about it.

"I have your number," she told Wyn. "I'll give you a call sometime."

"Wynona, are you coming?" Suzanne DeJong shouted from across the street. "I've got too much to do to wait around for you, young lady!"

Toni gave the girl a sympathetic look. "Better go, Wyn. I don't want to get you into trouble with your mom."

"Doesn't take much," Wyn muttered, sullen once again. She thrust her hands in her jeans pockets and crossed the street without looking back. Toni's heart went out to her.

The meeting with Suzanne had not been particularly pleasant; the woman was pretentious, demanding, and completely self-absorbed, reminding Toni of her own mother in ways that pushed all her buttons. She'd only made it through the interview by reminding herself of the hefty check she'd get if she could pull this wedding off. She didn't know yet how much the check would be; she'd held off giving her client an estimate by telling her she couldn't even guess the fee until she'd located a facility and hired all her subcontractors.

She looked at Danny. "How about lunch, Munch?"

Danny was caught off guard. His mom had never started the game before. He walked beside her down the street, thinking hard, then looked at her with a grin. "Name's not Munch, Crunch."

Toni laughed and pulled him to her side, ruffling his hair. He leaned into her for a moment, then pulled away, racing ahead to the car.

Toni had plenty to keep her busy throughout the rest of the day. After lunch, she put in a call to Cheri Vail, the wedding coordinator at Tomahawk Community Church who she'd been assisting over the last year. Cheri listened to the information she'd acquired from Suzanne and made a couple of suggestions. "Good luck, Toni. You've got your work cut out for you!" she said before hanging up.

She got definite "yeses" from Henry Gillette and Katie Castle to provide the music, and from Marie Quaid to make the wedding cake, and left messages for several other contacts about catering, flowers, and photography. Most of the afternoon she spent on the phone to hotels, churches, halls, and private facilities, trying unsuccessfully to find a location that might satisfy Suzanne DeJong and accommodate a hundred guests.

After dinner—just she and Danny, as Pop was gone on a senior outing for the day—she settled on the living-room sofa with a copy of the *Portland Bride's Resource Book* and a stack of bridal magazines, hoping for a spark of inspiration.

"Hey, Mom, look at me!" Danny interrupted for what seemed like the hundredth time. Toni sighed and looked up to see that he'd changed into his pajamas and a pair of cowboy boots. He did a somersault across the living-room floor and crashed into the coffee table. Brannigan barked sharply.

"Danny! Be careful!" Toni said irritably. "Can't you see I'm *busy?*"

At her sharp tone, Danny literally erupted. Toni could only stare at him in shock as he kicked the sofa where she sat, shouting, "I hate you!" He looked so out of control she was afraid he was going to physically attack her, but he turned and raced down the hallway instead, the Irish setter at his heels. He slammed his bedroom door behind him.

Toni couldn't move for several seconds. Everything she'd felt during the meeting at Danny's school came crashing down on her again...

She jumped up, her fists clenched and her jaw tight. She wanted to scream or to beat on something. Suddenly she remembered Danny beating on the wall with his pillow when he'd wet the bed last week. She grabbed the crocheted afghan from the back of the sofa and whipped it against the ragged overstuffed chair again and again. *"Uh, uh, uh!"* She grunted aloud with each hit.

Finally she let the afghan drop to the floor and stood in the middle of the room with her eyes closed, taking deep breaths and praying, *please God please God please God* silently, without knowing exactly what it was she was asking for. Composure, perhaps; slowly it returned. When she'd calmed down, she walked down the hall to Danny's room and knocked quietly at his door.

"Danny?"

Muffled sobs.

"I know you feel like you hate me right now, but I just want you to know I still love you. May I come in?"

"No!"

She hesitated. "All right. I'm in the living room if you want to talk."

Settling on the sofa, she leafed through bridal magazines and waited.

It took him ten minutes, and when he joined her, he didn't want to talk after all. He curled up in a ball with his thumb in his mouth and cuddled up against her. Toni sat with her arms around him, aching inside. She rocked him and talked to him without even knowing what she said, her touch and soothing tone more important than the words. *I love you,* they told him. When he finally fell asleep, she carried him to bed, pulling off his cowboy boots and tucking the blankets around him. Brannigan looked at her with soulful eyes. She patted the setter's head, whispering, "Watch over him, sweet puppy."

Pop came home tired and went straight to bed. Toni sat in the living room with her magazines and a pair of scissors, cutting out everything that smacked of "elegant and intimate." If nothing else in her life was going to work, this wedding *was.*

The tapping at her front door was so light she almost missed it.

There it came again, a little louder. She sat up, her heart beating faster. Who could possibly be knocking at this hour of the night?

When she saw through the peephole who stood on the other side of the door, Toni couldn't unbolt it fast enough.

"George!" She was so overwhelmed with emotion she couldn't have said anything else if she'd had the words.

The laugh lines at the corners of Georgine Nichol's deep brown eyes and the parentheses etched lightly at either corner of her mouth were the only signs that the woman standing on the front porch was ten years older than Toni was. Tall and willowy, she was the most unpretentiously elegant woman Toni had ever known. Her long wheat-colored hair was pulled back in a classic chignon; she wore full-cut pleated black trousers with low heels and a black turtleneck under her short camel-hair jacket. Strong, steady, and serene, George had always felt to Toni like a safe harbor.

"Figured if you could wake *me* up at midnight, I had every right to do the same. Are you going to invite me in?"

"George—" Toni said again but still had no other words. She took her suitcase and a large shopping bag, set them inside the door, and stepped aside to let her friend into the house. Then she opened her arms. Laying her head against Georgine's, she held on to her as if for dear life.

George held Toni like Toni had held her son two hours earlier, rocking her back and forth and stroking her hair. Toni didn't even know she was crying until she heard her friend say soothingly, "You cry all you want to, Toni. It's okay. You're okay. I'm here."

A sharp bark interrupted the scene just a moment before a small, scared voice inquired, "Mom?"

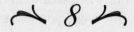

8

Toni opened her eyes to see Danny hunkered down in the hallway, his arms around Brannigan's neck. The look in his blue eyes reflected fear and uncertainty. He looked so forlorn, she thought, in the faded flannel pajamas he was finally outgrowing, his knobby wrists and ankles poking from the arms and legs like sticks from a scarecrow's costume.

She pulled away from Georgine, wiping her cheeks with the backs of her hands, then knelt down and opened her arms to her son. He let go of the setter and rushed to his mother, wrapping his arms around her neck and holding tight. He hadn't held on to her like that for so long.

Brannigan, released from Danny's hold, started barking and bouncing around the room as only a young Irish setter can do.

"Why are you cryin', Mom?" Danny asked against his mother's ear. "Are you sad? Did the lady hurt you?"

Before she could answer, Pop's voice interrupted. "Can't a tired ol' man get a bit o' rest around here? What in *tarnation's* goin' on?"

"I'm so sorry—I'm afraid I'm the one to blame." Georgine stepped into the light, a sheepish expression on her face. "It was the only flight I could get…"

"*Georgine?*" Doc rubbed his eyes and stared, then rubbed his eyes again. "Georgine Nichols! Well, if that don't beat all!" He hurried across the room and thrust out his hand, shaking the blonde's hand with vigor. "Ain't you just a sight for sore eyes! Why didn't you tell us you was comin'?"

Georgine smiled in response to Doc's enthusiasm. "I didn't know myself till yesterday. Doc, it's good to see you!"

"Ain't nearly as good as seein' you is!"

"Mom?" Danny asked again, his voice less fearful than curious now. "Why you cryin'?"

Toni's laugh came out as a hiccup through her sniffles. "I know it sounds crazy, Danny, but sometimes people cry when they're happy." She held him a little away from her and looked into his eyes. "The last time I talked to George, I *was* feeling sad and scared. So she came to see if she could make me feel better." She smiled at Georgine over Danny's shoulder.

"George is a boy's name," Danny said.

"It's really Georgine. George is her nickname." To her friend, Toni added, "Your timing couldn't have been better. You don't know how happy I am to see you!" She turned Danny around in her arms to face Georgine. "Do you recognize my big boy?"

"He's grown, but those eyes are unmistakable. You have eyes just like your mom's, Danny. Did you know that?"

He observed Georgine silently for a moment, then nodded with solemn certitude. "Yep. An' me an' my mom got the same hair, too, 'specially when I haven't had a haircut for a while, Grumpy says."

George nodded back, her brown eyes warm, accepting his observation gravely. How did she know what to do, Toni wondered, when she'd never had a child of her own? Danny needed time to warm up to people, to feel safe, and sometimes adults, even those with children of their own, didn't give him the chance. Georgine approached children in the same way she did everyone: relaxed, low-key, in a manner that respected them as people and accepted their level of interest in her, whatever it happened to be.

It was so unfair, Toni thought, that someone like George, who loved children so much and had longed for one of her own for years, had never had the chance to be a mother, while Toni, who was so undeserving...

She wrapped her arms tightly around Danny from behind. *No,* she told herself defiantly. *I won't listen to that. I'm Danny's mother. I love him. I'm different now. I deserve him.*

"I've had me a long day, Georgine," said Doc, standing in the middle of the living room fiddling with the sleeve of his plaid flannel robe. "You be here long enough we'll get to visit if I go on back to bed?"

"Till Tuesday. I thought I'd like to go to church with you tomorrow, if that's all right, and then take us all out for lunch after. How does that sound?"

"Good," Doc said with satisfaction. He waggled his bushy white brows. "Though we'll just wait an' see who takes *who* out for lunch."

"Please, George, come sit down." Toni gestured toward the worn sofa. "Danny, how about pouring George a glass of juice? I'll bet her wings are tired from flying all the way from San Diego." She let go of him and swatted his bottom toward the kitchen.

"Mom, you silly! She don't have wings!"

"*Doesn't* have wings," Toni corrected automatically. "Well, how'd she get here, then?"

"A nairplane. Or a car. Or on the train."

"A 'nairplane,'" Georgine confirmed, her gentle smile warming her face as she took a seat on the flowered sofa. "And a glass of juice sounds lovely."

Toni sat next to her as Danny skipped off to the kitchen. She put her arm across her friend's back and laid her head on her shoulder. "George, I can't believe you're here! You don't know what it means to me."

"I'd had a Portland trip planned for sometime this year anyway," Georgine said. "Your phone call last week just prompted me to get going on it. I made a few calls last week and have appointments set up for Monday and Tuesday."

"Appointments?" Toni perked up. "You mean for photo shoots? Oh, George! That would be wonderful! You'll stay here at the house, won't you? You can have my bedroom, and I can clear the stuffed animals off the extra twin in Danny's room."

Georgine laughed. "I'll accept your offer for the next couple of nights, but I haven't sold any business *yet!* I'm working on something. If I end up coming back—well, we'll see."

Danny came back into the room, walking with exaggerated care as he balanced a small glass filled to the brim with apple juice. He looked proudly at his mother as he set the glass on the coffee table in front of Georgine.

Toni smiled and patted the spot next to her on the sofa. "Thanks, sweetheart. Come sit by your mom for a few minutes, then it's off to bed with you again. Don't want you dragging around here and making us late for Sunday school in the morning!"

"Why don't you bring me that big plastic sack by the door first, Danny?" Georgine's brown eyes crinkled into a smile. "I think I just might find something for you in there."

A few moments later she pulled out a flat package wrapped in the Sunday comics and tied up with red ribbon, a curly bow cascading across the top. Danny wriggled the ribbon off the package, but instead of ripping into the paper as his mother expected, he held it up and studied it for a moment.

"Read me the funnies, Mom," he said.

"*Please* read me the funnies," Toni said.

Danny, not understanding she was giving instruction in etiquette, looked forlorn. "I can't. It's too hard." He dropped the package in his lap and hung his head. "I'm just dumb."

"Oh, *no*, Danny!" The pain to Toni's gut was as real as if she'd been delivered a physical blow. "Don't *ever* say that!" She wanted to put her arms around him and give him further reassurance, but something stopped her. She grabbed her arms and hugged herself instead. Was it ever going to end—these feelings of guilt that made her feel as if she were coming unraveled inside?

Suddenly she felt a hand on her own, covering the fingers clenched around her arm.

Georgine kept her hand on Toni's as she said to Danny, her voice sympathetic, "You sound really upset, Danny. It doesn't feel good when you *want* to do something, but you just can't figure out *how*, does it? I feel that way sometimes."

"You do?"

She nodded. "I felt that way just this morning when I walked out to my parking spot and discovered my car had a flat tire. I tried really hard, too. I got the book out, and I got the jack out, and I followed all the instructions—at least as near as I could make them out—and I could *not* figure out how to get that jack in the right place so it would lift my car! I was so frustrated!"

"What did you do?" Enthralled by Georgine's story, Danny seemed to have forgotten his own distress.

"Well, the girl next door, who's only seventeen—a *lot* younger than me, Danny, just a *girl!*—came out and saw me struggling, and she walked right over and said, 'Can I help you with that?' And she had my tire changed in ten minutes! Said she learned how in her auto-shop class at school and she was better than the boys at it. I felt pretty dumb," she finished.

"You did?"

"I did. But you know what? I'm not dumb. I'm just better at some things than others. I may not be able to change a tire like Cindy can, but I bet I take prettier pictures. Now—" Georgine sidled over, making a space on the sofa between herself and Toni. "Come on over here next to me, and let's see what we can make out of Garfield."

Toni watched the two of them together and listened in awe as her friend read the comic strip to Danny, stopping to comment on the pictures and helping him sound out several easy words. Her son was giggling with delight as if he hadn't been the picture of dejection just moments ago. As if he hadn't thrown the worst temper tantrum of his life just hours ago.

"You're wonderful with Danny," she told Georgine half an hour later after Danny had once again been put down for bed. He'd been as thrilled with the simple cartoon instruction book inside the package as he'd been with the wrapping, and he had refused to settle down till his new friend had promised to draw with him the next day. "You really need a kid of your own, you know?"

Toni regretted the comment the moment she saw the pained expression flit across Georgine's face. It lasted only a moment, but it reminded Toni once again how unfair her friend's childlessness seemed.

"I do love children," Georgine said. "Maybe I should be taking pictures of kids instead of clothes. Now—" She reached into the shopping bag at her feet and pulled out a beautifully wrapped package. "Something for you."

"For me?" Toni squealed. "George, you shouldn't have!" *You're here,* her eyes added. *I don't need anything else.* "What could it be?" she asked herself aloud as she tore into the wrapping.

"I remembered that story you wrote me about the swan

family at Red Rock Ranch," Georgine explained as the dark-haired woman lifted the gift from her lap. "And the promise God gave you the day you saw the swans for the first time."

"George, it's beautiful." Toni's fingers traced the silk embroidery on the square throw pillow. The deep blue pillowslip, patterned with an oriental gold filigree design, was embroidered in iridescent white with two swans, the graceful neck of the larger curved protectively over the head of the smaller. She turned the pillow over and read the words embroidered in a flowing navy script on a white panel: *He will cover you with his feathers, and under his wings you will find refuge.* It was the verse from the Psalms, as Georgine knew, that had finally made God real to Toni, had made his love accessible.

When Toni looked up at her friend, her eyes were brimming with tears. "George…" She shook her head, unable once again to find the words to express her feelings. "Thank you."

"I love you, Toni." Georgine slipped out of her shoes and curled her legs under her on the sofa. "I know the last week has been scary for you, but I also know how strong your commitment to recovery is. And I know how powerful our God is and to what lengths he will go to keep you safe."

"Yeah." Toni raised her dark, well-defined brows. "Like making me spill my purse all over the bar."

"Did you call your counselor?"

"I called my HMO to see about getting a referral. They'll let me know next week." She chewed at her lip, a nervous habit she was hardly aware of.

"Good. You can do this, Toni. God is with you."

"Sometimes…" Toni hesitated, then rushed on. "Sometimes I wonder why God would even bother with someone like me."

"You're feeling the way Danny feels about not being able to read, Toni. Is Danny any less precious to you because he isn't perfect? Do you love him any less?"

"But he *is* perfect." Toni shook her head. "I don't know how I can say that after the tantrum he threw earlier today, but it's true—to me, he's perfect."

"My point exactly," Georgine said. "You see him through the eyes of love. As God sees you. I know it's hard, but try to give yourself a break, Toni. You're just going through growing pains!"

Nodding silently, though still not convinced, Toni flipped the pillow back to its front. *I feel like the ugly duckling,* she thought as she stared at the lovely embroidered swans.

Ugly ducklings grow into beautiful swans, another voice reminded her.

An hour later as she quietly crawled into the extra bed in Danny's room, her arms were wrapped around the pillow. She stroked her fingers across the raised images as she lay on her back, staring at the ceiling in the dark.

Her first encounter with swans in the wild had been on an early morning walk at the clinic where she'd done her rehabilitation, high in the Centennial Mountains of southwestern Montana, the last refuge of the wild trumpeters.

She'd come across them suddenly, through a break in the trees, floating on the sunrise-colored water like a royal entourage: the cob in front, snowy white against the dark green of the trees across the lake, five fuzzy gray chicks in single file behind him, finally the pen, all elegance and grace.

Stopping, standing quietly, she had watched in astonishment as the scene played itself out: the cob herding his little family into a protected spot along the shore; he and his mate lowering their tails so the chicks, clambering over each other, could climb aboard; the little ones vying for position under the great curved wings of their parents—soft, downy wings that cradled, warmed, protected. The sight of the chicks' heads peeking from beneath the wings of their parents as they glided away had been pure delight.

She'd gone back to her cabin and picked up the Bible that Pop had sent her, as if guided. It had fallen open to the Psalms. One verse had stood out: "He will cover you with his feathers, and under his wings you will find refuge."

It was the first image of God that had ever made any sense to her; that had ever filled her with a yearning to know him. Whoever else God was, from that point on he'd become both mother and father to Toni, the ultimate provider of comfort and care to the wounded child inside who'd never been given enough of either.

She had spent many hours over the next several months sitting on the hill overlooking the nesting site of the great white birds, entranced by their grace and beauty, charmed by their play, fascinated by their interactions—yet sometimes, inexplicably, feeling almost overwhelmed by sadness as she watched. In some mysterious way, the swans had awakened her to her own longings, and in so doing, to her pain.

Much later in her recovery work she had come to understand. The trumpeters' devotion to family life had helped her grieve the losses of her past, the lack in her own childhood of the nurturing and protection that are every child's right.

When she finally made it home, she had vowed, things were going to be different. She was going to be different, make up for what she hadn't been and done so far. She was going to give her son the comfort, care, and confidence she'd never been given herself. Danny would nestle under her wing; she would hold him, carry him, protect him.

And as she'd watched the swans in flight in early autumn, long necks extended, snowy wings spread wide, she'd vowed that someday she would teach her son to fly.

Who am I kidding? she asked herself now, her heart heavy as she stared into the dark. *I don't know how to fly myself...*

9

Clark didn't think he'd ever seen anything as beautiful as Toni had been at Paper Chase yesterday morning. It wasn't just her exquisite face, her exotic, dusky eyes, her perfect skin, her raven's wing hair. A mannequin might be modeled after her exactly but would not possess her beauty.

What made her beautiful was the life force that energized her: her strength, her vitality. Excitement had resonated in her voice and flashed in her eyes as she'd told Ruth about the business opportunity that had presented itself to her, as if out of the blue. Clark didn't believe it had come out of the blue at all; opportunities came when people were ready for them. Toni's talents were wasted working as a clerk in a stationery store; even Ruth, who didn't want to lose her, agreed.

It scared him, how compelling he found her special brand of beauty. The fear hadn't diminished over the week and a half since they'd met, but his desire to spend time with her had increased exponentially. This morning the desire had just over-taken the fear, and he was ready to act.

He bounded out of bed to call her. They would sit together

in church; then they'd go out to lunch—maybe the Black Rabbit at Edgefield Manor, where they could stroll through the herb garden after, watch the glassblower at work, see if anything interesting was playing in the theater. Or maybe they could take a drive out the Columbia Gorge—the lodge at Multnomah Falls, or farther out, across the Bridge of the Gods to Skamania Lodge on the Washington side of the river...

"Toni?" he asked almost breathlessly when she answered the phone.

"Yes?"

"It's Clark McConaughey."

"Oh! Hi!"

Suddenly he was tongue-tied. Thirty-six years old, successful and sophisticated, practiced at the art of making dates—and he couldn't think of a thing to say.

"Hello?" Toni's voice was puzzled. "Are you there?"

"I am! Sorry. I was just calling to see—to ask—Toni, do you have plans for the day?"

"Well, yes...church, of course, and then I'm scheduled to work this afternoon. And—well, I have a special friend here from out of town for a few days. You'll probably meet George at Growth Group tomorrow night. Or..." She paused. "Would you like to join us for church this morning?"

"Oh. Thanks." *George,* he thought. *A special friend from out of town.* The information popped a hole in Clark's grandiose plans, completely deflating his excitement. An out-of-town boyfriend. That explained why she wore the wedding band, why she wanted to keep men at bay. She must get unwanted attention from every quarter.

Including his.

"Actually, I'm not going to make it to church this morning," he said. He wasn't in any mood to meet George, whoever he was. "I try not to work on Sundays, but sometimes when you've got a deadline…" He let the sentence dangle. It wasn't exactly a lie.

"That's too bad, Clark," Toni sympathized.

"Maybe I'll see you tomorrow night, then."

"I hope so. Good luck on your deadline."

"Yeah. Thanks."

After Toni hung up, Clark looked at the portable phone in his hand as if it were his mortal enemy. "I suppose you enjoyed that?" he said, then turned off the phone and went back to bed.

"That was the strangest call," Toni said to Georgine as she hung up the phone and sat down at the kitchen table to her coffee. Not even Pop was up yet to join them.

"What about?" her friend asked.

"I had the feeling, at first, he'd called to ask me out today. But by the end of the conversation it felt like he was making excuses *not* to ask me out. I can't figure out why he called."

Georgine perked up. "*He* who? Toni—have you been holding out on me?"

Toni laughed. "Not holding out, exactly. I have had other things on my mind, you know."

Her friend waved a hand. "Sobriety, your wayward son, a wedding to plan… Where are your priorities, girl! Tell me all about him."

She laughed again. "There isn't that much to tell, really. Clark's a friend of Ruth and Jack who's just moved back to town. He's in sales, I think—some kind of business seminars."

"Cute?" Georgine prompted.

"He was *very* cute with Danny on the boat last weekend. And even sat down to color with him at the store yesterday."

"Good. But you know what I meant by *cute*."

"A hunk," Toni acknowledged. "But more than that, he's got

this great *energy* about him. I don't know how to explain it, exactly."

"A 'Mr. Excitement,' huh?"

Toni shrugged. "Maybe it's just me. Come to Growth Group tomorrow, and you can check him out yourself."

"Believe me, I will," Georgine said. "And I might as well warn you, if I don't think he's good enough for you, I plan to send him packing."

"George, he hasn't even asked me out!"

"He's thinking about it. Believe you me," Georgine teased.

"Maybe I'd better warn *him* about *you*," Toni teased back. "Have yourself another cup of coffee. I need to get the men up."

Georgine's plans to take the Ferriers to lunch had been postponed to dinner, as Toni had to be at Paper Chase by noon. "I'll grab a burger on the way to work," she said as they walked to the parking lot after church. "Sorry I couldn't find someone to take my shift today, George."

"No problem! Danny and I have the afternoon covered—drawing cartoons after lunch, and then I thought I'd see if I could borrow him and Brannigan to shoot a roll of film. What d'you say, Danny?"

"Could we take Brannigan to Ramona's park?" Danny asked hopefully.

"I don't see why not—"

Toni interrupted Georgine, placing her hands on her hips and looking at her son sternly. "You know better than to ask that, Danny," she said. She explained to her friend that the boy and the dog had had an unfortunate escapade inside the store the last time they'd visited. "Brannigan's banned from the car for a while," she finished.

"Well, *that's* understandable," Georgine said cheerfully. "Bet I can get some good pictures right in your backyard. Danny, would you let me shoot my camera from up in your tree house?"

He looked at her dubiously. "You hafta climb a rope ladder," he said.

"I think I can do that. Unless you have a 'No Girls Allowed' rule?"

As far as Toni knew, Danny hadn't thought of such a thing, but apparently he liked the sound of it. "No girls, but a photog'apher's okay," he said.

"Good!" Georgine's dimple showed. "I say we drop your mom off at work and get on back to your house."

"Okay with me, Bee," Danny said, as cheerful as George.

"Bee?"

"Yeah, it's a game…"

Toni shook her head and followed George and Danny to the car.

Between customers throughout the afternoon at Paper Chase, Toni was able to reach Karen Hawes, who'd catered several weddings at Tomahawk, and Noreen Averill, who regularly provided beautiful floral arrangements for the church altar. Karen was thrilled at the opportunity to expand her business outside the church. Noreen had never done flowers professionally and was hesitant about the idea, but Toni's enthusiasm and genuine praise for her abilities won her over.

That left a photographer…

Georgine, Toni thought suddenly. Of course! If Suzanne was willing to pay "whatever it took" to get this wedding together, she'd simply include George's airfare in the photographer's fee.

Not that it was going to be easy talking her friend into doing a wedding. "*Bo*-ring" was George's one-word explanation for abandoning the wedding-photography business early in her career. But Toni had a feeling that Suzanne would go for George's highly dramatic style, not to mention all the tricks of camera angle, enhanced lighting, and makeup that were her stock in trade. Anything to make Suzanne look good. Besides, if George agreed to do the wedding, it meant she'd be back in town *soon*.

Before she could decide whether to call Georgine at home or wait till later when she could utilize all her persuasive powers, the store phone rang.

"Hi, Toni, how's business today?" Ruth responded to Toni's greeting.

"Hi, Ruth! Slow now, but I've had a couple of winter brides in to browse through the sample books, and the garden tea party stuff is selling well. Tying that promotion in with the Rose Festival was a great idea."

"I thought it might be! You did a nice job on the display, which helps. Hey—how are the wedding plans coming?"

"Believe it or not, except for a location, I've got almost everything covered. I just need to talk George into coming back up to do the photography. Of course, if I can't find a place for the party, like *yesterday*, I might as well forget it…"

"That's why I'm calling. I have an idea."

"About a location for the wedding? You've found someplace available? Ruthie!"

"It might not do at all for that fussy client of yours."

"At this point, she doesn't have much choice," Toni said. "Outdoors isn't such a great idea in the middle of June in Portland anyway. It could end up raining."

"That's the beauty of this place, Toni. You can be outdoors, or if it rains, you can be inside."

"Okay—what's the catch?"

"It's a boat."

"A *boat*? Oh!" Suddenly it dawned on Toni. "The *Snow Swan*!" Elegant, intimate, and preferably outdoors, Suzanne had said. What could be more elegant than the shiny brass and polished teak of the newly refinished salons? What could be more intimate than a cruise on the river with one hundred of your

100

closest friends? The upper deck would be wonderful for danc-ing. And if the weather cooperated, the ceremony itself could be on the sundeck.

"Ruth, what a fabulous idea! It's available on the fifteenth? I thought Jack's weekends were booked pretty solid through the summer."

"He had a cancellation just this morning for a six-to-nine slot. I know Suzanne was looking to do an afternoon wedding. Think you can sell her on the idea?"

"I *will* sell her on it," Toni said, her voice confident.

Ruth laughed. "I have no doubts! You could sell a bicycle to an octopus! Oh, there are a couple of bonuses, if you're inter-ested. Jack already had a bartender hired for that night, so he's available. And the party that cancelled had already contracted with a deejay and wanted to know if Jack would pass on his name if he booked another party."

"Perfect!" Bartenders and deejays were outside the realm of the church weddings she'd helped coordinate over the last year. Two less things to worry about if Jack already had them taken care of. "Oh, Ruth, I just can't believe how this is working out. It makes me feel… Well, it makes me feel as if God really does care about the details of my life."

"No question there. But don't sell yourself short, either, Toni. A lot of this has fallen into place because of the kind of person you are, because you like people and spend time getting to know them. And you inspire confidence. I don't know many other people who could have brought together all the people you have in the last two days."

"Really, Ruthie?"

"Really."

Toni felt inordinately pleased. "So when does Jack need con-firmation?" she asked. "And a down payment?"

"As soon as possible. And we need to get the order for the

invitations in *tomorrow*. Jack has copies of the rate schedule and a contract here at the house, by the way. Drop by after work if you want."

"I will."

"Good. Now—get off the phone and take care of my store, girl!"

Toni grinned. "Gotcha, Boss! And Ruth—thanks a million."

By Monday evening Clark had resigned himself to meeting George. He'd felt pretty stupid about missing church just because he didn't want to see Toni with her boyfriend. He had a feeling the people he'd met last week at Growth Group were going to be an important part of his life, and he didn't want to miss out on the chance to get to know them because of some silly infatuation. He'd get over it.

He arrived at the Bradley's a little early, hoping to have some time to talk to Beau before the others arrived. He liked the big, gentle man and had heard through the grapevine he played a mean tennis game. Perhaps they had other things in common as well.

A pretty, petite blonde carrying a squirming toddler was coming toward the door in response to his knock; he grinned at her through the etched glass of the window as she struggled with the lock.

"I still can't believe you're little Emily!" he told her, helping himself into the house as she tried to keep the toddler from wriggling out of her arms.

"Liz'bet," the child answered solemnly. She quieted and looked at him curiously, her brown eyes large and serious.

Emily laughed. "Elizabeth won't let anyone but her be 'little' around here," she said. "Lots of changes while you've been gone, Clark. Come on back to the kitchen. I've got Beau peeling veggies tonight."

She put Elizabeth on the floor. Set free, the little girl apparently couldn't think of anyplace she'd rather be than right by her mother's side. She reached up and grabbed Emily's fingers as they walked toward the kitchen.

"I didn't get a chance to talk to you much last week," Clark said as he followed her. "Are you still teaching?"

"I've cut down to half-time so I can spend more time with the baby."

"Who's here?" Beau looked over his shoulder from his spot at the kitchen sink. "Oh, hi, Clark! Nice to have you back again."

"Thanks. I know I'm early. Need some help?"

Beau wiped his hands on his chef's apron and extended his right arm. "Got it under control."

"How's life at the garage?" Clark asked as he shook Beau's hand.

"Let's just say I wish *I* could cut back to half-time, too," he said, scooping Elizabeth into his arms. She giggled as he bussed her loudly on the cheek. "Best thing I ever did, marrying Em and making a family." He grinned at his wife over the top of the little girl's head. "I recommend it!"

A knock came at the front door. "He knows he'd *better* say that," Emily said to Clark on her way past him to answer the door. A dimple appeared in one side of her cheek. They obviously adored each other.

Good for Emily, he thought. And Beau as well; they'd made a good match. Maybe such a thing was more possible than he'd thought…

The entire group was assembled within the next twenty minutes, and the dining table was loaded down with food. Toni came in wearing kitchen mitts and carrying a steaming dish of spinach lasagna, one of Clark's favorites. As he'd come to expect, laughter and excitement entered the house with her.

"Hi, Em!" she said, setting her hot dish on the tile counter in the kitchen. "Beau, you're looking good! Clark—" She smiled at him. "You must have caught up on your work."

She was dressed in a slim-fitting coral shirtdress that warmed her cheeks and made her exotic blue violet eyes stand out in contrast. Clark realized that every time he saw her he felt slightly stunned. How long would it take for that reaction to stop?

Taking off her kitchen mitts and setting them on the counter, she added, "Everybody, I want you to meet a very special friend who's here from out of town—Georgine Nichols. George, meet Emily, her husband Beau, *and*—" She opened her arms in a dramatic flourish. Beau took her cue and beat rapidly on the counter with his hands in an impromptu drumroll.

"My man of the hour, Clark McConaughey!"

⤙ *10* ⤙

Georgine! George was a *woman!*

Clark felt a sudden release of tension across his shoulders that he hadn't even realized he'd been carrying. At the same time, he felt his face redden—the curse of his fair-skinned ancestry.

"First I've heard about being 'man of the hour,'" he said in explanation to Toni's friend. "I was hoping at least for 'man of the week!'"

Georgine laughed, her warm brown eyes crinkling at the corners. "I'm not sure you'd want to take her on for an entire week," she said.

"George!" Toni protested.

"Well—how many men do *you* think could keep up with your energy for a week?" she teased.

Georgine was a svelte, sophisticated blonde who actually looked more Clark's type than Toni did—if he had such a thing as a "type." But in Clark's eyes, there was no comparison. As usual, Toni absolutely sparkled with life.

The sharing time after the potluck was livelier this week than it had been the week before. Chappie was excited that he was getting to do an entire six-week sermon series at church. As college pastor, he had duties other than preaching and wasn't often assigned to the pulpit. Doc was having a harder time saying good-bye than he'd anticipated in his last days of work at Columbia River College. Jack, having been through the same experience within the last year, encouraged and empathized with him. Katie shared a story about a girl in one of her classes who'd come to her about a family problem Katie had been able to help her with.

"What's going on with you, Toni?" Chappie asked after several others had talked about the current status of their lives. "You seem pretty keyed up tonight."

She laughed, a low-pitched musical sound that bubbled out of her. "You're right, I am!"

As she had Saturday in the stationery store, Toni glowed with enthusiasm as she shared the unexpected request she'd received from a stranger to plan her wedding for her. Clark didn't know everything that might be involved in such an undertaking, but he knew how much preparation went into the seminars that were part of his work. A formal wedding must be ten times the prep.

He listened with interest as she reported she'd talked her client into a wedding on the *Snow Swan*, even though it was available at a different time of day than Suzanne had originally wanted her wedding. He could imagine how persuasive Toni would be in a sales position.

"So," she finished, "this morning Suzanne signed the contract, and then I hand-delivered the order for the invitations to a new printer in town who's been after the Paper Chase account. He promised to have them done by Thursday afternoon. *Engraved!* Unheard of. If I have to stay up all night Thursday, I'm getting those things in the mail Friday morning."

"A wedding on the sternwheeler!" exclaimed Katie Castle, a

106

cute redhead Clark remembered as having a beautiful singing voice. "That sounds so romantic."

"Hope you're not thinking about leaving me so you can get remarried on the *Snow Swan*," Keith, her tall, athletic husband teased.

She crooked her arm through his and leaned her head against his shoulder. "No…but how about an anniversary party?"

"First anniversary coming up," Ruth explained to Clark in an aside.

"Do you forget that you've committed us to a *camping trip* the week of our anniversary?" Keith said, rolling his eyes. "You're looking at our anniversary party right here, Katie Milady." His expansive gesture covered everyone in the room.

"Katie, you're kidding!" Mary Lewis looked distressed. "Why didn't you say something earlier? I don't think we can change our reservations now…"

"It's okay, really, Mary," Keith interrupted. "Our anniversary's the night before we leave." He waggled his eyebrows comically. "I've got something special planned; don't worry about that."

Katie narrowed her eyes. "If you've got something planned, I think I'd *better* worry," she said.

Clark sat back against the cushions of the sofa, resting an ankle over his knee. *Another couple who by all appearances seems well matched,* he mused. If he wasn't careful, this group was going to turn his cynicism about marriage on its ear.

"Speaking of the *Snow Swan*," Jack interjected, "I have an invitation to extend. How about Rose Festival fireworks from the sternwheeler Friday night?"

Toni clapped her hands. "Jack, that's perfect!"

As the others joined her in enthusiastic agreement, Clark overheard Toni explain to her friend Georgine that Portland's annual Rose Festival opened with "the absolute most glorious fireworks spectacle you've ever seen in your entire life," launched from a barge on the Willamette River downtown. *She is so alive,* he thought, watching her from across the room.

"The Rose Festival's so fun, George!" she was saying. "The navy ships come in, and we have a Starlight Parade and then the Grand Floral Parade, the floats all covered with roses, and a carnival and all kinds of music, plus the Dragon Boat races... Maybe you could stay a few extra days?" she coaxed.

Georgine laughed. "Ever thought about going to work for the Portland Visitors Association?" she asked. "Or the Portland Chamber of Commerce?"

Clark found his way to Toni's side as the group broke up later in the evening. "Fireworks on the *Snow Swan* sounds fun, doesn't it?" he said, trying to sound casual. "Going to be there Friday night?"

"Wouldn't miss it. You?"

"I'll be there." He smiled at her, then turned to Georgine. "George—I can't tell you how happy I was to meet you tonight."

"Well—thank you!" Toni's friend looked a little taken aback at the fervency of his comment.

Clark didn't care in the slightest. Imagine, George being a woman!

Thursday evening found Toni at Emily Bradley's home once again, this time armed with wedding invitations. The printer, true to his word, had completed the order on schedule, and Toni was pleased with his work. The stationery was simple and elegant, a flowing black script on a white linen weave stock. Whatever her shortcomings, Suzanne did have impeccable taste.

Ruth, Katie, and Emily had volunteered to help Toni address the invitations. With four of them working, she'd have no problem getting them out by the next morning. Her client was cutting things close, but she wouldn't be able to complain—at least not legitimately—about Toni's efforts.

"Has Georgine gone back home?" Emily asked as they sat down to work.

"For now. But she's coming back to shoot the wedding in mid-June."

"Great! Is that what she does in San Diego?" Katie asked, reaching for a handful of envelopes from the box in the middle of the table.

"She's done a few weddings, but really she's a fashion photographer. That's how I met her." Toni handed address lists to the three women as Katie distributed the envelopes. "A couple of her old friends from San Diego have relocated to Portland to start a mail-order business—a line of children's play clothes. They want George to work for them, handle the art direction for the catalogs, but she's not sure she wants to give up photography." Toni sighed. "I would be *so happy* if she moved to Portland!"

"She seems like a nice woman," Ruth said.

Toni nodded. "An understatement if I ever heard one."

"What about Clark, Ruth?" Emily asked. "I've been dying to find out more about him."

"He's a doll, isn't he?"

Agreement all around, though Toni held back from making any comments.

"And you've only seen him in his networking uniform," Ruth said. "You should see him all dressed up."

"*Networking* uniform?" Emily asked.

"I swear—he has three entire wardrobes. *Organized* in his closet."

Toni gasped in mock amazement. "He's *orderly?*" she said. "Are you *sure?*"

Ruth laughed. "I kid you not," she said. "He's got expensive business suits, silk ties, and Italian leather shoes for leading seminars and making sales calls, casual slacks and pullover sweaters like you've seen him wear for networking, and since he works at home and can wear whatever he wants there, its either shorts and a T-shirt or sweats. Looks pretty good in those, too, by the way."

Katie sighed. "I can imagine..."

"Katie!"

"Oh! Not as good as Keith, of course." She grinned. "What exactly is it he does for a living, Ruthie? I haven't quite figured that out."

"Sales of some kind, I gathered," added Emily. "He could pretty much sell *me* anything!"

"Believe it," Ruth responded. "Clark sold cars to pay his way through college, and he once went for twenty-three days selling a car *every day*. Not your run-of-the-mill salesman! What he's doing now, with his father and two other partners, is marketing, developing, and delivering custom business seminars for banks and large corporations. It's perfect work for him; it combines his background in finance and industry, his marketing skills, his research and writing skills, and his love of the spotlight. He is *not* the type to fade into the background!"

"Never a dull moment," Toni said dryly.

"Never." Ruth finished an address with a flourish of her pen.

"And he's *single!*" said Emily. "Ruthie, why didn't you tell me about him when he was still living in Seattle? My sister Abby's up there, y'know."

"Now why didn't I think of her earlier?" Ruth said. "I've been introducing him to nice single women for years, but nothing's ever come of it."

"He won't survive as a single man at Tomahawk," Emily said with certainty. "Too many available women. Really *nice* available women."

Ruth laughed. "If that was all it took, Clark McConaughey would have been married a long time ago. There've always been available women."

"So what's his problem?" Toni asked.

"No problem. He's just never decided marriage is what he wants. If he ever does, I don't think he'll dillydally. Once Clark decides he wants something, he goes for it with all he's got. And usually gets it."

"So what's he like, Ruth?" asked Emily. "Underneath the smooth exterior?"

Ruth straightened the stack of envelopes in front of her. "Clark is just the best, that's all. Cream of the crop. Intelligent, interesting, caring, kind—he was always wonderful with Sunny, who was determined for years she was going to marry him. Independent, gregarious, self-assured without being arrogant like successful men can be..."

"You make him sound like a god," Toni snapped.

The other three women looked at her in surprise.

"Sorry," she said sheepishly. "He just sounds a little too good to be true, know what I mean?"

"Well, I have to admit I'm prejudiced," Ruth said. "And he does have his faults. I just don't think it's my place to talk about them." She smiled wryly. "You get to know anyone, their faults show up eventually."

Some of us sooner than others, Toni thought tiredly. *Some of us have more and bigger faults.*

Why even bother to be interested in a man like Clark McConaughey? She could never measure up...

"These look fabulous, ladies," Toni said an hour later as she slipped the finished invitations, stamped and sealed, into the envelope boxes. "Maybe we should start our own little business," she added, tongue in cheek. "Marketing, developing, and delivering custom envelopes. What d'you say?"

~~~~~

When Toni called Suzanne the following morning to tell her the wedding invitations were in the mail, the phone rang half a dozen times before anyone answered. Then it was Wynona.

"She's not here," the girl said shortly.

"Could you tell her the invitations went out this morning? I promised I'd let her know."

"I guess."

Toni hesitated, then commented, "You sound upset. What's wrong, Wyn?"

"Nothing much. I hate my mother, that's all." Wyn's voice was hard and angry.

"What happened?" Toni asked gently.

"She never keeps her promises!" the girl burst out. "Never. She promised we were going shopping to pick out my maid of honor dress tonight, but now she's going out with Frank instead. I hate him. He's fat and old and disgusting, and he wants me to call him Dad. No way. I don't even wanna be a stupid maid of honor."

Toni was silent, thinking fast. She understood well what Wyn was feeling. Even the words were familiar. But Suzanne was her client here; she'd be walking a thin line taking sides with her daughter. "I'm sorry, Wyn," she finally said. "You must be really disappointed." She paused, then added in a lighter tone, "Does this mean you'd be free to baby-sit tonight?"

"Really, Toni?" The girl's voice colored suddenly with hope. "You need me?"

"I could use your help." The idea hadn't occurred to her till now, but she liked it. "Danny and I've been invited to watch the Rose Festival fireworks aboard the sternwheeler *Snow Swan*, where your mom's wedding is going to be," she explained. "It would be really nice if you could come along to watch Danny so I could spend some time with my friends without worrying about where he is or what he is doing. How about it?"

"Fireworks on a boat? In the middle of the river? Cool!"

Toni smiled at Wyn's excitement. "But I don't know if my mom will let me."

It is amazing how quickly one's excitement can be deflated, Toni thought.

"Let me talk to her," she said. "D'you know what time she'll be home?"

Within an hour, Toni had made the arrangements with Suzanne, who seemed hardly to care where her daughter spent her time as long as she didn't bother her mother. Toni felt her anger mounting every time she had to deal with the woman. Thank goodness she'd be through with her in a couple of weeks.

The phone rang just as she was leaving for work later that morning. "Ms. Ferrier? Ellen Shaw. I just have a minute here before I have to be back in the classroom, but I thought I'd try to catch you. We'd like to schedule an appointment to discuss Danny's test results with you."

Toni's stomach tightened. She couldn't face that lineup of specialists again; they were worse than a firing squad. "I'm very busy the next few weeks, Mrs. Shaw. Couldn't you just tell me over the phone?"

"We really need your input. We could make the meeting before school instead of in the afternoon if that would make it easier for you."

You don't understand! Toni wanted to shout. *There's nothing you can do to make it easier!*

Ruth and Toni arrived at Paper Chase at the same time, Ruth to work in the office paying bills and Toni to open the store. The older woman studied the younger with concern as she let them both in the front door.

"Toni? You feeling all right? You don't look well."

"The truth? I feel lousy."

"Why didn't you call? Come on in—let's see if we can't find someone to cover your shift."

"No!"

Ruth looked taken aback by her sharp tone.

"I mean, I doubt anyone's available…"

"Look, if worse comes to worse, *I* can watch the store today and pay bills tomorrow. There's no sense you working when you're sick."

"I'm not sick, Ruth. I need to keep occupied."

Ruth looked at her with a puzzled frown and said nothing.

Toni shoved her purse beneath the counter, then pushed aside the curtain to the storage area to hang her jacket.

"We have half an hour till the store opens," Ruth said from behind her. She brushed past Toni to get to the desk set up in the back corner of the narrow room. "Start a pot of coffee, get the cash register set up, then report to me before you finish opening duties."

"Sure."

Ten minutes later Toni stood nervously next to Ruth's desk, chewing her lower lip. Ruth looked up, peering over the top of her reading glasses. "Get yourself a cup of coffee, and pull up the chair," she said.

"I've still got to get the floor vacuumed," Toni protested.

"I'll help. Right now, I want you to relax."

They sat in silence for several minutes, sipping at their coffee, Ruth looking as laid-back as if she were lounging on the deck of a cruise ship and Toni feeling absolutely seasick.

"It's Danny," Toni finally said.

"Ah."

More silence.

"Remember the meeting I had with his teacher a couple of weeks ago?"

"The night of your dad's big retirement to-do. I thought that was it. You were an hour and a half late for dinner after that meeting. What happened?"

A lump in her throat, Toni gave Ruth a brief sketch of her experience at Danny's school. She didn't include where she'd found herself afterward. "Mrs. Shaw called this morning. I think they want to put him in special ed."

"Good. He'll get all the help he needs to be successful."

"You don't get it, Ruth! There's nothing *wrong* with Danny. He just marches to his own drummer, that's all. They have no right to label him 'retarded' or 'learning disabled' or whatever they're calling it now!"

Ruth ran a finger around the rim of her coffee cup and stared off into space. "I remember when the doctors first told us Sunny had Down's syndrome," she said after a moment. "I

116

didn't believe them, even with Sunny's obvious physical symptoms. I *wouldn't* believe them, not for weeks. Turned out my denial wasn't about Sunny at all. It was about *me*. About feeling guilty."

"What d'you mean?"

"I was almost forty when I got pregnant with Sunny," Ruth answered. "Jack and I'd been married a year, and I wanted a baby more than anything. It wasn't as common back then for a woman my age to bear a first child, but I was healthy. The doctors warned us that the incidence of birth defects increased as the mother's age increased—particularly Down's syndrome. Jack wondered if we oughtn't adopt a child instead of trying to get pregnant, but I wanted a baby of my own. Besides, that kind of thing always happens to someone else, I told myself. Wouldn't happen to us."

Toni was silent.

"Is this about Danny or about you, Toni?" Ruth gently asked.

Toni closed her eyes and stretched her neck in a slow circle, trying to loosen the tightening muscles. "Both," she finally admitted, opening her eyes. "It's not the same as it was with you and Sunny, Ruth. There's nothing you could have done to prevent Sunny's handicaps except not have her. And I know from what you've told me you were never sorry you had her. Well, I'm not sorry I had Danny either, but I am sorry *how* I had him. Danny's having problems because *I screwed up*."

She brushed away a single tear escaping down her cheek. "I'm not lying to myself anymore, Ruth." Her voice was choked. "I know what I've done to Danny."

Ruth reached over to wrap her fingers around Toni's. "And I know you've done everything you could for him the last two years," she said. "You know that God's already forgiven you, don't you, Toni? Can't you accept his forgiveness?"

Toni shook her head sadly. "I've tried, Ruth. But the plain fact is, accepting God's forgiveness won't make a lick of difference for Danny."

Ruth was silent for a moment. Then she said, "I wish you'd felt free to talk to me sooner. This can't be easy for you to deal with."

"I thought I'd be okay. I *am* okay."

Ruth shook her head. "Dealing with your feelings about Danny is a major thing, Toni. You don't *have* to be okay about it."

"I talked to Georgine when it first happened," Toni said. "And I'm still waiting to hear about a referral from the HMO to see a counselor. But I know what they're going to say. If I'm not actively drinking again, I'm not covered." Her mouth twisted in a humorless smile. "Maybe I should go on a bender."

Ignoring the cynical suggestion, Ruth said, "Not covered unless you've relapsed? That's ridiculous! Surely not."

"I tried to get in once before, last Christmas when I was feeling depressed. I was scared I *was* going to relapse." She shrugged as if it didn't matter. "They said they couldn't help me."

"What did you do?"

"Went to see Chappie instead." She looked across the desk at Ruth, sudden hope leaping inside her. "I don't remember everything he said, but I remember it helped. And I remember he prayed with me."

"Will you let me pray with you?" Ruth asked, her voice gentle.

Toni swallowed the lump in her throat and nodded.

Ruth closed her eyes and prayed simply, "I love Toni, God, and it hurts me to see her in pain. I know it hurts you, too. Open her up to your healing love. Give her peace in the knowledge that you're working in her life even through the pain."

Yes, Toni thought, squeezing Ruth's hand. *Thank you, God, for being with me even when I forget you're there.* She took a deep breath and felt as if she were inhaling the very peace her friend had prayed for her.

"Amen," Toni murmured. Then, opening her eyes, "Thanks, Ruthie. I needed that reminder. What would I do without you?"

"We all need each other, Toni," Ruth answered gently. "What would *I* do without *you?*"

The sky was overcast but the night warm as the *Snow Swan* pulled away from the dock at nine o'clock that evening with a capacity crowd. The boat would cruise the Willamette for half an hour before docking along the seawall for an unfettered view of the fireworks that traditionally kicked off Portland's annual Rose Festival.

At Clark's suggestion, Jack had given away a boatload of tickets for the fireworks cruise as a promotional gimmick, some of them through the local public broadcasting station for their membership drive and some through the corporations he'd identified as possible clients for on-board meetings and seminars. He'd even hired a deejay; the varnished teak deck of the upper salon made a great dance floor.

Again at Clark's suggestion, Jack also had his relief captain working tonight so he could mingle with the crowd. "Connecting personally with potential clients is essential if you're going to sell them on the boat, Jack," Clark had pointed out. "They see you, they like you, they're having fun, they think about having their next meeting or company party on board."

"Why is it your ideas always cost me money?" Jack grumbled.

"You've got to spend money to make money."

"Yeah, yeah." But he'd gone along with Clark's ideas.

The crowd, a good mix of personalities ranging in age from mid-twenties to probably mid-fifties, with a handful of kids thrown in, buzzed with energy. The bar on the lower deck was already busy. Clark bought himself a cola and climbed the stairs to the upper deck.

He wasn't surprised to see that the sundeck was the place of choice for the kids. Danny Ferrier was one of them, leaning over the railing next to a somewhat frightening teenager, a girl with garish red hair and a row of rings and studs in one ear. When she turned to say something to Danny, Clark saw that her eyes were heavily made up and she had a ring in her nose to go along with her earrings. She definitely stood out in the crowd of conservatively dressed revelers.

"Looks like you disapprove of my choice in baby-sitters," an amused voice behind him said. He turned to see Toni standing there, looking as beautiful in faded jeans and a bulky scarlet sweater as she did dressed up for work.

"Was I that obvious?" he asked sheepishly. "I try not to judge on appearances, but some people make it difficult." He tilted his head in a puzzled expression. "She *does* seem an odd choice," he admitted.

"Wyn's the daughter of the bride I'm working with. Danny likes her. Goes a long way with me."

Clark nodded. "She's a pretty girl once you get past the weirdness."

Toni smiled at him, and he forgot all about Danny's baby-sitter. Forgot everything except Toni. "I hope you don't think me too forward for saying it," he said before he could stop himself, "but you really are one of the most beautiful women I've ever known."

She looked uncomfortable at the compliment, shifting her eyes away from his. "Thank my genes." Then, recovering, she tossed him a mischievous grin. "You're not so bad yourself."

He laughed. "Thanks, I think! Have you ever thought of modeling?"

"Been there, done that. It's not the world for me."

"Really? I did some modeling for a couple of local sportswear companies when I was in college, and I always thought it was kind of fun."

"Once in a while, maybe. As a full-time career, no." Her eyes slid away from his again. "It was life in the fast lane in L.A. I don't want any part of it anymore."

"Oh?"

She ignored his invitation to elaborate. The deejay, warming up the crowd behind them with his patter, started a big-band disc and invited Ruth and Jack to start the first dance. The captain led his wife out on the floor and swung into an energetic foxtrot as the crowd clapped.

Toni cocked her head at Clark. "Care to dance?"

"How could I possibly turn you down?" He finished his drink and set the empty cup on a passing waiter's tray, then took her hand to lead her onto the floor; it felt cool in his, her fingers long and slender. He involuntarily tightened his grip.

They danced well together, Toni following his lead effortlessly, as graceful as he'd imagined she would be. He kept his moves as impersonal as possible for the very reason he wanted to draw her close: she was intoxicating, too desirable for comfort. Once she was in his arms, he didn't want to stop dancing.

"Only one dance?" she pouted as he led her off the floor. "It's such fun, and I don't often get the chance."

Too busy fighting off predators? he wondered. He suddenly realized she wasn't wearing the gold band on her finger. Did she feel safe with him, then? *He* certainly didn't feel safe with *her.*

"We can dance again later," he said. "We haven't had much time to get to know each other. I thought we could have a drink and talk."

"As long as you promise another dance," she agreed.

Clark led the way downstairs, paid for a couple of colas at the bar, and guided Toni to the stern of the lower deck. The lighting, the low ceiling, the soft patina of the wood, and the gentle swish of the paddle wheel created an intimate atmosphere in the salon. The music piped in from upstairs was muted enough that they could carry on a conversation, but loud enough they had some privacy in the close quarters. He found a spot at one of the tables and pulled out a chair for Toni.

"She's a beautiful boat, isn't she?" Clark asked, just to say something. "Bet you didn't have any trouble convincing your bride it would be the perfect place for her wedding."

"Actually, Suzanne hasn't been an easy sell on *anything*. I think it's her way of maintaining control."

"What's the deal with her three-week time line on the wedding?" asked Clark. "Last-minute decision or poor planning?"

Toni rolled her eyes. "Who knows? She pays the bills; I don't ask questions."

"Don't forget I have lots of business experience. I'd be happy to give you some pointers if you need some advice."

"Thanks." Her blue violet eyes sparkled. "Though something tells me your advice doesn't come cheap."

He grinned. "According to Jack, it isn't cheap even when I give it to him free. Tonight's cruise for instance…"

Toni listened with interest as Clark explained why he'd encouraged Jack to give away tickets for the fireworks cruise. "Investment in advertising is one of the smartest things a small-business owner can do," he finished. "Jack has a beautiful boat and great potential for making it pay, but unless people know about it, he's not going to make it."

"Well, you *sound* like you know what you're talking about," she teased.

He laughed. "Forgive me if I sound like a know-it-all. One thing my father drilled into me early on was to act as if I knew what I was doing no matter what. Sound advice, believe it or not. Whenever I practice it, I find out I really *do* know what I'm doing!"

"Where's your dad now?"

"Seattle. Moved there maybe a dozen years ago. Six years ago he formed Command Performance, Incorporated. We do corporate training."

"And you're a partner now, Ruth says."

Clark arched an eyebrow. "She does, does she? And what else does Ruth say?"

"Only that you're one notch down from God," she teased.

He felt himself redden. "Ruthie does tend to exaggerate, doesn't she?"

"Only time will tell," Toni answered dryly. "And your mom? She's still alive?"

"Alive and superficially well in San Diego with her fourth but not necessarily last husband. I doubt she'll ever find anyone who satisfies her."

"At least she marries them."

"What?" Clark didn't understand the cryptic comment.

"My mom was always living somewhere in California with her fourth, or fifth, or sixth but not necessarily last *boyfriend*. Which means I was, too."

"You didn't grow up with your father?"

"Didn't even know him till I was fifteen. Or didn't remember, anyway. I was two when they divorced. Pop was supposed to share custody, but my mother picked up and left without telling him. He never found us."

"You're kidding! So she basically kidnapped you."

"Basically. Then barely paid any attention to me till I got to an age where she thought I was trying to steal her boyfriends.

Believe me, no attention was better than the attention she gave me then. Eventually she shipped me back to Pop." Toni seemed lost in her own thoughts for a moment. Clark didn't interrupt.

"You're an only child, then?" she finally broke the silence.

"Not exactly."

"'Not exactly'? What does that mean?"

"I have a half brother, Will. Ten years younger than I am. About your age, I'd guess. Twenty-six?"

Toni nodded. "You never lived with him?"

"For a few years, when he was a baby. Molly and Royce— my mom and dad—shared custody of me for a few years. I helped take care of Will when I was at Molly's." He grinned. "Even learned how to change diapers! But Willis Sr. didn't care much for me. Molly made her choice, and it wasn't me."

"That must have hurt. What were you, thirteen or fourteen?"

He nodded.

Toni got that faraway look in her eyes again. "That's when things got crazy for me, too," she said softly.

A loud crackle through the sound system interrupted their conversation. Jack's voice came over the intercom: "Fireworks are scheduled to start in five minutes. If you'd like to make your way to the upper deck..."

Clark grabbed Toni's hand and pulled her toward the stairs. "We'll finish this conversation later," he promised over his shoulder.

~ 12 ~

Toni stood on tiptoe in the crowded upper salon, craning her neck as she searched through the windows for Danny and Wyn on the sundeck. "I see them," she told Clark, pointing. "Think we can get out there?"

"Follow me." Clark grabbed her hand once more and pushed his way through the crowd, polite but forceful.

"Pretty good at getting what you want, aren't you?" Toni teased him as they joined Danny and Wyn at the starboard railing. The *Snow Swan* was anchored next to the harbor wall between the Morrison and Hawthorne Bridges.

Even in the gathering gloom of night, she could see that both banks of the river were crowded with spectators. Blinking white lights outlined the rides at the amusement park set up in Waterfront Park. She'd have to try to find time to take Danny to the Fun Center; maybe this year she could talk him into the scarier rides that she'd always liked best.

"Hi, Mom," Danny said.

"Hi, guy." She sidled in next to him. "Didn't save us much room." She smiled at the girl standing next to her son. "Is he being good for you, Wyn?"

"Huh? Oh…yeah." Wyn was staring unabashedly at Clark.

Toni smiled to herself. She'd have guessed Clark's clean-cut good looks would have been unappealing to the grunge-inspired girl, but Wyn's mesmerized expression said otherwise. "Wyn, I'd like you to meet Clark McConaughey. Clark, Wynona DeJong."

"How do you do, Miss DeJong?" Clark said politely. "Toni tells me you're baby-sitting tonight. You must do a good job if she trusts you with her son."

Wyn nodded and looked away, suddenly shy.

Clark punched Danny's arm playfully. "Having fun, Dan-the-Man?"

Danny grinned. *That* nickname was going to win him a friend for life, Toni thought.

A loud whistle cut through the chatter around them, and a bright explosion suddenly lit the sky, the boom coming a fraction after the sparkling red-and-gold streamers burst from their hot center and arced up and out in long octopus arms. Danny, jumping with excitement, grabbed his mother's hand as a single loud crash of cymbals came over the outside speakers. Then the music took off on a wild ride as a trio of star shells blew just seconds apart from each other, casting eerie light and color on the underside of the high cloud cover. The show was on, music and fireworks together creating a breathtaking fantasia of light and sound.

Toni felt Clark at her back, not so close as to be touching, but close enough that she could feel his warmth in the cool night air. He wasn't much taller than she was, maybe three inches, but his solid strength behind her made her feel protected.

Protected. Besides Pop and Jack and the other men in her Growth Group, safety wasn't something she'd often felt in the presence of men. She knew that part of her comfort with Clark was his friendship with Ruth and Jack and Chappie. In some ways, he seemed an extension of the established group of friends she'd slowly come to trust over the last year and a half.

In other ways, Clark still felt slightly dangerous. How could that be, that one person could inspire such opposite reactions as safety and danger?

Or was the rush of adrenaline she felt when she was near him something other than fear? She'd loved whirling with him on the dance floor, not just because he was a good dancer and she liked dancing, but because there was something about him that sparked her to life in a way she'd never experienced before. She liked the way she felt around him; he energized her, exhilarated her.

You also liked the way it felt to be high, she reminded herself. She shivered involuntarily.

"Cold?" Clark asked in her ear. She shivered again.

A moment later his jacket was around her shoulders. Again she was mindful of the paradox: On one hand, the gesture felt protective; on the other, the weight of his jacket on her shoulders felt like an unfulfilled longing she hardly dared acknowledge. Longings could consume one so...

She took a deep breath and cleared her mind of conscious thought. For a little while she let herself be only sensation: a receptor of the popcorn explosions of color, of the beat of the music, of the acrid smell of gunpowder, of the feel of the rail, smooth under her palms, and of the almost imperceptible motion of the boat beneath her feet.

The sky exploded in one final burst of light and color and sound. Toni's breath caught in her throat at the spectacular display, and then she was cheering and clapping with the rest of the crowd, carried away on a wave of excitement.

A few minutes later the paddle wheel started churning. Toni pushed away from the railing and grabbed Danny by the hand when the deejay put on an energetic song. She pulled him through the crowd and into the salon for a lively dance. "Come on, Clark, Wyn," she called. "Join us!"

Wynona was thrilled—maybe a little *too* thrilled, Toni thought. She certainly wasn't trying to hide her crush on Clark. He threw Toni a look of pleading desperation over Wyn's head. Toni threw him back a grin and a wink, spun Danny in a breathless circle.

After a couple of songs, she took mercy on Clark and asked Wyn to take Danny downstairs to the bathroom.

"The *head*, Mom," he said impatiently.

"Right. The head." She fished a pair of dollar bills out of her jeans pocket and handed them to Wynona. "How about getting a soft drink for each of you? We'll be back to the dock in no time; you can wait for us downstairs."

Wyn was reluctant to leave her dance partner, but she finally followed Danny to the stairway, dragging her feet.

"Took your time," Clark grumbled. He grabbed Toni around the waist and pulled her onto the dance floor. "And just what was that wink all about, huh?"

Toni smiled up at him with an innocent expression. "Just thought you were a cute couple, that's all."

He groaned. "Very funny. Fifteen years older and a dozen less earrings, she *still* wouldn't be my type."

"Oh? And just what *is* your type?"

He pushed her away a little and looked down at her face, his sandy brows drawn together in a mock frown. "Are you flirting with me, Antonia Ferrier?"

"I *must* be out of practice if you can't even tell!"

He laughed. "Just checking. I notice you aren't wearing the wedding ring tonight." He hesitated, then added, "Feeling okay about hanging out with me?"

She turned her head away to gaze out the window for a moment. She'd taken the ring off and put it back on several times before finally relegating it to her jewelry box tonight.

And the fact was, she was feeling *very* okay about hanging out with Clark.

Turning back to him with a smile, she answered, "I will be okay if you stop asking questions and just dance!"

"Done," he said, pulling her close as the deejay put on one last slow song.

They swayed to the music, not needing words.

Toni couldn't say no when Clark asked if she'd go out for a cup of coffee after she'd gotten Wyn and Danny home, even though she had to open at Paper Chase the next day. She didn't want to say no.

They met at midnight at an all-night diner near Toni's house and drank decaf and shared a hot fudge sundae, and later a grilled ham and Swiss on rye, and later still an order of onion rings. They talked about inconsequential things and laughed at nothing, leaning toward each other over the table, once in a while touching in the almost unconscious way people do when they like each other. They outlasted their tired waitress and had far more energy than her 2:00 A.M. replacement.

"Tell me more about your brother," Toni finally prompted. "I *dreamed* about having a brother or sister when I was growing up."

"My half brother," Clark corrected. "And believe me, Will is no dream. More like an ongoing *nightmare*."

She looked at him in surprise. It didn't seem the kind of thing he would say.

"He's a drunk," Clark told her, his gaze direct. "Worse, he won't admit it. 'Nothin' wrong with me another drink won't fix.' One of his favorite lines."

Clark's voice betrayed not a glimmer of sympathy. Toni's heart quickened with anxiety. What would he say if he knew

129

about her own problems with addiction? Or did he know? Her history wasn't exactly a secret around Tomahawk.

"You said earlier you didn't grow up with him," she said. "When did you find out about his drinking?"

Clark's fingers began an agitated tattoo on the tabletop. "Yeah, I didn't see him much when he was growing up, at least not while Molly was still with Willis. But by the time I got back from Seattle with my MBA—I was twenty-four, Will fourteen— Molly was on her third husband, and Will was in a lot of trouble: skipping school, failing most of his subjects, sneaking out at night. I found out later he'd already been drinking and smoking pot for a couple of years."

Toni nodded without commenting. Sixth grade had been the year she'd begun her own path of substance abuse. There was always plenty of alcohol available at home, and her mother was drunk so often she didn't notice if the levels in her bottles were a little lower than they'd been the time before. Toni was smart enough never to finish a bottle off.

"I got Will involved in Royce's Youth Entrepreneurial Services," Clark continued.

"Did that help?"

"For a while. He was a little in awe of Royce, I think—of Royce's success. His own father was a drunk, too, and a ne'er-do-well who got by on his looks and charm and couldn't hold a job longer than a tick's life span." Clark wrapped his hands around his coffee cup and stared down into the dark liquid, silent for a moment.

"What helped Will the most," he went on, "was introducing him to Jack and Ruth—they took him in the same way they'd taken me in. He really adored little Sunny." Once again he paused.

"It sounds as if everyone adored her," Toni said.

He nodded. "She was sweet, undemanding. Generous with

her affection. Sometimes I think she was the only person Will ever allowed himself to love."

Toni nodded again. Love was a dangerous thing to feel for a kid whose daily diet was rejection. "He must have been devastated when she died."

"He was. We all were, of course, but Will completely fell apart. At least Jack and Ruth and I had our faith to fall back on. Will didn't believe in God—especially after Sunny died. And—he saw the accident. She died in his arms."

"Oh, no! How horrible!"

"It was."

"That's when he started drinking again," Toni said. It was a statement, not a question.

Clark nodded. "I don't think he'd ever stopped entirely, but it got a lot worse. He dropped out of school. Molly kicked him out of the house half a dozen times, but she always let him come back home. Will was a master manipulator—still is. He knew how to play her."

"Did he know how to play you?"

"I wouldn't let him. I tried to step in and play the father role, which of course went over like a lead balloon. He *still* resents me for 'interfering' with his life."

"Do you see him now?"

"Once in a while. I won't be around him when he's drinking, and to tell the truth, I don't like him very well when he's sober either. The universe revolves around Will and what he wants. Other people don't matter except to fill his needs."

"'King Baby,'" Toni said, recognizing her addicted self in the description.

"King Baby?"

"A practicing addict is King Baby. He demands what he wants when he wants it."

"You sound like you have some experience."

131

Toni hesitated. It was a natural time to tell him about her own struggles with addiction…

"My mother," she said instead.

Clark reached across the table to take her hand. "I'm so sorry you had to grow up with that, Toni." His voice was filled with compassion. "Is she still living?"

"As far as I know. We haven't had contact for years," Toni answered flatly. "And as far as I know, she's still drinking." She pulled her hand away from Clark's, uncomfortable with the direction of the conversation.

Clark seemed not to notice her withdrawal. "When Molly married Willis Sr., he'd been dry for over a year," he said. "After he'd fallen off the wagon more times than she could count on one hand, she finally left him. 'Once a drunk, always a drunk,' she told me. I don't hold out much hope for Will even if he does decide to dry out."

"You're not giving much credit to the millions of people who've made recovery a way of life," Toni said sharply.

He looked at her in surprise. "Do you know anyone like that?"

"One or two. They work hard at it."

Clark shook his head doubtfully. "But how do you know they're not going to relapse? If not today, tomorrow or next week or ten years from now? How do you know they're going to make it?"

She was silent for a moment. They were questions she'd asked herself. "You don't," she finally said. "Recovery's about faith."

~ 13 ~

It was after four in the morning when Toni crawled into bed, exhausted, for a few hours of sleep before work. The evening had been so wonderful until that last conversation. For once she was attracted to a decent man—a decent man who wasn't sure recovery from addiction was possible.

Well, maybe he was right. Maybe she was only fooling herself.

No, she told herself, wrapping her arms around the embroidered pillow Georgine had given her. For the first time in her life, she *wasn't* fooling herself. In the midst of her addiction she'd lied to herself constantly, the way Clark's half brother Will was still lying to himself. She wasn't in denial anymore; recovery was about self-honesty as well as faith.

She remembered being in denial even as she started her rehabilitation at Red Rock Ranch. The first assignment, less than twenty-four hours into the program, was a written self-assessment in response to a series of questions.

My name is Antonia Taryn Ferrier, she'd written. *I'm a model. I'm here because my friend Georgine is worried about me. I had a little accident a couple of weeks ago, but I'm fine now. I can quit whenever I want to.*

Oddly, she even remembered the taste of the rubber eraser as she chewed on the end of her pencil, her brow furrowed as she had tried to focus on the guide sheet for the assignment. It had taken her half an hour to complete the first three questions, and the guide sheet was three pages long. She had needed a drink.

The next question, after several readings, had finally registered: *Who, besides yourself, has your addiction most harmed?*

She'd stared at the question numbly. Her addiction? She got a little toasted once in a while—all right, more than once in a while—and when cocaine flowed as freely as sugar, it was pretty darned hard to say no. But she knew her limits. The night George found her on the floor of her hotel room was a fluke. She hadn't been paying attention to how much she was doing. Normally she was a responsible user.

It's my choice to use, and it doesn't affect anybody else, she'd finally written.

Toni knew about fooling herself. She'd done it for years.

But faith had given her new eyes. God was making an honest woman out of her.

Once again Ruth and Toni met at the door of Paper Chase.

"Toni, you really *do* look sick today," Ruth said, squinting at the younger woman as she let them both in the front door.

"And here I thought I'd done such a good job with my makeup this morning!" Toni slipped her handbag off her shoulder. "Just tired," she said, then added without thinking, "Clark and I went out for coffee after the fireworks last night, and we overdid it."

She cringed inside as Ruth arched her brows. Now why had she let that cat out of the bag? She'd never hear the end of it.

"How late?" Ruth wanted to know.

"I didn't get to bed till four this morning," she admitted. She ducked behind the front counter to stash her handbag and hide from Ruth's reaction.

"I noticed you getting pretty cozy on the dance floor last night," Ruth said, her voice alive with curiosity.

"We just talked, Ruth," Toni said firmly.

"So?" the older woman prompted.

"So what?"

"So how'd you and Clark get along?"

"Anybody ever tell you you're nosy?"

"Often! I'm not, really. Just *interested*."

"Right." Toni sighed. "We got along just fine. For the most part. Look," she said, sidestepping around her boss, "I've got to vacuum this morning. It never did get done yesterday."

Ruth followed her into the back room. "What about the *least* part?"

Toni laughed. "You just don't give up, do you? Okay, Ruthie, here's the scoop: He's a great guy, but I really don't see a future for us." She swung the heavy commercial vacuum cleaner out from its spot against the wall and started to wheel it out front, but Ruth stood in her path.

"You don't? Why not?"

Toni's voice came out sounding brittle. "One, I'm a drunk, which he doesn't yet know. Unless you've told him. He isn't particularly fond of drunks. Two, I haven't found men in general to be all that dependable. Three, I'm not so sure *I'm* dependable. May I get through, please?"

Ruth stepped aside but followed her out on the floor again. "One, you're not a drunk; you're a *recovering* alcoholic," she said from behind her. "And I *haven't* told him, by the way. That's for you to do. Two, Jack's dependable, Chappie's dependable, Keith and Beau are dependable—need I go on? Three, *you* are my *most* dependable employee."

Toni plugged the cord into a wall outlet. "Ruthie, he told me about Will." She stood, facing the other woman with her hands on her hips. "Not only is he unsympathetic, he isn't really sure an alcoholic can change."

"Toni, you're living proof an alcoholic can change."

"May I do the vacuuming now?"

"No."

Hugging her arms across her chest, Toni looked at the floor and waited.

Ruth said nothing.

Finally the younger woman looked up again, tossing her head to shake the hair away from her face. "I can't guarantee any more than one day at a time, Ruth," she said. "You don't know. You just don't know how hard it is. Even if I never take another drink—what if I'm like my mother in other ways? What if I can't commit? What if I make promises I can't keep?" She shook her head. "It's better if I never get involved."

"You can't help but get involved, Toni," Ruth said quietly. "You're a beautiful, passionate woman whose whole *life* is about getting involved. You can't keep men at bay forever with a thirty-five-dollar wedding band. Why not see what it feels like to get to know a decent man?"

"You don't get it, Ruthie!" Toni's voice reflected her exasperation. "Why would any decent man ever be interested in me?"

"Oh, honey!" Ruth's expression was pained. "You don't even know how special you are, do you?"

Toni ignored the question. "Besides—how would I know a good man if I saw him? I'm a bad judge of character. Look at my track record."

"You had some close calls with a couple of jerks when you first got out of rehab, but you *saw* what they were; you resisted their flash and dazzle and sent them packing. And as far as knowing that Clark's a good man—well, has your Aunt Ruthie ever steered you wrong?"

Toni shook her head mutely, her eyes brimming with tears. How could Ruth love someone like her, who might but for the grace of God have been the drunk who killed her only daughter?

And why would any decent man who had a choice want to take on someone with Toni's past? Once Clark knew, he'd be out the door faster than Brannigan after the postman.

Nonetheless, when Clark called that evening to see if she and Danny might like to go to the Rose Festival Fun Center with him after church the next day, Toni accepted eagerly. She might as well make the most of it while he was still around, she philosophized. After all, nothing was guaranteed...

"You're welcome to sit with us for the service," she invited.

"Thanks," he said. "I just might do that."

She changed her outfit three times Sunday morning before settling on a butter-yellow floral print dress that looked like spring, especially when she added pale-blue button earrings, a white straw hat, and strappy white sandals.

"Too much?" she asked Doc anxiously, responding to his expression when she walked out to the living room where he and Danny were waiting. "I know Tomahawk isn't really a dress-up kind of church..."

"You look beautiful, Mom!" Danny said. He sounded a little awestruck.

Doc nodded. "Just su'prised me, is all. I remember your mama in a hat like that, way back before you was even born."

I'll try not to let that ruin it for me, Toni thought. "I just thought it would be fun to dress up for once," she said.

"Could I wear my tie?" Danny asked unexpectedly.

"Don't you remember how itchy wearin' a tie gets?" his grandpa asked in surprise.

"I wanna be dressed up like Mom is."

Toni grinned on the way out the door. Danny and Pop were both wearing ties. "Must be my civilizing influence," she teased her father.

"We had to be fittin' thorns for such a rose as you're lookin' this mornin', Toni," he said, his blue eyes twinkling.

Toni, feeling unaccountably happy, put an arm around each of them as they walked to the car.

She was pleased when Clark slid into the pew next to her at church fifteen minutes later. He was dressed up, too, wearing slate blue slacks and a peach-colored dress shirt with a colorful silk tie. Doc greeted him with a nod of his head and a cheery smile. Danny wanted to sit next to him, which surprised and delighted his mother. Her son's behavior was so erratic lately; she never knew what to expect.

Clark had a pleasant singing voice, Toni noted as they shared a hymnal for an opening song, holding it low so Danny, between them, could see it, too. *More than I can say for myself,* she thought. Music was definitely not Toni's gift, but she loved the hymns and choruses she'd learned at Tomahawk and always joined in energetically. "Anythin' worth doin's worth doin' with all you got," Pop said on occasion. Toni lived by his philosophy.

"Please turn in your Bibles to Matthew, chapter five," Chappie said from the pulpit after announcements had been made and the song leader retired to his place on the facing bench. "We'll be reading the Beatitudes aloud each Sunday for the next few weeks. Simple words and simple concepts which I hope will become increasingly rich with meaning as we explore them together…"

Danny wanted to share the pew Bible with them, and even

though Toni knew he wasn't able to follow along, she humored him. The reading specialist who'd been working with him had told her to engage him in as many activities that encouraged reading as she could come up with. "*Wanting* to read is the first prerequisite for *learning* to read," she'd said. "Do what you can to make him want to learn."

After the Scripture reading and a brief prayer, Danny slid past Clark to go to Children's Church, and Clark moved closer to Toni as she pulled a pencil from the holder on the pew in front of her. She removed the bulletin insert with Chappie's sermon outline printed on it.

Toni didn't ordinarily take sermon notes, but when Chappie spoke, she tried to jot down a point or two; she always felt as if she learned something practical she could take away with her. Clark, too, pulled a pen from his pocket and prepared to take notes.

But forty minutes later Toni realized she hadn't written down a thing, nor could she remember much of what Chappie had said. What she knew she would remember was the sharp crease in Clark's dress pants, the golden hair on the back of his large hands, his blunt fingers and well-kept nails, the musky smell of his aftershave. Clark's sermon notes, as clean and white as hers...

Frowning, she shifted her body away from him on the pew and tried to concentrate on Chappie's closing words.

"The life of faith is a *new way of seeing*," the minister was saying. "A new perspective that challenges our priorities and values."

The comment caught Toni's attention. It's what she'd been learning over the last two years in recovery—new ways to see. Different priorities. Different values.

For a recovering addict, perspective was everything.

"Come back next week expecting to learn new truths as we explore the countercultural nature of this most familiar of passages, the Beatitudes," Chappie said. "Christ's teachings were not the status quo in first-century Palestine, and they are not the status quo now. They were revolutionary in their own culture. They still are meant to turn contemporary culture on its ear."

Toni wished she'd been listening. It sounded as if she'd have enjoyed the sermon.

She glanced down at the one line she'd written on her notes: *The life of faith is a new way of seeing...*

Recovery, too, was about learning to see with new eyes.

Clark, Doc, and Toni were talking to Chappie at the doorway when Danny raced up the stairs just inside the front doors, dragging Keith Castle behind him. Katie followed, panting. "Danny! Keith! Slow down! I can't keep up with you!" she gasped.

"Wimp," Keith laughed, winking down at Danny.

"Hi, Mom!" Danny called. "Guess what? Kee an' Irish are goin' to the Fun Center today, too! Can they come with us? Please?"

"Duty calls," Toni said to Chappie, rolling her eyes. "I'll call tomorrow to find out when you're open, okay?"

"Great! I look forward to talking to you, Toni. Good to have you here, Doc, Clark." He turned away to greet a couple who'd been waiting.

"Now—" Toni smiled a greeting at Keith and Katie and looked down at Danny. "What's it all about, child-mine?"

"Kee an' Irish said they'd take me on some rides so you an' Clark could get mushy if you want to."

Toni looked up, her mouth open in a startled *O*. Keith and Katie had been on the *Snow Swan* Friday night, too. Had she and Clark been that transparent?

Clark's lightly freckled face was crimson, and Keith was

140

shaking his head, one hand over his eyes. Pop looked as if he might break into a laugh at any moment.

Katie laced her fingers through the thick auburn hair at her temples and said sheepishly, "I confess. I really did say that. To Keith. I didn't expect to hear it repeated." She dropped her hands and tousled Danny's curly hair affectionately. "Silly me!"

Keith slid his hand down his face, then crossed his arms over his chest, his head still shaking. "My wife!" He sighed. "Sorry, but I can't do a thing with her," he said sadly.

Katie punched him lightly on the shoulder. "Of course you can!" She stood on tiptoe and lifted her face for a kiss. "For instance…"

"Mmm-m," Keith murmured.

Toni laughed. "Speaking of mushy! Sure you want a kid hanging out with you?"

"Only if it's Danny Bananny," Keith said, pulling Katie close with one arm and Danny with the other. "He understands us!"

"Scary thought!" Toni would be forever grateful to Katie, who had freely given her time and love to Danny when Toni had been incapable even of considering her son's needs. And Keith—he'd been like a son to Pop. "As far as joining us today—well, it's Clark's party." She put an arm through his and cocked her head. "Want a chance to get mushy with me?" she teased.

He growled in his throat and waggled his eyebrows. "I've been dreaming of the day…" he teased back. Didn't take him long to recover from embarrassment, Toni noted, smiling up at him. She liked that; she liked the way he rolled with the punches.

Keith and Katie exchanged a glance, as if very pleased with themselves.

"How about Grumpy?" Danny said. "Grumpy'd have fun on the rides."

"Why not?" Clark started to say.

"I'm afeard your grandpa's stomach'd fly away an' not come home ag'in if he ventured on one o' them rides," Doc put in quickly. "You young 'uns have your fun an' let an ol' man have some peace an' quiet. You two want to go on ahead with Clark now? I can take your car on home, Toni."

Danny jumped with excitement. "Yeah! Let's go!"

"Not in your good shoes and a tie," Toni told him. "Or me in a straw hat and sandals, for that matter." She glanced at Clark again. "You brought something casual to change into, right? Want to follow us home?"

"Or Danny could come with me to show the way."

Danny nodded, grinning. "I'm a good nag-i-vator," he said proudly. "Mom says so."

Keith grinned crookedly. "You and Katie have something in common then, Danny. She's really good at that 'nag' part."

He escaped having his ears boxed only by grabbing his wife in a hug that pinned her arms to her sides. "Meet you at your house in half an hour. We're doing lunch at the waterfront, right? I'm sure Fast Eddie's has a food booth."

"Blue Mountain smoky spareribs, here we come!" Clark said, tossing his car keys in the air and catching them. "Danny, what are we waiting for?"

⌒ *14* ⌒

The afternoon was a blur of images for Clark, like a reel-to-reel movie played on an old projector that was out of focus and out of control. There was the house on Dearborn Street, the only one among its shabby neighbors with a fresh coat of paint, a surprising lavender with trim in white and forest green. Colors by Toni, painting by Keith Castle and friends. The yard was neatly kept, the roses just beginning to bloom, the lawn mowed and the flower beds bright with color—gardening by Doc.

The furniture inside was an eclectic mix of secondhand pieces, painted white to stand out against the hardwood floors and the rich, jewel-toned walls: amethyst in the living room, ruby in the dining room, emerald and sapphire in the bedrooms, topaz in the sunny kitchen, all trimmed in gleaming white. Colors *and* painting by Toni. Plants everywhere. Pictures everywhere. Pillows so plentiful that the worn condition of the sofa and overstuffed chair in the living room almost escaped Clark's notice. Color, life, light. Toni's stamp on everything.

He drove the five of them to the festival center at Waterfront Park. Traffic, horns, making a game of beating the lights,

Danny's first Chinese fire drill. Finally, a place to park and a five-block walk to the river, all of them carried along in the festive crowd like lemmings to the sea, pouring across Front Street, flooding into the festival-center grounds.

Sweet and smoky spareribs, corn on the cob dripping with butter, flaky biscuits, sweet-potato pie—the last crumbs saved for the gentle, giant Clydesdale pushing its velvet nose into his hand. Tiny ballerinas, some not more than three years old. School bands beating and blaring. A swirl of people shouting, laughing, buzzing with color and energy. Jugglers and mimes and clowns. Katie's red hair swinging. Keith's head always visible above the crowd. Danny sure to be between them, basking in their attention. Silly rhymes, silly games, silly songs.

And Toni. She made him dizzy. She made him feel alive in ways he hadn't known. Her dazzling smile and easy laugh; the swing of her arm as they walked; her long fingers threaded through his—soft, warm, fitting so well, so naturally. The casual elegance of her outfit, dressed-up shorts in some kind of silky fabric, black with white dots, and a matching sleeveless top that crisscrossed from her shoulders, wrapped around her back, and tied at the waist.

Toni slamming up against him on the "Super-Fantastic Fun Rides"—the wild rides, the ones only the two of them wanted to go on.

The "I dare you!" look she gave him in front of the karaoke stage.

His "Dare you back!" answering grin.

The two of them suddenly on stage, each with a microphone, the crowd whistling and clapping, Danny cheering. Toni couldn't carry a tune, Clark already knew from standing next to her in church, but she didn't let it hold her back.

Drawing a deep breath, she belted out the first lines of the song on the video monitor. Clark came in right on cue.

Bows, thrown kisses, an impromptu dance as they left the stage. Energized by the applause and the laughter, high on each other. What a match they were!

"Yay, Mom!" Danny shouted as they jostled through the crowd. "You guys were awesome!"

"Hot!" Keith agreed.

"A tough act to follow," Katie said. "No way I'd get up there now!"

"Not a bad show for someone who can't carry a tune in a bucket," Toni answered, breathless with laughter.

"Want some ice cream to soothe those vocal cords?" Keith asked.

"Sounds great!"

"We'll stand in line," he said, indicating Danny as well as Katie. "In the meantime, *your* mission—should you choose to accept it—"

Clark and Toni both broke into the *Mission Impossible* theme as Katie laughed and Keith finished, "—is to save us front-row seats for the puppet show."

"I don't know if that's safe," Katie said. "I'm afraid we'll get back to find these two up on stage stealing the show from Kermit and Miss Piggy!"

Without warning, Toni grabbed Clark's hand, lifted it, and pirouetted under his arm. Taking his cue from her, Clark took hold of her other hand as well and spun her around till she stood with her back to his front, her arms crossed at her shoulders. Simultaneously they threw back their heads in dramatic poses.

Katie laughed. "See what I mean?"

Toni gracefully rotated out of Clark's grasp. "We'll be good, won't we, Clark?" she said, once again dazzling him with her smile. She tugged at his hand. "Come on, let's go be Super Seat Savers!"

When Clark looked back over his shoulder, Keith was whirling Danny in the air. He set him back on the ground, out of breath and giggling, and the boy reached for his hand as they set off for the ice-cream booth. Clark felt a touch of envy. Keith and Danny clearly shared a very special relationship; the man might have been the boy's father, the way they interacted.

I wonder if Danny could ever accept me as a father figure?

The thought startled him. *Slow down, Clark!* he cautioned himself. It was pretty soon to be thinking about fatherhood; he'd known Toni less than two weeks. He hadn't even kissed her. Still, there was something that felt so *right* about her...

"Hey, Toni—"

She laced her fingers through his and swung his arm. "Hey, Clark!"

"Tell me about Danny's father."

She stopped short, abruptly withdrawing her hand from his and crossing her arms in a classic gesture of self-protection. "What do you mean?"

Clark was startled at the instant change in her demeanor. She'd pulled into herself like a sea anemone poked with a stick. A crease appeared between her brows; her mouth was tight and strained. His innocent request had somehow switched her energy from happy to hostile, and he didn't have a clue as to why.

He'd been feeling so close to her, so connected. Now he felt suddenly cut loose and set adrift. "Toni, what's wrong?"

"Danny doesn't have a father," she said shortly, not looking at him.

Clark was hardly aware of the people streaming around them, jostling against him, as he tried to make sense of Toni's withdrawal. "You mean he's dead?"

"I mean that Danny is *my* son; he's never had a father."

"His father hasn't been involved in Danny's life at all?"

146

She finally looked at him, her eyes sparking with anger. "Why do you keep using that word? How explicit do I have to get? Danny doesn't have a father. I wasn't married. I don't even know who the *sperm donor* was!"

Clark wondered if he looked as dumfounded as he felt. His mouth opened, but nothing came out. Finally he took her elbow without saying anything and guided her toward the stage where the puppet show was scheduled to begin in twenty minutes. The front-row chairs were already beginning to fill up.

He sighted a place near the center aisle several rows back and led her there. "You sit here on the aisle, and I'll move down. We can save the seats between us for Danny and Keith and Katie." His tone was neutral.

"Need to put a little space between us?" Toni's voice was bitter.

Clark's mouth tightened in anger, but he held his tongue. *I don't have to put space between us,* he thought. *You've accomplished that already.*

"What's the matter?" she goaded, her voice low but intense. "All of a sudden I'm not good enough for you?"

"Look, Toni, I admit, I need a little time to get used to this, but give me some credit, would you? So Danny doesn't have a father. So you made a mistake nine years ago. Nine years ago! I think I'm a big enough man to deal with that."

Toni shook her head, not looking at him. "Look, you don't know the half of it. If you did—" She shook her head again. "I'm your worst nightmare, Clark."

"*What* are you *talking* about? Toni, give me some kind of clue here! We were having a great time, then all of a sudden—"

She leaned across the empty chairs between them. "Look at me, Clark."

He met her gaze, then felt the anger draining out of him as he held it. What was lurking in the depths of her beautiful blue violet eyes? It wasn't anger. Hurt? Fear? Shame?

"It's not just that Danny doesn't have a father. He hasn't had much of a mother, either," she said tiredly, all the fight suddenly gone out of her. "Pop had to file for custody just to keep him safe from me, to see that he was cared for." She stopped, looked away. "I'm an alcoholic, Clark."

Shock was too mild a word for Clark's reaction. He struggled to keep his expression neutral as he tried to think of something to say. How could this be? Why hadn't Ruth warned him?

You didn't want Ruth to know you were interested, he reminded himself.

"I'm...surprised," he finally said. "Surprised you didn't tell me sooner," he added. "When we talked about Will and your mother." He rubbed his nose with his forefinger, an unconscious gesture he used when he was nervous, which wasn't often.

"Don't you see?" She looked at him briefly, long enough for him to see the extent of her distress, before she turned her face away. "I didn't tell you because I know how you feel about—about *drunks*. And—I wanted you to like me."

He was silent for a moment. "You're not a drunk, Toni." He hesitated. "Are you?"

"'Once a drunk, always a drunk,' is the way I've heard it said." There was no life in her voice.

Clark rubbed his nose harder. "It's only my experience, Toni—with Will and his father." He shrugged his shoulders helplessly. "Maybe I don't know everything. Recovery's about faith, you told me. Maybe I just need to learn." But he could feel himself shrinking away from her in his mind. She seemed suddenly alien to him. Where had that earlier sense of connection come from? How had he felt that he'd known her?

She shook her head. "Clark, I doubt you've ever done anything in your life to be ashamed of. *I'm ashamed of everything in my past.* How could you possibly understand?"

~~~~~

Later that evening, by the time she'd finished an almost hour-long phone conversation with a very disagreeable Suzanne DeJong hashing out more details of the wedding, Toni was exhausted. From the earliest hours of the day, she'd been at fever pitch emotionally: anticipating the time she'd spend with Clark, sharing the church service with him, throwing herself into the fun at the festival center.

Then blowing it with Clark. Completely blowing any possibility of anything special ever happening with him.

Danny had finally rescued her from further embarrassment at the festival center by racing up with an ice-cream cone in each hand and promptly dumping a scoop of Very Berry onto her rayon dry-clean-only shorts. Unfortunately, she'd taken out her frustration on her son, who then refused to sit next to her and pouted angrily all the way through the puppet show. Clark had been gallant enough to hunt down a bottle of seltzer water and a handkerchief so she could try to get the purple stain out before it set.

After the show she'd knelt by Danny's chair and apologized: "I was wrong to yell at you for spilling the ice cream, Danny. I know it was an accident. Mommy was upset about something else, and she took it out on you. *I* took it out on you," she had corrected herself. She had hesitated. "Give me a hug?"

He had, but it was a stiff, reluctant hug.

The life had gone out of the party, and everyone had agreed it was time to go home. Clark had walked them to the door of the house after Keith and Katie had driven away. "Tell Clark thank you, Danny," Toni had instructed as she unlocked the front door.

"Thanks, Manx!" Danny had shouted and disappeared through the door to tumble on the living-room floor with a wildly barking Brannigan.

"Name's not Manx, Banks," Clark had called after him. Toni had turned her head to look at him, startled. She hadn't told him about the game.

"You hear it enough, you pick it up," he had answered her unspoken question. "You and Keith both did that with him today."

"We did? I don't even notice anymore." She had crossed her arms, sliding her hands up and down her bare arms against the late afternoon chill. "Well, I'd better go," she had said, her eyes avoiding his. "Thanks for taking us today. I had fun."

"I did, too." He had crossed his arms, unaware he was mirroring her defensive posture. "See you around?"

"Yeah," she had said. "See you."

"Ruth, don't even ask," Toni warned the next morning when her boss came in to cover the closing shift. "I don't want to talk about it."

"About what?"

The look Toni shot the older woman must have spoken volumes; Ruth let her be for the rest of the day. Toni felt lethargic, her high energy and naturally ebullient personality subdued to such an extent that she wondered if she might be coming down with something instead of being merely depressed.

Merely depressed? she scoffed to herself. There was nothing *mere* about the hole she'd fallen in; her depression was the size of a moon crater, at least. She still had Danny's problems weighing on her, though she'd managed to put them aside in her excitement about her developing relationship with Clark. Now that she'd put the kibosh on that, her burden of anxiety seemed doubled.

At least this time she hadn't found herself in a bar with a drink in her hand. That said something.

At the end of her shift, Toni quietly thanked Ruth for her understanding.

"I love you, Toni," her boss said, giving her hand a quick squeeze. "I want to know what's going on so I can do whatever I can to help. But I understand your need for space, too. Just know I'm here if you need me, okay?"

Toni nodded wordlessly, her eyes shining with unshed tears.

Ruth hesitated, then asked, "Have you talked to Chappie? He really is a wise man. I think he could help you work through things…"

"I called him this morning," Toni said. "We have an appointment later this week. But Ruth—" She shook her head sadly. "I just don't see how anything can change."

But picking up Danny from school a few minutes later gave her hope. He climbed into the front seat of the Valiant with a happy grin, a story about a new friend, and an imaginatively illustrated writing project with a gold star. "Good for you, sweetheart!" she told him. When she leaned over to hug him, he actually relaxed into her arm for a moment. Toni felt her spirits lift. Her son's receptiveness was probably temporary, but at this point she'd take whatever she could get.

She pulled onto Dearborn Street a few minutes later just in time to see a UPS truck backing out of the driveway of their neatly kept yard. It wasn't an unusual sight; Pop often ordered tools and gadgets from catalogs that used United Parcel Service delivery.

What *was* unusual was the sight of Pop sitting on the sofa staring at an unopened box in the middle of the living room instead of tearing into it. Normally he was like a kid at Christmas when a package came.

He looked up when Toni opened the front door. "*There* you are!" he said as if he'd been waiting a long while.

She tossed her purse on the dining table. "Came right from

work and school. What've you got there, Pop? Some new gizmo?"

"I wanna see, Grumpy!" Danny said. "Open it, open it!"

"It's been real hard not to," Doc admitted, stroking his white beard, "but I can't rightly say as it's my priv'lege openin' this here crate. Ain't addressed to me."

"Not addressed to you?" Toni leaned over the back of the sofa and saw the name felt-penned in black on the large wooden crate: *Antonia Ferrier.* She frowned in puzzlement. "What in the world?"

D anny was practically jumping with excitement. "Open it, Mom!"

"Got the tools all set," Pop told her, holding up a crow-bar and a claw hammer. "Need some he'p?"

She smiled. Thank goodness for Danny, pill that he was sometimes, and Pop—steady, loving, always there. Dependable. Safe.

"I wouldn't know the first thing about using those tools, Pop," she said. "You go ahead. I can see you're as anxious as Danny."

She peered at the return address but didn't recognize the name or the street number. Who did she know in Pasadena, California? Coming around the sofa, she sat on the edge and leaned forward as her father began to dismantle the box. Obviously he'd been "studyin' on it"; he knew exactly where to go in.

"I can't imagine what it could be…"

Doc dropped one side of the crate. A river of foam "worms" poured out onto the faded rug.

"What is it, Grumpy?" Danny asked.

"Don't rightly know just yet," he answered. "Looks like a whole 'nother box inside, but all covered up in bubble wrap. Here's somethin'." He carefully removed a large manila envelope taped to the top of the inside box and handed it to Toni, then set to work dismantling the rest of the crate.

She frowned at the unfamiliar handwriting as she undid the metal clasp. The envelope contained a smaller sealed envelope and a single sheet of paper. She removed the paper first. *City of Angels Hospice,* the letterhead read. A short typed message and a signature at the bottom: *Sister Mary Alice.*

Toni felt a sudden overwhelming sense of dread. She stared at the letter, tried to read it, but the words all ran together and she couldn't make sense of them.

"Well, I'll be jiggered!"

Toni looked up. Pop had cut through the bubble wrap and pulled it aside.

"What *is* it, Grumpy?" Danny pleaded.

"I declare, Toni!" Doc's voice was filled with wonder. "If it ain't the weddin' chest I give your mama on our honeymoon!"

Toni stared. Sitting in her living room in Portland, Oregon was the only beautiful item she remembered from her California childhood. She hadn't seen the intricately carved oriental chest, its finish aged to a warm patina, for almost a dozen years. She knelt by it, her hands tracing the scene on the lid: a willow overhanging a curved wooden bridge, a swan beneath it; a graceful woman in a flowing robe, her hair pulled up in classic Chinese style, her almond eyes peeking over an open fan; a man in the garb of an ancient Chinese warrior kneeling before her. A garland of carved blossoms bordered the scene.

Toni had always loved the chest. It had been not only the most beautiful item in the string of shabby houses she'd grown up in, but also the only item she remembered being always in her life, the only thing her mother always took with her wherever she went. A symbol, Toni realized now as she gazed at it, of the constancy she'd never had as a child but had always longed for.

"Bought it in San Francisco's Chinatown on our honeymoon," Doc said quietly. "It was the only thing your mama wanted from the divorce—that and cash money. I didn't know it, but she was fixin' to leave with you. Didn't have room to take much with 'er." He looked over at Toni kneeling next to him. "First time you hauled yourself up, still not a year old, was on that chest. Learned to walk pullin' yourself around it, you did."

"Pop—" Toni shook her head. "What's it doing here?"

"The letter don't say?"

She gazed at the sheet of paper in her hand, crumpled now where she'd been gripping it. "I couldn't read it. Here, you see." She thrust the letter at him.

Doc squinted at the paper, his eyes rapidly covering the page. His hand dropped to his knee. He stared at the carved wooden chest without saying anything.

"Pop?"

"She's gone," he finally said. His voice was very quiet.

"Gone?"

"Mina's gone to her grave."

Mama is dead. Toni was silent for a moment, trying to sort out how she felt. Easy enough, she decided in short order; she felt nothing.

"Sister Mary Alice says Mina's dyin' wish was for you to have her treasures. The chest an' all what's in it."

"I don't want it."

"T'other letter's from your mama, Toni. She wrote it at the end."

"Not interested."

Danny, who'd been listening to their exchange with a puzzled expression, finally interrupted. "*Who* died? Grumpy, who?"

"Your grandma, Danny Boy. Your grandma who never had the chance to know you."

"Oh, *please,* Pop. She could have *made* a chance to know him," Toni said impatiently.

"She died like Ruggles did?" Danny asked. Before Brannigan, before Toni had come on the scene again, Danny had lost a dog to old age. Ruggles had been more than just a pet; he'd been her son's best friend. Pop had told her Danny had had a hard time dealing with the loss until Brannigan appeared.

At Doc's nod, Danny added, "That's real sad, isn't it?"

"It's always sad to say good-bye," Doc told him.

Diplomatic, Toni thought. Doc had said his good-byes to Mina years ago. So had she. Only it had been more like *good riddance.*

And that is the last I'm going to think about my mother today, Toni told herself. She got up from her knees and sat on the edge of the sofa. "Danny, have you fed Brannigan yet today?"

He looked surprised. "Ain't time yet."

"Oh." She didn't even bother to correct his grammar. "Well, I'll bet he'd like a treat. How about you find him a dog biscuit and take it outside while I see what I can put together for the potluck tonight?"

When he was gone, she leaned back into the cushions of the sofa, her hands threaded through her hair, and closed her eyes. "Pop, you can do whatever you want with Mina's chest. And with her letter. I'd be happier having them out of sight."

"You sure you don't want to look through 'em, Toni? Mebbe it'd clear up some things between you. Mebbe it'd be good for us to talk some about Mina."

Toni put her hands over her ears and shook her head. "Don't want to look; don't want to talk; don't want to know. I'm *done* with Mama, Pop. She's gone, and I'm done."

Doc looked at her sadly. "Wish I could b'lieve it," he said, laying the manila envelope on top of the beautiful piece of furniture.

The chest was too heavy for an old man and a young woman to move very far. Toni helped Doc lift it to a place against the wall of the living room until he could get some help to carry it upstairs to the attic. "We c'd ask Kee an' Chappie to come by after Growth Group tonight," he suggested. "Not too out of the way for either of 'em."

She nodded. "I'm sure they'll help. You ask them. I'm not going tonight."

"Not goin'? But—"

"I'll make a pasta salad for you to take. I just can't do it tonight, Pop." Not after this. And not with the likelihood Clark would be there. Unless he was planning to bail out, too, of course...

Doc stroked his beard in thoughtful silence for a moment. "Might be the best thing for you t' be with friends tonight, Toni," he said slowly.

"Might be. But I need some time alone."

"You c'd come just for the dinner..."

"Please, Pop—"

He put up his hands. "All right, then, Toni. You've made up your mind. I'll give ev'rybody your regrets."

First on Toni's agenda after Doc and Danny left was a call to Georgine. The answering machine picked up. Toni's heart sank. "George, I wish you were home—"

"Toni? Is that you?" George's voice was breathless. "Just got in. What's up?"

Once again her friend put everything else aside as Toni poured out her heart.

157

"I'm so sorry, Toni." The voice on the line hesitated. "Are you going to be okay?"

"If you mean am I going to stay sober—I have every intention to. I can't say more."

"I'll be praying for you."

"Thanks."

"So…" Georgine paused again. "Clark first. You're sure it's all over with him?"

"Let's just say the atmosphere was *chilly* when he left. Why in the world would he bother with me, George?"

"Because you're strong, intelligent, beautiful, and caring, maybe? He'd be a fool not to give you a chance."

"Maybe he'd be a fool to *take* the chance."

"*I* don't think so," George said. "Toni…the letter from your mom. Do you think it might be an apology? An attempt to reconcile with you before she died?"

"I don't know. I don't *want* to know." Closing her eyes, Toni laid her head on the back of the sofa where she sat with the phone to her ear. "*If* it was an apology, it's too late." She pushed the hair away from her forehead with her free hand. "I don't want to forgive her."

Georgine was silent.

Toni gave her head a shake and added almost as if to herself, "I don't see how I could."

Clark had gone back and forth in his mind all day about whether or not to attend Growth Group at Beau and Emily's. The argument imposed itself between every phone call, in the middle of paragraphs at the computer, even mid-sentence as he ordered a sandwich for lunch at the deli down the way.

A part of him shouted to stay away. He wasn't ready to see Toni. Even after her stunning revelations yesterday, even after

158

their intensely awkward good-bye, he was certain that seeing her again would make him as weak-kneed and dizzy as he'd felt every time he'd seen her, from that first glimpse of her dancing gracefully across the window at Paper Chase to his last glance of her the night before, standing on her front porch as still and pale as a statue as she watched him drive away.

He wasn't ready to feel weak-kneed and dizzy, he told himself as he changed from the sweat suit he'd been wearing in the office all day to a pair of khaki trousers and a beige-striped shirt.

What have you been doing with her, then? he asked himself as he pulled a textured olive sweater over his head. He hadn't been ready when he'd first met her, either. Yet something had compelled him to make excuses to see her, to be with her, to talk to her—something that grew stronger after each time he did.

He wasn't feeling in the least bit sensible about her. And if there was anything he needed to feel right now, it was sensible. He shouldn't see her until he had things sorted out in his mind, he thought as he combed his hair and brushed his teeth.

Toni's disclosures about her past had completely thrown him. *Talk about challenging priorities and values!* he said to himself as he locked the door to the apartment and started down the three flights of stairs to his car in the parking garage.

She was right; he hadn't done much in his life he was ashamed of. Did that mean they shouldn't have a romance? Should he view the disaster at the festival center as a sign from God that Toni wasn't right for him?

Right for him! A *romance!*

Slow down, Clark, he told himself for the second time in as many days.

All right, then. Could they even be friends? Did her past make it impossible for him to understand her, as she'd suggested?

But, God, I want to understand! he pleaded, hardly knowing he was praying. *And I want to know that she's all right...*

Which is why you're on your way to Beau and Emily's, came the answer.

He looked out the window in surprise. He was headed east on Interstate 84, and he hadn't even realized he'd made the decision.

He passed the exit for Paper Chase and the next exit, which would have taken him to Will's apartment.

How hard had he worked at understanding Will?

He dismissed the question as soon as it entered his mind.

Exiting the freeway another few miles down the road, he stopped by a grocery store to pick up a loaf of French bread and a tub of butter. As he stood in the checkout line he tried to rehearse how he would act, what he would say when he saw Toni. Even in his mind he was bumbling and tongue-tied.

When Doc and Danny showed up without Toni a few minutes after he'd arrived at Beau and Emily's, he was as much relieved as disappointed. Then, when Doc revealed at dinner the reason Toni had stayed home was that she was "feelin' out of sorts," he was upset and anxious. Had she stayed away because of him?

A little later, after the kids had disappeared into the basement and the adults gathered in the living room, Doc shared more specifically. Clark felt his emotions shifting once again as the bearded, white-haired man told the group about the UPS delivery earlier in the day and the letter from Sister Mary Alice at City of Angels Hospice.

"I'm feelin' sad," Doc concluded. "Sad about the way Mina died without a soul t' love 'er. Sad about her livin' that way, too. Such a waste, it was. Makes me so proud of my Toni for pullin' herself out o' the pit the way she has." His voice broke, and he paused to compose himself.

"Toni's pretendin' it don't affect her that her mama died, but I'm afeared it's brought up all the bad blood between 'em in 'er mind. Says she don't want t' talk about it. Can't force 'er to, I knows that. I'd be obliged if you all would pray she'd work it through somehow. Don't know everything that Mina did and didn't do when she had Toni all those years, but it ain't hard to figger there's lots t' be forgiven. Toni's not done it. I'm just hopin' she don't take 'er anger to the grave like Mina took 'er shame."

I could have been there for her, Clark told himself. *If I'd have let myself.*

If she'd have let you, another voice reminded him. It wasn't just he who had pulled away, and it wasn't just Toni. Neither of them knew how to handle the fears her self-disclosure had brought up. Distance seemed the safest bet.

Chappie led in prayer for Doc and Toni, and several others joined him. Clark sat quietly, agreeing in his heart but not comfortable expressing his thoughts aloud.

"Clark, you've been quiet tonight," Ruth said to him as the group broke up an hour later. She'd worked the closing shift at the store this evening and come in halfway through dinner. "Anything going on you want to talk about?"

"No, I—" He stopped. Maybe it was time to let someone in on this. Someone who knew him. Someone who loved him. "Ruthie, would you have time to stop somewhere for a cup of coffee before you go home?"

"For you I always have time. Let me call home so Jack knows where I am. He couldn't come tonight. There's an all-night coffee shop on eighty-second if you want to follow me."

Ten minutes later they were settled into a booth with steaming cups of decaf on the table in front of them. Clark stared into his coffee, feeling as awkward and tongue-tied as he had when he'd been trying to practice what he'd say to Toni. It was so unlike him not to have words at the ready.

He should have known that Ruth wouldn't let his uncharacteristic restraint get in her way.

"It's Toni, isn't it?"

~ 16 ~

Startled, Clark jerked his head up to meet her eyes. "She hasn't said anything, has she?"

"As if that's the only way I'd know something was going on between the two of you! I didn't just fall off the cabbage truck, you know," she said tartly.

Clark smiled for the first time all day. He felt himself relaxing in Ruth's familiar presence. Having her tease him about his interest in Toni seemed the least of his worries now.

"*That's* for sure!" he gibed, raising his eyebrows.

"You leave my gray hairs and wrinkles out of this, Clark McConaughey!"

Clark raised his hands in a gesture of mock defense. "Hey— *I* didn't mention gray hairs and wrinkles!"

"About Toni…" Ruth prompted. "What happened between you yesterday?"

What *had* happened between them yesterday? Excitement. Energy. A certain sense of breathless wonder as they explored and discovered each other. Then the withdrawal. And then the bombshell.

He didn't say that to Ruth, however. "I don't know what's

going on, Ruthie," he said instead. "With Toni *or* with me. I thought that something special was happening between us. I know it sounds trite, but before yesterday I felt as if I'd known her for a long, long time. As if she'd been a part of my life forever and I just didn't know it; I just hadn't run into her yet. Does that make any sense at all?"

"Make sense! Clark McConaughey, are you telling me you're in love with Toni?"

"Of course not!"

He couldn't be in love with her—could he? He'd only known her for two weeks of real time, and he was thirty-six years old, and he'd never been in love. Not really.

So how would you know falling in love from an upset stomach? a voice inside his head niggled. *You've got to admit you've never felt about anyone the way you feel about Toni Ferrier...*

"To tell the truth, I'm not sure what I'm feeling, Ruthie," he admitted. He quirked a grin. "*Something,* for sure—I've been through an entire bottle of Pepto-Bismol in the last two weeks!"

Ruth laughed. "Didn't I tell you?"

Clark sobered. "You know me, Ruth. You know my history with Will and his father. You know how I felt when Sunny died at the hands of a drunk driver. How could I ever be in love with an alcoholic?"

"Ah, so that's it. I wondered how long it would be before she got around to telling you."

"Why didn't *you* tell me, Ruth?" Clark asked, his voice on the edge of accusation. "If you saw that I was interested?"

Ruth looked out the window for a moment before answering, her gaze unfocused. "It wasn't my place," she finally said.

"You've talked to *her* about *me.*"

"Only about the obvious. How wonderful you are."

"I'm not so sure she believes you anymore." Clark looked at Ruth directly. "She hasn't said anything about me?"

"She let it slip on Saturday that you'd gone out after the fire-works Friday night and stayed up talking till the wee hours. I confess—I pried after I found out." Ruth took a sip of coffee, eyeing Clark over the rim of her cup.

"And?"

Ruth lowered the coffee mug, keeping her fingers wrapped around its warmth. "She told me you'd talked about Will. That you had no sympathy for him. That you didn't think an alcoholic could ever change."

He winced. That must have hurt like salt in an open wound. No wonder she'd been defensive. No wonder she hadn't felt safe enough to tell him about her own history with alcohol.

"I was telling her my truth, Ruthie. All I have to go on is Will and his father."

"A pretty small sample, don't you think?" Ruth asked gently.

"Maybe so, but it's what I know. How do I know Toni's different? How do *you* know?"

"I *don't* know. I believe."

Toni's words came back to Clark: *Recovery's about faith.*

"From the evidence of her choices over the last two years, *I believe* that Toni has set her course in a new direction," Ruth continued. "I believe she knows what she wants, and she knows what she has to do to get it. Addiction isn't it. Relationship is."

"What d'you mean?"

"Addiction is about escape; relationship's about engaging. Toni's addictive use of alcohol was a way to disengage from a life that probably, from the little I know, must have felt like hell itself. She didn't know when she started drinking that she was opening the door to another hell. Out of the frying pan, into the fire, as they say."

"Ah, yes—the ubiquitous 'they.'"

Ruth ignored his flippant remark, recognizing it for the distancing strategy it was meant to be.

165

"Is this about Toni or about Will?" she asked instead.

"What d'you mean?" he asked again.

"I mean if you didn't have the experience you've had with Will, would you be so upset about finding out Toni's a recovering alcoholic?"

"I don't know," he answered honestly. "I suppose I *am* afraid she's like Will or his father. You know Willis Sr. supposedly quit drinking six or seven times. 'I can quit whenever I want to!' he used to tell Molly. And he would—for a week. Maybe a month one time. But he never *really* quit."

"He wasn't willing to face the consequences of his choices," Ruth said. "It's hard, but Toni's done it. She keeps on doing it. She feels such shame for her past, Clark. It colors everything. She doesn't trust herself, which makes it mighty hard to trust anyone else."

Clark nodded. "I know. She told me she was ashamed of everything in her past. She told me I could never understand."

"In some ways, maybe that's true. In other ways... Well, it would be my guess, knowing what you've been through with Molly, that you could relate to her feelings about her mother. Mina's death is going to be a big deal for Toni, Clark. She hasn't forgiven her. She's going to need all the support she can get to deal honestly with the feelings that are bound to surface."

Can I do that for her? Clark wondered. *Can I set aside my fears and be there for her?*

"How long has she been clean and sober?" he asked cautiously. "Almost two years, you said?"

Ruth nodded.

"Not very long."

"That depends on your perspective. It probably feels like a very long time to Toni."

Clark nodded. It probably felt like a lifetime to Toni.

"She doesn't go for the easy escape anymore, Clark. She

166

tackles her problems head-on. She is by far the bravest person I've ever known." Ruth's voice was filled with admiration. "I do believe in Toni," she reiterated. "And you know what else I believe?"

"What?"

"I believe that God is bigger than her addiction. I believe that he is bigger than her shame. And I believe she's learning to rely on God to help her through her problems. Alcohol isn't an option anymore."

Clark met her gaze. "Are you telling me I shouldn't be concerned about her past?" he asked. "Surely you reacted, too, Ruthie—when you found out she was a recovering alcoholic."

"I didn't have it sprung on me the way you did, Clark," she admitted. "When she first came back to Portland after her rehabilitation program, Chappie Lewis called me about giving her a job. I knew about her background before I met her."

"And you hired her anyway?" Clark shook his head. "Didn't you worry about hiring someone just out of rehab?"

"Of course I did. I hired her on probation, same way I do all my clerks. After three months I stopped worrying."

"You really did?"

"I really did. Toni's almost hyper-responsible," Ruth said. "And she's smart, creative, energetic, personable—a superb salesperson. Toni doesn't sell stationery, she sells herself. I keep telling her she's much too talented to be working for me, for what little I can afford to pay her; she doesn't quite believe it yet. She's a natural at business, Clark. With a little self-confidence, she could do anything she wanted to. When I first hired her, I thought I was doing her a favor. Now I feel as if she's doing *me* a favor by staying on."

"That's quite a testimonial, Ruth. You trying to sell me on her?"

"I'm not saying a relationship with Toni would be easy," she

167

answered. "Or even that you *should* pursue her. What I am saying is that she's a very special person and that she deserves respect. More than that—she deserves love."

"We all do."

Ruth reached across the table and took his hand. "Yes. You deserve it, too, Clark. But you've got something going for you Toni doesn't. You believe in yourself. You always have.

"Toni's strong, and she has strong support, and I've watched her faith grow steadily over the last year. What she doesn't have is much faith in herself. Someday, the right man is going to help her find that faith, too—make her realize how special she is, how much she has to offer.

"I don't know if that person is you or not, Clark. I think that you and she could be very good together. You're a splendid match in energy and drive and creativity. It's obvious sparks fly when you're around each other.

"But there's more to a relationship than chemistry. Can you nurture each other's souls?"

"Ruth," Clark said, feeling lost, "how in the world would I know how to nurture somebody's soul?"

"Love is a grand teacher."

The following week was one of the craziest, most confusing that Toni could remember in the last two years.

Keith and Chappie dropped by Monday night to move her mother's carved oriental chest to the attic; Katie came in to say hello. Her expressions of condolence and her concerned questions made it clear that Pop had shared more than just the basics about Mina's death. She wished he hadn't; she wanted no more from anyone than to be left alone. She most decidedly *didn't* want to talk about her feelings.

Tuesday morning when she went in to get Danny up for

school, he rolled over on his stomach, pulled his pillow over his head, and refused to get out of bed. "Not goin' to school," his muffled voice informed her.

She sat down on the edge of his bed and rubbed his back through the blankets. He squirmed away. "Are you sick?" she asked. When he didn't answer, she took her hand off his back and massaged her own forehead instead. She didn't have the energy to fight him. "If you're too sick for school, you're too sick to play outside," she said shortly. "I'll let your grandpa know."

The phone rang while Pop was in the shower and she was in the middle of making breakfast, still in her robe and slippers. "Clark. Hello." Her feelings on hearing his voice were mixed: happiness, hope, embarrassment, fear.

"Hi, Toni. I wanted to say how sorry I am about your mother's death."

"Thanks for calling, Clark, but…well, *I'm* not sorry at all. She hasn't been a part of my life for years. When she was, she wasn't much of a mother. I can't say I'm feeling any great loss."

"Still…if you need to talk…I can be a pretty good listener when I put my mind to it."

"Thanks." There was an awkward pause, interrupted by a piercing blast over Toni's head. She turned around to see black smoke pouring out of the toaster. "Oh, no!" she groaned, dropping the phone and leaving it to dangle as she jerked the electrical cord from the wall and grabbed a towel to fan the smoke alarm.

"Toni?" Clark's tinny voice came through the dangling receiver. "What's going on?"

She continued fanning with one arm and grabbed the phone with the other. "Sorry, Clark, minor emergency. Gotta go!" She hung up without further ceremony.

Doc came racing into the kitchen in his plaid robe, his hair

169

still dripping from the shower. "It's okay, Pop," she answered his alarmed query. "I burnt the toast, is all. Must have accidentally bumped the dial." She stopped waving her arms. The alarm started to sound again. This time Danny came running.

Sighing, she raised her arms to fan the air beneath the ceiling device once again. "Pop, could you check the eggs, please?"

Too late. They were a rubbery mess.

She sighed again. "Danny, get out the cereal bowls," she said irritably. The look she gave him added, *And you'd better not give me any guff.*

When the alarm continued to shrill every time she stopped fanning, she had Pop get her a chair, climbed up on it, and disengaged the batteries. "Remind me to put the batteries in again before I leave for work," she said as she opened the casements to air out the kitchen.

She pulled cereal out of the pantry and milk from the refrigerator and fixed a bowl for Danny.

"Danny says he's not going to school today, Pop," she told her father, pouring herself a bowl of Raisin Bran. "I'm too tired to fight him. Could you make sure he stays quiet and doesn't go outside today?"

Doc peered at his grandson, who was wolfing down his bowl of Trix. "Don't look sick to me, Danny Boy. What's goin' on?"

He shrugged and didn't answer, but when Doc persisted, he threw down his spoon and shouted, "I hate school! Leave me alone!" Then he pushed away from the table and ran off to his bedroom, slamming the door behind him.

Toni shook her head, feeling helpless. "See if you can figure out what's wrong, Pop. Maybe he'll tell you. I can't get anything out of him."

She ended up being late for work, the first time since she'd started at Paper Chase. Ruth didn't say anything except, "Would you like to take some time off this week, Toni?"

"No!" She couldn't afford to take time off.

Wednesday before work she went in to Danny's school, ready for a fight. "Danny doesn't need special education," she said without ceremony. "What he needs is a little respect."

"We're not suggesting—"

"He refused to go to school yesterday," Toni interrupted. "It took my father nearly all day to discover why: Some of the kids are calling him dumb."

"No wonder he didn't want to be here!" said Mrs. Shaw. "I'll watch for it now that I know. I can probably already tell you which students are involved."

"But it's already happening, and you *didn't* know!" Toni said in exasperation. "You can't see everything. I remember how cruel kids can be. How's it going to help to put Danny in the dumb classes? He'll never want to come to school!"

"It's entirely up to you whether or not you enroll Danny in special education, Ms. Ferrier," the learning specialist explained patiently. "But we don't have dumb classes. All our children receiving special services are mainstreamed into the regular classroom for most of the day. If you agree to his placement, Danny will continue to be pulled out for his sessions with the reading specialist, but my aide and I will be in his classroom on a regular basis to assist him in whatever ways he needs. Other students, too—some special ed identified and some not. We're very low-key. Danny won't feel as if he's being singled out."

The specialist's matter-of-fact explanation made Toni more willing to listen to her recommendations. It helped that only Mrs. Shaw, the counselor, and the learning specialist were present at the meeting this time. She didn't feel quite so intimidated.

According to Mr. Gibbons, Danny's tests indicated his problems were less severe than they'd feared. Toni was profoundly relieved to hear that his IQ was above average. His reading disability had been confirmed, however, and the

171

school psychologist had written in his report that Danny quite possibly was mildly ADHD—attention deficit hyperactivity disordered.

"You'll want to make an appointment with his pediatrician," Mrs. Shaw told her. "The doctor may want to put Danny on medication to help him focus so he'll be better able to learn. But there are also some behavior-modification techniques we can teach you so that what we're doing at school can be reinforced at home. Would you be interested?"

"Oh, yes!" Toni responded eagerly, excited to hear there was something she could do to help her son. Lately she'd been feeling like a helpless bystander, watching him flounder, feeling as if it were her fault, and not being able to do a thing about it.

The counselor added, "I'll be visiting with Danny every week so that he has a chance to talk about his feelings. If kids are calling him names, we'll find out about it right away." He paused. "But we'd also recommend that you get him into counseling outside the school setting. We're convinced his emotional issues are interfering with his learning more than anything else."

Toni nodded, a lump in her throat.

17

Contrary to her original intent, Toni ended up signing all the paperwork for Danny to begin receiving special services in the fall. She came away from the meeting feeling subdued but hopeful. She still wasn't crazy about the idea of enrolling her son in special education, but she was willing to give it a try. If it didn't work, she could always pull him out, they assured her. That option made her feel as if she had at least some control.

She halfway expected Clark to call at Paper Chase sometime that day. He didn't. *Why would he?* she asked herself as she walked to her car after work.

But he called yesterday to see how I was.

He's a nice man. Doesn't mean he's interested in you in the way you're wishing...

What exactly was it she was wishing?

She dismissed the question without exploring it and tried to think about what she wanted to say to Chappie when she got to the church for their appointment.

"I don't know where to start," she said after she'd settled into the chair across the desk from the minister, a cup of hot coffee in her hands.

"You've been feeling scared and overwhelmed, you told me on the phone," he prompted her.

She nodded. "It was all about Danny, to start with. I signed the forms this morning to place him in special education." She told him about the initial meeting with Danny's teacher and the roomful of specialists, the meeting where she'd first been forced to face the consequences for her son of her own past choices.

"It was all so unexpected, Chappie, even though I'd seen some of the signs myself. I hadn't wanted to admit that anything was wrong with Danny. If I did, I'd have to admit it was my fault. That day in the meeting... I couldn't bear hearing all the problems he was having, knowing I was responsible for them." She took a deep breath and told him with great embarrassment about ending up after the meeting in her old hangout with a drink in her hand.

Chappie nodded. He didn't seem at all shocked, as she'd expected him to be. "You were feeling guilty and ashamed. A heavy burden," he commiserated. "It must have felt almost too heavy to bear. And you were worried about Danny on top of it. You did what you'd always done to try to escape from your pain. It's understandable, Toni." He looked at her curiously. "You were late to your dad's retirement dinner that night, but you didn't act drunk."

"I wasn't. I didn't have the drink."

"Toni, that's wonderful! That you got as far as sitting in a bar with a drink in your hand and still resisted the temptation—good for you!"

Toni shook her head, remembering her fingers around the bucket glass, remembering the weight of it in her hand as she lifted it. If she hadn't been such a klutz with her purse...

"What does it matter now, Chappie? It's the past I can't change." She turned her direct blue violet gaze on him. "I tried not to drink during my pregnancy, but I did. A lot more than I should have. I neglected him after he was born. Spent money on booze instead of baby formula. Left him alone. Thank God Pop was there to rescue him...

"I don't deserve Danny. I don't deserve Pop, or friends like Ruth and Jack, or a man like Clark Mc—"

She stopped, dismayed.

Chappie let it go. "But what you do now *does* matter, Toni. What you do now matters most of all." He leaned forward in his chair, his elbows on the desk, and steepled his fingers. "No matter what you've done in the past, *right now* you have the opportunity to carry out God's will for Danny."

"I don't know what you mean."

"What do you suppose *is* God's will for your son?"

"I don't even know what his will for *me* is!"

"You do," Chappie said gently. "It's in your heart, if you'll listen. God has a vision for you, Toni, as he does for Danny. As he does for all of us. I believe his will for us is that we be loved. His vision is that we be nurtured and cared for; that we feel safe to explore and express all of who we are; that we in turn love and nurture and care for the people he brings into our lives."

"So when I love my son, I'm carrying out God's will?"

"Yes! And wallowing in guilt and shame doesn't help you do that."

"No, it doesn't," Toni said slowly. "I don't feel very loving when I'm feeling ashamed. But Chappie, I don't know how to let those feelings go. I know in my head that God's forgiven me. I just don't *feel* forgiven."

Chappie nodded. "I know. I've been there. It takes time for our feelings to catch up to our faith. The irony is that even though God sees us through the eyes of forgiveness, clean and perfect, we *are* unworthy. All of us. Not because of what we've done. Just because in comparison to God, no matter how good we are, we will never measure up to him.

"So we can focus on our unworthiness and dig ourselves deeper and deeper into a pit of despair, or we can focus on the specific choices we made in the past that had destructive consequences—like the ones you've told me about—and resolve to never make those choices again.

"You're doing that, Toni. The past can't be changed. But you're choosing to do the right things now—to make your life and the lives of the people you love better *now*. You're choosing to rely on God for the strength to change your present. One day at a time."

One day at a time. Maybe it was all anyone could do.

Chappie prayed with her before she left, but she was so preoccupied with her thoughts, she couldn't have said five minutes afterward what it was he'd prayed. Her own prayer was simple: *God, I need you. Teach me. Guide me. Amen.*

That night she slept fitfully, waking from dream after vivid dream filled with scenes of horses racing, wild birds soaring, a dolphin playing; of herself watching, weeping, longing to run, to fly, to swim, not able. Chained to a post, trapped in a cage, carrying a burden bigger than herself...

It was as if in opening up to Chappie, Toni had loosened images and feelings wedged away for ages in her brain, hidden, unexplored.

Sometime in the early morning the dreams changed. Now she clung to the mane of the horse as it raced against the wind, wrapped her arms around the neck of the wild bird soaring in the sky, lay across the dolphin's back as it dove into the sea. Then she fell into a deeper, dreamless sleep and didn't wake till Doc came in and shook her, worried that the buzzer on her clock had been droning on and on. Oddly, she was instantly alert and felt refreshed and exhilarated.

As if adventure lay before her.

~ ~ ~ ~ ~

That afternoon, Clark dropped by Paper Chase. Toni couldn't deny the pleasure that washed through her when she looked up to see his friendly, open face. He was wearing a gorgeous raw silk jacket, beige, over a pale sage green shirt, with a quirky Mona Lisa tie. His own smile was less enigmatic and more expansive than the one on the face of Michelangelo's famous lady.

He didn't *look* like someone who was ready to turn tail and run. Maybe she hadn't scared him away after all.

"How's it going, Toni?"

"Hangin' in there. You?"

"Good—great! I just pulled a major coup—wanted to tell someone in person. Is Ruth working?"

Her heart plummeted. *Of course. He came in to see Ruthie, not me.* "She took the day off. Want me to leave her a note?"

"Nope." He grinned and pulled a bottle and two wineglasses from behind his back. "If she were here, one of us would have to drink from a coffee mug. Unacceptable. Inelegant."

She stared at him. "Clark, you know I can't drink—"

"Sparkling cider," he interrupted, holding the bottle up so she could see the label.

"But I'm working. I really shouldn't be—"

"Please?" he interrupted again. "I need someone to help me celebrate."

She laughed, the sound bubbling out of her as the tension she'd been carrying around for days began to break up and release. She realized too many days had gone by since she'd really laughed. *It isn't natural to go so long without laughing,* she thought.

"I'd love to. Are you going to tell me what it's all about?"

Clark set the wineglasses on the counter and peeled back the foil on the bottle before pulling off the plastic cap. "I—" he poured the cider with a flourish into one of the glasses and handed it to her—"have just landed—" he poured the other glass and set the bottle on the counter—"*Olympic!*" He lifted his glass triumphantly.

"Clark! Really? The biggest sports-shoe company in the world?" She lifted her glass to clink it against his.

"It's a really exciting project. Two years worth of training sessions for their site managers—worldwide." He lifted his glass to Toni's and took a sip of the sparkling cider. Toni followed suit.

"I don't know if you've read about it, but Olympic's been getting some bad press about their overseas factories," he went on. "We're going to address the cultural and ethical issues that are causing the problems. It's right up Manny's alley. One of my partners," he added in explanation at her puzzled look. He took another sip. "I'm going to make it in Portland, Toni."

"Of course you are!"

Their eyes met. Electricity sparked between them. They raised their glasses to each other again. "To success," Clark said, grinning.

It suddenly occurred to Toni that she was going to make it, too. She was going to stay clean and sober. She was going to do what she needed to do for Danny. She was going to find a way to make a good life for them…

"To success," she repeated and took a long swallow of the effervescent cider.

Clark, his voice alive with energy, told her about his project as if she knew exactly what he was talking about, as if she were his peer, his partner. She didn't understand all of it, but enough to see the possibilities. Enough to know that connection and creativity excited him as much as they did her.

"Would you like to come over for dinner?" she suddenly asked.

He grinned. "Yes! But only if you'll let me help."

~ ~ ~ ~ ~

The evening was a dizzying blur of fun and laughter. Jokes and stories flowed freely over their dinner of homemade pizza, and even Danny put aside his sullen antagonism to join in with the grown-ups. Last week his class had gone to see the fleet of navy ships anchored at the Willamette River harbor-wall for the Rose Festival, and he recounted the field trip with enthusiasm. "They had destroyers and an ammo ship and three fast...fast frig..."

"Fast frigates," Clark helped him out. "With guided missiles. I went down to see them, too, Danny. Interesting, wasn't it?"

"They were real cool," Danny agreed.

After dinner Brannigan came in, and the games came out: Yahtzee, Clue, and a boisterous card game called nerts that Toni said was one of her favorites. Clark caught on fast and matched her competitive spirit gleefully, slapping cards down right and left. Danny and his dog were both bouncing off the walls by the time they finished their last game.

"Time for bed, Danny," Toni finally said. "Scoot, now."

Danny balked. "I'm not sleepy," he argued.

Toni took a deep breath and let it out in a long sigh. "Tell you what," she said. "You go brush your teeth and get into your pj's, and we'll read your chapter book out here on the sofa tonight. If you get one of those old towels from the bottom shelf of the linen closet, you can even hold Brannigan on your lap. How's that?"

"Can Clark read to me?"

"I'd be honored," Clark said before Toni had time to ask.

Doc excused himself when Danny reported back to the living room with minty breath, wearing his new sailboat pajamas. "I'm awful tired," the old man said. "Toni, you'll close up the house when Clark gets goin'?"

"Sure. 'Night, Pop."

"'Night, Doc,'" Clark echoed.

"'Night, Grumpy,'" Danny chimed in.

Doc, his blue eyes twinkling, smiled through his beard at the three of them sitting in a row on the sofa, Clark holding a copy of E.B. White's *The Trumpet of the Swan*, and Danny with his arms wrapped around Brannigan's neck.

"'Night, all," he said.

Danny fell asleep before Clark had finished a chapter. Clark glanced at Toni and saw that she was nodding off as well.

"Falling asleep on me!" he teased. "Hope you're relaxed and not bored."

She smiled sleepily. "Relaxed," she answered him. "Want to help me get Danny to bed?"

Nodding, he coaxed the dog off the sofa and lifted Danny easily into his arms.

"Where to?" he whispered.

Leading him down the hallway and into the nearest bedroom, Brannigan padding behind her, Toni switched on the bedside lamp and pulled back the blankets. When Clark had deposited Danny on the bed, she tucked the blankets around him and gently kissed his forehead. The Irish setter leaped up, circled once, and settled at Danny's feet.

"Danny's lucky. You're a good mom, Toni," Clark told her as they returned to the living room.

She stopped so suddenly he nearly ran into her from behind. "Toni?" he said, noting with puzzlement her bowed head and the slump of her shoulders. He touched her shoulder lightly. She lifted a hand to her mouth, and as he moved around her, he saw that tears were streaming down her face.

"Toni?" he said in alarm. "What's wrong?"

She shook her head, as if unable to talk, and dropped onto the edge of the worn sofa. Clark sat down next to her, gingerly at first, but when Toni looked over at him, her dusky eyes swimming beneath thick black lashes wet with tears, it seemed the most natural thing in the world to move closer and take her in his arms. She didn't resist, but she didn't relax either.

Her mother? he wondered as he held her, resting his chin on the top of her head. Was she finally acknowledging her feelings about her mother's death?

She pulled away after a few minutes, wiping her eyes with the backs of both hands. "I'm getting your shirt all wet," she sniffled. He'd discarded his silk jacket long ago.

"It'll dry." He sank back into the sofa, touching her lightly on the shoulder once more. "C'mere," he invited.

Without looking at him, she leaned back into the sofa, her back against his side. He curled his arm around her protectively. "Want to talk about it?" he asked quietly.

"I'm sorry for getting so emotional," she started to apologize.

"It's okay, Toni," he hastened to assure her. "You don't need to apologize to me."

"It was—it was your compliment. That Danny's lucky. That I'm a good mother."

He felt confused. Why would a compliment make her cry? "Well, you are," he said. "The way you—*invite him in,* I guess is the way I'd describe it. Even when he's not behaving just the way you want him to. It's obvious you love him, Toni. And that you take delight in him. What better gifts could a mother give a son?"

She rotated around to face him, a smile lighting her beautiful features. "Thank you, Clark."

He wanted to kiss her, but something told him if he did, he wouldn't be able to stop. Kisses weren't what she needed right now. A listening ear was.

His heart went out to her as she told him about the problems Danny was having in school, about his recent placement in special ed and the recommendation he receive counseling.

"The last few weeks have been my hardest since I stopped drinking, Clark. I worried for a while, when things felt so overwhelming, that I was going to slip back into—into my old habits. But God has protected me."

Clark remembered what Ruth had said about Toni, that she was strong, that her faith in God was growing. Looking at her now, feeling her warmth against him, how he wanted to believe it!

"What's been hardest for you in all this?" he asked.

She didn't hesitate. "Knowing it's my fault. Knowing the choices I made in the past are still affecting Danny's present—and *my* present. Knowing the consequences will never go away."

"That must really hurt."

She looked as if she might cry again. "I'm trying to let it go," she said, her voice cracking. "But it's hard."

Clark squeezed her shoulder in silent support. After a moment, Toni added, "I had a good talk with Chappie yesterday. He reminded me that when I keep beating myself up for my past mistakes, I keep myself from doing the one thing I *can* do for Danny to make things right."

"And what's that?" Clark asked.

She looked away. "Loving him."

Clark pulled her closer. "You're doing it, Toni," he murmured into her hair. "You're doing what's best for him even though it's hard for you. You're a wonderful mom."

He gently turned her face toward his. Now was the time to kiss her.

But she placed a hand on his chest and pushed away. "Clark…I don't know."

"What don't you know?"

"When you left on Sunday, I thought—that is, you seemed so—are you sure?"

"I was blown away, Toni. By what you told me and by the way you threw it at me. It felt as if you were attacking me and running away from me at the same time. I admit, I felt like running, too. I had to think it through." He paused. "I suppose I should warn you I talked to Ruth about it," he added sheepishly.

"You did! What did she say?"

"She thinks you're wonderful. She thinks we would be good together."

"She does?"

"She does," he said, stroking the side of her face with the back of his hand. "So may I kiss you now?"

"What about Will?"

His mouth slipped into a grin. "I have absolutely no desire to kiss Will."

She laughed, and his heart lurched in response.

"I mean—if you don't think Will can change, why would you think I can?"

He cupped her chin in his hand and leaned closer.

"Maybe I've been wrong about Will. As for you—well, some things you just have to take on faith."

The kiss was so sweet he wanted to cry.

He started to draw back, but she leaned into him at just that moment, and something leaped in his heart. Then he was lost in a kiss so wild and wonderful he knew he had to leave now or he'd never want to.

～ 18 ～

Toni sat curled up on the sofa for a long time after Clark left, her arms wrapped around her knees and her bare toes dug in between the cushions. For a while she simply enjoyed the afterglow of Clark's presence: remembering the feel of his arms around her while she talked, his safe, protective arms; reliving the kiss that promised her so much...

Did she dare believe its promise? Would he love her? *Could* he love her? Could he put aside his preconceived ideas enough to even *know* her?

Ruth had assured her that Clark was a good man. Her friend's confidence in him went a long way toward overcoming Toni's distrust. She'd been afraid of men who generated much excitement; they hadn't been good for her. But the energy between her and Clark felt like clean, healthy energy. She wanted to believe that Clark would be good for her.

Still—he was a salesman, after all. A good one. A smart one. His intuition was sharp, his observation skills honed; Ruth said he could express his clients' desires better than they did themselves. Once that was done, the sale was easy.

Was that what he'd done with her? Figured out what she

185

wanted before she'd even figured it out herself? It seemed clear for the first time in her life, what it was she wanted. Someone to share both her triumphs and sorrows. Someone to listen, to understand, to encourage, to want her beside him on a mutual journey of faith and love. Someone whose touch made her tremble. A peer, a partner. A father for Danny.

Were his warmth and openness real, or were they only part of his sales pitch? She remembered Ruth's story about him selling cars to put himself through college. How much could she trust a man who'd sold a car every day for twenty-three days, for heaven's sake!

And what did he want from her? A man always wanted something...

Too many times in the past, Toni had fooled herself about people. Wanted something so badly she'd blinded herself to the truth. Believed she was loved when she was only being used. She couldn't afford to do that anymore. She wasn't the only one who stood to lose; she had a father and a son who counted on her.

Don't let me make a mistake here, God, she prayed silently. Even with Ruth's endorsement, she was going to need to be careful with Clark. Go slow. Get to know him before she did anything so rash as fall in love.

Guide me...

She was glad Clark was out of town on business Friday and Saturday. The physical distance made it easier to keep her perspective. So he was like a son to Ruth and Jack. So he seemed to have the respect of Chappie and the other members of her Growth Group. So he'd been sweet and caring when she'd gotten emotional. So his kiss made her toes curl...

He was still a virtual stranger. There was still too much she didn't know.

It didn't keep her from dreaming, of course. More than once over the next two days Ruth caught her staring out the window with a faraway look in her eyes. It was so unlike her, Ruth asked once again if she was feeling all right.

"Ruthie..." Toni said instead of answering the question. "Do you really think Clark and I would be good together?"

"Oh, so that's what this is all about!" Her boss looked pleased. "So the two of you have ironed everything out?"

"I don't know as I'd say *everything*," Toni said. Then, impatiently, "Well, do you?"

"Do I what?"

"Think Clark and I are a good match?"

Ruth smiled, her hazel eyes warm with affection. "In some ways, perfect. It remains to be seen, as I said to Clark, how good you'll be at nurturing each other's souls."

"What does *that* mean?"

"Encouraging each other's growth. Holding each other up, letting each other go—knowing when to do which. Challenging each other to explore undeveloped aspects of yourselves. Creating a safe place to do so. The tasks of love."

"Whoa!" Toni's eyes widened. "Ruth, you're scaring me!"

"Really? I don't mean to," the older woman said. "I just want you both to be as happy in marriage as Jack and I have been. Whoever you end up with. But..." She grabbed one of Toni's hands between both of hers and held it tightly. "I'm so glad you've decided to give each other a chance!"

On Saturday Toni made the final calls to confirm the services for Suzanne DeJong's wedding, now only a week away. Final, that is, barring any last-minute changes the woman might decide she wanted. A distinct possibility, if her demands so far were any indication. Toni was thoroughly enjoying coordinating the details of the wedding, but working with Suzanne was a definite challenge.

She'd loved brainstorming ideas with her subcontractors, however, to come up with products and services that suited her finicky client. If everything came off as planned, it was going to be an absolutely elegant wedding.

Toni had discovered she was very good at pointing out possibilities and encouraging self-confidence in the women she'd pulled together to do the wedding. *Ironic,* she thought, *seeing that self-confidence isn't my forte...*

When Suzanne had complained, after viewing snapshots, that Marie Quaid's cakes were "pedestrian," Toni had suggested Marie use real flowers to adorn the cake, an idea the decorator had embraced with enthusiasm. Her "practice" cake, adorned with roses and baby's breath, had been gorgeous. Even Suzanne had agreed.

Noreen Averill had called Toni in a panic when she found out the wedding was going to be on a *boat*. How were flowers going to fit into the scheme of things? The two of them had ended up going shopping and purchasing a latticework arch, which Noreen had painted white and entwined with lifelike vines of silk ivy. With the addition of fresh flowers the evening of the wedding, the arch would make a beautiful backdrop for the ceremony, either on the sundeck if the weather cooperated or in the upper salon.

"We'll still need the corsages and boutonnieres, the bride's bouquet, and maybe one nice arrangement for the guest-book table," Toni had told Noreen.

"Piece of cake," she had said, much relieved.

Suzanne had made some catering changes, after Karen Hawes had given Toni her bid and the contract had been signed, that increased the food costs by almost 50 percent. Toni had been firm but polite with the bride. "If you want squab and giant shrimp, I need the extra money now." She'd gotten it with only minor complaints and passed it on so Karen could do her job.

Henry Gillette was playing classical guitar for the ceremony, including a fifteen-minute prelude, the processional, and an accompaniment to Katie Castle's solo of "The Lord's Prayer." An odd choice on Suzanne's part, it seemed to Toni. She doubted the woman had any interest in the Lord or prayer.

The one thing Toni's client had been thrilled about from the beginning was having Georgine as the wedding photographer. Toni had showed her some of Georgine's work in a glossy fashion magazine. She hadn't batted an eye about the price of the photographer's work.

"Georgine is willing to do your makeup for an extra fee," Toni had told her. "Believe me, she knows all the tricks of the trade. These photos will be works of art. *You* will be a work of art."

"Perfect!" Suzanne had exclaimed, not complaining as she wrote Toni another check.

Her last call on Saturday was to Suzanne herself. "Everything's set on this end," Toni told her client. "You *do* have someone to perform the ceremony, right?"

"Judge Halpern," she said proudly as if Toni should know who he was. "Of the Superior Court. A friend of Frank's."

"Great. All I need from you now is Frank's address to pass on to Georgine—she'll meet you there at four o'clock—"

"Make it three," Suzanne interrupted. "Maybe she can do something with Wyn."

"—and a check for the balance when I meet you on the boat before the wedding," Toni concluded as if the woman hadn't interrupted. "Any questions?"

Of course she had questions. And comments, most of them delivered in a haughty tone Toni supposed was meant to make her feel like the hired help.

Oh well, she told herself as she hung up half an hour later, letting the woman's snobbery slide off her. In point of fact, she *was* the hired help.

Toni's eyes lit up with pleasure when Clark slipped into the pew next to her Sunday morning. Once again, Danny squirmed between them for the singing and the Scripture reading.

She remembered how little of the sermon she'd heard the week before with Clark sitting next to her. *God, please help me concentrate,* she prayed. Chappie had told her at the end of their meeting on Wednesday that his sermon for this morning addressed some of the same issues they'd talked about. She was anxious for additional insights.

"Christ, we ask that you would be our present teacher as we look into your written word today," the minister prayed after the children had been dismissed for their own program. "Let us see the world through new eyes. Amen."

Toni pulled the sermon notes from the bulletin and reached for a pencil.

"Happy are those who recognize their poverty of spirit," Chappie began, paraphrasing the first beatitude, "for all the riches of God's kingdom belong to them." He looked around the congregation. "Christ begins his Sermon on the Mount with this profound paradox: The poor are rich. The empty are full. Those who are nothing, are everything. The paradox defies all logic; how can both be true?

"Remember from our sermon last week that Christ presented the Beatitudes to his followers as a *new way of seeing.* If this is true, what is it he wishes us to see differently? What does the first beatitude teach us about what's most important in life, about what is truly valuable? How does it challenge our cultural values and priorities, as I suggested last week? What does Christ mean by 'poverty of spirit' and, conversely, by his promise of the 'kingdom of heaven'? These are the questions I've struggled with this week to prepare for today's sermon."

Toni chewed thoughtfully on the end of her pencil. As a recovering addict, she knew what it was like to be spiritually empty, to long so for something to fill that emptiness that she'd nearly destroyed herself trying. It seemed to her it was the pain of her spiritual poverty that had driven her toward drugs and alcohol—certainly not toward happiness.

"The word that helps me best understand poverty of spirit," Chappie went on, "is *humility*."

Humility? Thinking about her failures and her weaknesses? That didn't make sense to Toni, especially after her conversation with Chappie earlier in the week. It was the times she realized how far she still had to go that she felt *least* happy—most overwhelmed and hopeless. She glanced at Clark next to her as he crossed his arms over his chest, his pen moving in unconscious agitation between his fingers, a slight frown wrinkling his brow. She wondered what he was thinking.

Chappie continued, "Now, humility's gotten a bum rap in our culture. I think that's because people don't really understand what it means. And I think the church has to take some blame for that. Humility's been made very unattractive by the church—'Christian worm-ism,' I've heard it called."

He swept his eyes over the congregation. "Friends, God doesn't want us to crawl on our bellies through the mud bemoaning our unworthiness any more than he wants us to boast about our greatness. The fact is, people who think *too* highly of themselves usually have other people waiting in line to take them down a notch or two, but people who think of themselves as worms normally don't get an argument."

Toni barely noticed the ripple of laughter that swept through the congregation as her mind grappled with the minister's words. "We often hear sermons on the dangers of boastful pride," he continued. "The angel Lucifer was thrown out of heaven for his pride. A proud and boastful spirit is decried in

Scripture. But in my experience, *beating* oneself up is more common and more dangerous than *puffing* oneself up. More dangerous because it is more insidious—because it *masquerades as humility*. Self-abasement is what's given true humility such a bad name.

"A person who refuses to accept acknowledgement for his or her accomplishments seems false to us and is often just as arrogant and self-important as one who boasts about his accomplishments. The man puffed up with pride says, 'I can do anything'; the one who wallows in false humility says, 'I can do nothing.' In both cases, *self-will* is operating. And self-will is the antithesis and enemy of true humility. 'Worm-ism' isn't humility. True humility doesn't say, 'I can do nothing,' nor does it say, 'I can do everything.' True humility cuts through both extremes to say, 'I can do *something*—with the help of God.'"

Writing furiously, Toni saw from the corner of her eye that Clark was leaning forward, listening intently. *Something in Chappie's sermon must be hitting a nerve for him as well,* she thought.

"When self-will is operating in our lives, we are making ourselves our own gods, and in so doing we stunt our spiritual and emotional growth. Poverty of spirit—true humility—is essential if we are to be mature and healthy people."

Okay, Chappie, Toni thought. *So if the feelings I described to you this week aren't true humility, what is? And how do I get to it?*

Chappie proceeded almost as if he could hear her thoughts. "One requirement for true humility is seeing ourselves as God sees us. Seeing ourselves in a way contrary to what we see through the lens of our culture or the lens of our past—misshapen lenses that distort clear vision, make us myopic, encourage self-absorption.

"First, we live in a culture that teaches us to value independence and self-sufficiency to such an extent that we shut God and everyone else out of our lives. Please don't misunderstand me. I'm not suggesting it's wrong to strive for independence and self-sufficiency—only to strive for them above all else. To be addicted to them. To make personal success by our culture's standards the ultimate goal of our lives."

Toni's head jerked at the word *addicted*. She was startled Chappie had used the term. It was a strong statement.

"Second," he continued, "focusing on the mistakes and failures in our past can also keep us from developing our relationships with God and others. Again, don't misunderstand me. Reflecting on the consequences of our past mistakes can bring insight that helps us make better choices for the future. And certainly there are those who refuse to look at their failures at all, who numb themselves to the pain of their past by lying to themselves or by using substances or behaviors addictively. Hiding from our feelings of inadequacy isn't the answer. But miring ourselves in them is never productive.

"Seeing ourselves from God's eyes means seeing ourselves in perspective," the minister said. "For some, that means letting go of self-importance; for others, learning self-acceptance. In any case, it means understanding our need for God and other people. There is a hunger at our core that all the success in the world can't begin to satisfy, nor can all the things we use and abuse in order not to feel our sense of failure—because the hunger is a spiritual hunger. It can be assuaged only in relationship—in the true meeting of souls.

"We are created to need God. We are created to need each other. All alone, we are inadequate. No matter how hard we try to convince ourselves otherwise, we know that at an elemental level we are incomplete. And we will not begin to grow emotionally and spiritually until we accept our inadequacies, and allow ourselves to feel the pain that accompanies them."

Toni felt a lump forming in her throat. *But I know I'm inadequate, God. I know I need you, and Pop, and Danny, and Ruth, and*

Georgine. She tapped her pencil unconsciously against the paper in her lap. *What I've done to Pop and Danny can never be undone. I know I'm unworthy. And believe me, I feel the pain...*

Again, Chappie seemed to be reading Toni's thoughts. "Understand that poverty of spirit is not about intrinsic unworthiness; God makes it clear in Scripture that we are incredibly valuable. We are created in the very image of God, 'fearfully and wonderfully made'; even the hairs of our heads are numbered. He has loved us with an 'everlasting love.' He knows the plans he has for us, plans to make us prosper, to give us hope and a future."

I am incredibly valuable!!! Toni scribbled on her sermon notes, underlining the words. She didn't know if she believed it, but she knew she wanted to.

"When we see ourselves as God sees us, we see both our glory, 'a little lower than the angels,' and our weaknesses," Chappie went on. "God sees our shortcomings, our disobedience and willfulness. But he loves and accepts us despite our weaknesses—despite the mistakes we make. He sees beyond them. He sees our potential. He sees the best part of us."

What does that mean? Toni wondered. *What is my best part?*

"Still," Chappie's voice once more broke into her thoughts, "even at our best, we don't begin to approach the glory of God. Though made in his image, we are still only infinitesimal sparks of light in contrast to his eternal, all-consuming glory—like the brief light of a single match in comparison to the radiance of a thousand suns. Poverty of spirit is not a matter of our unworthiness per se but an understanding of our unworthiness in comparison to God."

Chappie took a sip of water from the glass on the podium before continuing. "One important requirement for developing true humility, then, is seeing ourselves in perspective. How do we go about doing that? By practicing the other requirement:

seeing God. By getting to know him. By spending time with him, letting our relationship with him unfold. Poverty of spirit, in fact, is a natural consequence of seeing God—of beholding him in all his glory and his awesome power.

"In order to experience true humility, in other words, we must stop focusing on ourselves—on either our achievements or our failures—and focus on God instead. Remember, the opposite and enemy of humility is self-will, whether in the form of self-love or self-hatred. Developing humility is a process of de-centering and re-centering. I am not my own god; only God is God."

Who is at the center of my life? Toni wrote on her notes. *God—or myself?* She chewed on the end of her pencil as Chappie continued.

"Clearly, in God's eyes I am important. I am special. But I am not more important than anyone else. I am not superior. Neither is anyone else more important nor more special than I. In God's eyes I am not inferior. He sees us all on an even playing field.

"And so we come to a second and third paradox. One, we are persons of infinite worth, and at the same time totally unworthy of the mercies God bestows on us. Two, while each of us is unique, a creature of singular and infinite potential, each of us is also ordinary, sharing with our brothers and sisters all the traits and experiences that make us human. We are all capable of the same heights. We are all capable of the same depths."

Chappie was the father of seven children, Toni reflected, a wonderful father who loved and guided and protected his sons and daughters, who made his relationships with them a priority. Was he saying that even he was capable of doing what Toni had done? of putting his children in danger? of deserting them? She shook her head. God might see them on an even playing field. She knew she didn't.

She looked down at her notes. The words she'd underlined earlier jumped out at her: *I am incredibly valuable!!!* Next to them she wrote, *I am incredibly unworthy...*

"When we finally come to a place where we recognize and accept our poverty of spirit," Chappie said, "we open ourselves to all the riches of the kingdom of heaven promised to us in the first beatitude. The riches that make life worth living, that give us purpose for getting out of bed in the morning, that make every day a new adventure. Love, joy, peace, hope. We develop a sense of gratitude, a recognition that life is an incredible gift. Gratitude makes us ever more humble. Our increased humility makes us ever more able to experience God's bountiful gifts.

"The cycle continues. The paradox makes sense: 'Blessed are the poor in spirit, for theirs is the kingdom of heaven.'"

I feel unworthy, Toni thought. *I feel ashamed of what I've done to Danny and how much I've hurt Pop. But it isn't the humility Chappie is talking about,* she realized. *It is its enemy, its opposite.*

How could she ever see herself the way Chappie said God saw her—infinitely valuable, even if flawed? How could she ever accept herself the way he said God accepted her?

How could anything ever be right in her life with her past mistakes staring her in the face every day?

Clark had been prepared to tune Chappie out the minute he heard the word *humility*. He was glad he'd paid attention long enough to understand that the minister didn't mean it the way he'd feared.

If anyone had a corner on "Christian worm-ism," as Chappie called it, it was the church Clark had tried for a while in Seattle. It hadn't taken him long to figure out that his self-confidence, as well as the fact he'd been financially successful, were considered suspect—if not downright sinful. Except when they'd begun their building-fund drive, of course...

He bristled again when Chappie mentioned independence and self-sufficiency in a less-than-flattering light a little later in his sermon. They were words Clark saw as highly descriptive of himself. Even after the minister had clarified his comments, Clark felt resistance. Some part of him knew his resistance meant something was going on inside he didn't want to look at. It was true that career success had always been important to Clark, but it had never been his ultimate goal. Had it? Certainly he enjoyed the outward trappings of success. But the more important rewards for his work were the things he'd learned, the people he'd met, the feeling that he was contributing to others. No one had the right to make him feel guilty about being successful.

But maybe your life isn't about independence and self-sufficiency, some part of him said. *Maybe it's about your need for control...*

Clark frowned, not wanting to listen to this inner voice, but unable to ignore it. *Life isn't always clean and neat the way you want it to be,* the voice prodded. *Sometimes it's messy. Maybe you don't want to get your hands into the muck of it. Maybe you've been hiding behind your work and your money...*

He shifted uncomfortably as Chappie talked about interdependent relationships, about the universal human need to be spiritually connected to other human beings. He'd been taking care of himself for so long now, and doing it so well, that he rarely felt any sense of urgency in his relationships. Was he fooling himself? Was his intuitive response to Toni Ferrier when they'd met—his sense of incompleteness, his inexplicable need to know her—a message from God? A sign that he wasn't as self-reliant as he'd thought?

Glancing at Toni, he was startled by the pained expression on her face. She looked as if she were trying not to cry. He looked away again, quickly, afraid to see more evidence of her distress. Afraid of how it made him feel.

He remembered how it had felt to hold her. He wanted to put his arms around her again, comfort her for the nameless sorrow welling up in her eyes, for whatever pain it was that pinched her mouth.

He closed his eyes but saw her image still in his mind. She was enchanting, as fresh and lovely as spring in a lace-trimmed dress the same delicate rose as the flush along her cheek, her dark hair curling around her face, her lashes thick and black around those exotic, dusk-colored eyes. He'd asked her in their long, late-night conversation after the fireworks about her ethnic heritage, wondering what combination of genes could have created such exquisite beauty. "I'm a mutt," she'd said, with a touch of self-deprecation he found strongly appealing in a woman so beautiful. "French, Czech, Russian, Portuguese, with an Indian princess somewhere way back in the mix," she'd told him. "Or so I'm told."

There was a certain abandon about her none of the pieces of her heritage seemed to explain. "How about Gypsy?" he'd asked.

Her smile had been mysterious. "Who knows?"

He opened his eyes again. This was ridiculous. He needed to concentrate.

"An increased sense of gratitude, then, is one sign we're developing humility in our lives," Chappie was saying. Clark wondered what he'd missed, how long his mind had been wandering. The last thing he'd written on his sermon notes was, *Created to need each other. Do I believe this?*

"A second sign of true poverty of spirit," Chappie went on, "is a growing willingness to serve others. Without humility, we serve ourselves—that old self-will kicking in again. When humility is operating in our lives, we are able to truly serve others—to be sensitive to their needs and to do what we can to help and encourage them.

"The problem is, what *looks* like service to others may instead be *self*-serving in ways of which we're not even aware. Let me caution you about two patterns of activity that might look like ministry but are counterfeits in the same way self-abasement is a counterfeit of humility."

Once again Chappie drank from the glass of water on the podium before continuing his sermon. "A big part of my ministry for many years now has been counseling with individuals about their spiritual journeys. Over the years, I've talked with many, many people who believed they were serving God by suppressing their own personalities to meet the needs of others, by becoming doormats, by allowing others to run roughshod over them. That's not service, friends. Allowing yourself to be used and abused serves the best interests of no one.

"Another group of people I've counseled with," the minister continued, "usually because they're burnt out, or their families are falling apart, or they've reached a crisis of faith, are those who seem the most obviously committed to serving God and others. These are the deacons/Sunday school teachers/youth workers/whatever-the-church-needs-at-the-moment people. The ones you'll find in church every time the doors are open. The ones who seem to give and give and give until it seems impossible they'd have anything left to offer.

"Sometimes these are the ministers, the missionaries, the inspirational speakers—those who've given their lives to what we call full-time ministry. And sometimes these people aren't serving God at all. *They're serving their own addictive needs.*"

The auditorium seemed to Clark suddenly noisy—whispering, papers rustling, pencils tapping. Chappie seemed to hear it, too.

"'What?' you say. 'Are you saying people can be addicted to the *church*?'" His eyes roamed over the congregation. "'But, Chappie, people have addictions to *bad* things! Drugs, alcohol, gambling. Surely you can't be serious!'

"The truth is, it's not just the drugs or the alcohol or the gambling that are bad for us—it's the *addictive use* of any substance or activity. If we're prone to addiction, as most of us are, there are plenty of socially acceptable ways to 'feed the need,' most of which go completely unnoticed. As a culture, we're in denial. Even as conscientious Christians, we're in denial.

"Anytime we use a substance or activity to keep from dealing with our failures or our feelings, to make us feel better for the short term, to try to fill an inner emptiness that only our relationship with God can fill, we are using that substance or activity addictively. It doesn't have to be drugs or alcohol. It might be work. It might be eating. It might be shopping. It might be exercise.

"And yes—" Chappie continued. "Christian ministry can be used as addictively as any of those activities. How do I know?" He was silent for a long moment, head down, his hands gripping the sides of the podium.

"I've been there myself," he finally said, raising his head. "I've ignored my health, my family, my friends, and most of all *my relationship with God* because I desperately *needed* to be doing something that looked like service on the outside in order to feel okay about myself on the inside. I wasn't *choosing* ministry. I *needed* it."

The church was as quiet as a windless afternoon, as if the congregation were collectively holding its breath.

Again, Chappie took his time before continuing. "I've never talked about this part of my life in a public forum," he said. "But as I prepared for today's sermon earlier this week, God made it clear that it was time. Someone out there needs to hear about my pain in order to confront their own. Someone needs to understand the pain that drives someone they love."

Will's image suddenly flashed through Clark's mind. He pushed it away, frowning. What was there to understand? Will was weak. He'd never amount to anything…

"It took a crisis in my family life to make me realize my addiction to church work was destroying everything most important to me," Chappie said. "It took a very brave act by my dear wife, Mary, who loved me enough to confront me with her own pain. Even now, a dozen years later, every day, sometimes every hour, I ask God to help me understand my motives when I think I'm serving others. It's only at that level I can know for sure.

"Like an alcoholic, I'm in recovery, one day at a time, still fully capable of using supposedly spiritual activities to serve myself instead of serving others. I've engaged in Christian service addictively for the same reason people use substances addictively: because I felt spiritually hungry and didn't understand how to satisfy that hunger. Yes, even as a minister."

Clark's head was pounding. He'd always seen addiction in terms of Will and Will's father. He'd always seen the problem as character weakness. Could there be something more to it? Could Will actually be more in tune with his spiritual nature than Clark was? Could his addiction be seen as a hunger, a horribly misguided search for God?

What about Toni? How had she managed to end up on the path of sobriety? Could it be that someone—Doc, Georgine, Ruth, Chappie—had recognized her hunger and shown her another way to feed it? Acknowledged her search and guided her to a new way? Toni had people in her life who loved her. Who had Will ever had? Maybe Sunny...

Chappie was saying, "What I learned—not easily, I might add—is that true service isn't about our needs. It's about our gifts. It's about relationship, about connection at the deepest levels. It acknowledges both our own and others' intrinsic worth. True service doesn't place us beneath others, servants with no rights of our own; nor does it place us above others, kings casting bread to the peasants below. True service equalizes. It recognizes what we get back from our giving.

"If we are to be free to serve, we can't deny the feelings of unworthiness that force us into the role of 'rugged individualist' or make us doormats or drive us to addiction. What we must do is put those feelings in proper perspective. Instead of hiding our feelings of unworthiness and trying to escape their pain, we must learn to deal with them instead.

"We may be only humble jars of clay, but we are jars of clay

202

that hold 'the light of the knowledge of the glory of God.' In our hearts we hold the treasure of God's glory and power. And because we have this all-surpassing power in residence in our hearts, we can say with the apostle Paul, 'we are hard pressed on every side, but not crushed; perplexed, but not in despair; persecuted, but not abandoned; struck down, but not destroyed.' Though we are poor in spirit—no, *because* we are poor in spirit—we have all the riches of God dwelling in us.

"Poet Noel McInnis writes, 'Be loving of your empty times as well as of your full ones. No one has ever had a filling without an emptying to give it room.' In those words the poet explains the paradox of the first beatitude: 'Blessed are the poor in spirit, for theirs is the kingdom of heaven.'"

Chappie closed his Bible and said quietly, "Let's enter now into a time of prayer and meditation…"

Clark bowed his head, moved and humbled by Chappie's confession and the insights the minister had gained from his experience. *What is it you want me to learn, God?* he prayed.

Once again Will's image flashed through his mind. This time he held it.

~ 20 ~

The week leading up to Suzanne DeJong's wedding flew by for Toni. She saw Clark twice more, once in the evening for dinner and a movie, once in the morning before work for a long walk in Waterfront Park. On the days she didn't see him she talked to him on the phone—long, rambling conversations about nothing and about everything.

She was especially pleased to hear that after Chappie's sermon Sunday, Clark had made a vow to himself to spend more time with his half brother, and when he did, to try to listen more and judge less. She couldn't help but feel that the better Clark understood Will, the better he would understand her.

"You might want to attend an Al-Anon meeting or two," she suggested. "Pop would probably take you. He started to go to the meetings while I was in rehab, to try to figure out what to expect and how to deal with me when I got out. He still goes once in a while."

It was Danny's last week of school before summer vacation. She managed to slip away from work for an hour to attend his class party, an effort rewarded by Danny's happiness to see her there. His report card was no better than she'd expected, but she was coming to terms with her son's placement in special ed, accepting it philosophically and trusting it would help him be more successful next year.

She decided she could afford a new outfit for the wedding and took herself shopping one evening after work. The fitted navy column dress she found on sale, with its white collar and piping, was very feminine and also had a nautical flair. *Perfect for the* Snow Swan, she thought as she pirouetted in front of the mirror to see it from all sides.

Georgine flew in on Friday afternoon. They spent the evening catching up. George told Toni about the progress of Child's Play, Incorporated, her friends' new catalog business out of Portland.

"Their product is a line of fashionable, high-end clothes for children. The outfits are well-made, and Felice's designs are darling, but what I really love about the concept is this buy-back plan Marilu and Marty want to install after they get going."

"Buy-back plan?"

"Yeah. When kids outgrow the clothes, their parents can return them to Child's Play for credit. Then the used clothes will be distributed to needy children, both here in the U.S. and overseas."

"Oh, George, it sounds like the perfect kind of company for you to join! And I'm not just saying that because I want you to move to Portland, either."

"I'm thinking about it pretty seriously. Now—"

Toni interrupted with a squeal of delight and an excited hug for her friend.

Georgine returned the hug, smiling at Toni's exuberance. "Now tell me what's going on with Clark," she said.

Toni immediately got "all dreamy-eyed," as Georgine described it, and told her friend in detail about the events of the last two weeks. "We're besotted," she finished, sighing dramatically. "Both of us."

"As long as it's mutual," George said, grinning. "I'm really happy for you, Toni."

Saturday dawned overcast with light sprinkles, but the forecast was for clearing in the early afternoon. By the time Georgine set out for the groom's house, where Suzanne and Wyn, her sole attendant, were getting ready for the wedding, the clouds had broken up and a warm sun dried the pavement.

When Toni had expressed concerns about logistics for the wedding—setting up the latticework arch, getting the tables on the lower deck positioned for the guest book and gifts in the forward section and for the caterer in the lower salon, setting up chairs in the upper salon for the ceremony and taking them down again for the reception—Clark had offered his assistance.

She'd hesitated. "Only if you let me pay you," she had told him.

He had protested. "Toni, I'd be happy to help."

She had shaken her head. "I really need to know I can do this on my own, Clark. I've got an idea, and it all depends on how this wedding turns out. How well I do at it. If I pay you to be my assistant, then it's still my show."

"All right," he had said grudgingly. Then he had brightened. "Can I use the money to take you and Georgine out afterward?"

Toni had laughed. "I guess once I pay you, I can't keep you from spending your money any way you want to! That would be lovely, Clark. I'd like you to get to know George. She's wonderful."

"You're pretty wonderful yourself," he had returned.

It scared her a little how good his words had made her feel.

To say Clark was impressed by Toni's handling of the wedding was like saying Moses had been impressed by the burning bush. Awe was a more accurate description of his feelings.

From the archway on the sundeck, intertwined with white roses, calla lilies, ivy, and white twinkle lights, to the beautifully decorated cake, to the squab and giant shrimp in the buffet, there was no question that Toni had achieved "elegance and intimacy," as Suzanne DeJong had requested. The women she'd recruited from the church to do the flowers, the cake, and the catering looked like they'd been doing weddings for years. Henry's classical guitar and Katie's contralto solo added just the right touch to the ceremony.

Only someone of Toni's intelligence and boundless energy could have planned and pulled together a wedding like this in only three weeks. She was amazing: playing charming hostess, graciously engaging with the wedding guests, yet all the while aware of both the big picture and the smallest details.

She made sure every aspect of the event ran smoothly: seeing that the groom was in the right spot before the music began, that the processional started at the right moment, that the reception line moved efficiently, that the chairs were folded up and hidden away by the time the deejay called for Suzanne and Frank to dance the first dance.

Everyone was impressed, especially the bride. "Well, miracle of miracles," Toni said when Suzanne had the groom write out a check for a hefty tip as the boat docked at the end of the wedding cruise.

"No miracle about it, Toni," Clark said, shaking his head in admiration. "Suzanne just knows a good thing when she sees it. If there's a miracle here, it's you."

Toni gave him a spontaneous hug, her blue violet eyes sparkling with energy. She could hardly keep still; she was so wound up. "I did good, didn't I?" She laughed. "Listen to me! Maybe Chappie's words are sinking in. Anyway, I can't *wait* to tell you my idea."

"So tell me! I'm all ears," Clark said, returning her hug.

"Not yet. When we go out. I want George to hear, too."

"I thought you couldn't wait to tell me," he grumbled good-naturedly.

"Toni—" a voice interrupted from behind them.

They both turned to find a radiant Wynona smiling shyly at them. Between Janna Blaine, the hairdresser who'd recommended Toni to Suzanne, and Georgine, Wyn had been transformed. Her hair was still red, but a subtler shade that warmed her skin and brought out the ginger in her brown eyes. It was curled and pulled up in a loose swirl with tendrils artfully escaping at the nape of her slender neck.

The black eyeliner she usually wore had been replaced with a smudge of light brown, the cakey black mascara with a single coating of dark brown. It was impossible to tell if the glow on her cheeks was makeup or excitement or the sheen reflected from the deep rose silk of her long, slim dress. In the context of her new look, even her nose ring was elegant.

"I thought maybe I'd come to church on Sunday," Wyn said, glancing at Clark from beneath her lowered lashes before turning her attention to Toni. "If it's still okay for you to pick me up?" she added anxiously.

Toni smiled at her warmly. "I'd be happy to, Wyn. Invitation's still open for the camping trip next week, too, if you decide you want to come. I know Danny would love to have you along."

"Thanks." She grimaced, and for an instant she looked like the old Wyn. "Mom and Frank would probably be happy to get rid of me for a couple of days."

"By the way…" Toni cocked her head to one side. "Have I told you how beautiful you look tonight?"

Wyn blushed and looked down, hands clasped behind her back. "About a hundred times."

"Oh! Why do I keep forgetting?"

"As stunned as I am, I guess," Clark interjected. Then he added in a teasing tone, "Don't tell your mom, Wyn, but I think you outshone the bride tonight."

He was immediately sorry he'd said anything. The look Wyn shot him could only be described as adoring.

Clark and Toni started final cleanup as the last guests left the boat. The caterer and her assistant had already completed most of the messy work, and when Georgine joined them after her final dockside shots of the wedding couple, it took only another ten minutes to finish up.

Ten minutes more and the three of them were settled at a window table at Atwater's, on the top floor of Big Pink, Portland's tallest downtown building. Georgine sat back in her chair with her coffee cup and watched the tuxedoed pianist as he played a medley of romantic tunes. Toni rested her elbows on the table and sat with her chin in her hands, staring out over the city lights. Clark couldn't look at anything but Toni.

"Atwater's isn't the kind of place people in my income bracket get around to very often," she'd told him in the elevator on the way up.

"It's the kind of place you deserve, Toni," Clark had told her, squeezing her hand. *You deserve all the best,* he thought. And he wanted to be the one to give it to her.

He interrupted her musings as their waitress set a shrimp cocktail appetizer on the table. "Okay, Toni. This idea you've got us all curious about. Out with it!"

A panoply of emotions played across Toni's lovely features. Clark watched her face in fascination. Her cheeks were flushed and her eyes bright. She was excited about something, but at the same time hesitant, not completely sure of herself.

"All right," she said, "but if it's a stupid idea, please tell me. You guys are the experts."

"It's a business idea?" Clark asked.

Toni nodded. "Yeah." Another deep breath. "Okay. Here's what I think. I think there are a lot of women out there who don't have the time to spend on all the little details that go into making a wedding happen. They have lives they can't just put on hold like brides used to do when they got married at nineteen or twenty. They work, they exercise, they volunteer, they keep a house, they might have kids."

"That's true," Georgine said. She raised a pale eyebrow. "I think I know where you're going here. You want to plan weddings?"

"More than that. Run a complete wedding service. For the *Snow Swan*." She looked from Clark to Georgine and back to Clark.

"For the *Snow Swan*. Hmm." Clark looked at her speculatively. "Have you talked to Jack about this idea?"

"No. I wanted to get some feedback first."

"What do you mean by 'complete' wedding service, Toni?" Georgine asked.

"I mean that other than a couple of consultations and a few follow-up phone calls, the bride wouldn't have to do another thing except write the check and show up in her wedding gown with the wedding party at the right time on the right date. I'd do everything else."

"Aren't there businesses out there that already do this sort of thing?" Clark asked.

"Some. Not many get as involved in every aspect of the wedding as I'm thinking about. First, I wouldn't just plan the weddings; I'd *design* them. Meet with the bride to get an idea of who she is and what kind of *feel* she wants her wedding to have. Then come up with a concept that suits her. Like the look I came up with to make Suzanne's wedding 'intimate and elegant.'" She stopped, her expression begging for encouragement.

Clark gave it to her. "You did a primo job, Toni. Your client couldn't have been more pleased. So…after you came up with your concept, you'd carry it through like you did for today's wedding?" he prompted.

"Yes!" she answered eagerly. "I'd do everything that had to be done to make the wedding happen. Find appropriate suppliers, coordinate their services, coordinate the wedding itself. I'd be in on the whole picture from beginning to end."

"Maybe set up a package deal?" Georgine joined in. "So your brides know up front how much it would cost them? Most people don't have the kind of unlimited resources Suzanne DeJong had."

"Maybe. On the other hand, a package deal might limit my clients' choices. It couldn't cover someone like you, George, if they wanted really special photography."

"Maybe you could offer several packages at different prices, Toni," Clark said. "And options within each package."

"Maybe…" She chewed her lower lip thoughtfully. "If I could develop a large enough network of suppliers and subcontractors, I might be able to keep the flexibility I want and still be able to standardize my prices."

As Toni went on to explain several other ideas she'd come up with for the *Snow Swan* wedding business, Clark listened with growing admiration. Her agile mind and her creativity more than made up for her lack of education and experience. Ruth was right; she was a natural businesswoman. On top of that, her energy and excitement were contagious.

"It's an interesting idea, Toni," Clark said when she'd finished. "I see real potential." He leaned forward, resting his elbows on the table. "Have you thought about how you'd advertise your service?" he asked. "To run something like that for the sternwheeler, Jack would have to put some cash into marketing."

"Well—no. I guess I figured Jack would handle that."

"Never figure someone else is going to be willing to spend their money," Clark said wryly. "Especially Jack. But if you *could* sell Jack on the idea..." He dropped a hand to the table and drummed his fingers, looking toward the window, his eyes far away. Then he focused once again on Toni. "Have you worked out any numbers? Do you know for sure that Jack could make money doing wedding cruises? More money than he's making now? Enough more to justify, say, twenty thousand dollars in advertising and promotional materials?"

"*Twenty thousand dollars!*" Toni looked stricken. "That much?"

"I know it sounds like a lot, but money for promotion and advertising is some of the best money a new business can spend," he said. "You can offer the best wedding services in the city, but if no one knows about them, you're not going to survive."

Toni shook her head. "I can't ask Jack to spend that much!"

"Not all at once," Clark hastened to assure her. "That's spread out over a year. You need a business plan, Toni. If you could show Jack a projection of the money your service would bring in during that year..."

"I'm already lost. I wouldn't have the faintest idea how to go about making projections or writing a business plan."

"But I know how."

She rolled her eyes. "I can't afford you, Clark."

He waggled his eyebrows. "I'm sure we could work something out. A kiss here and there, a home-cooked meal once in a while, maybe a batch or two of homemade chocolate chip cookies..."

"Clark! You'd really help me?"

"Absolutely. It's a good idea, and I think it would be great for Jack's business on the *Snow Swan*. He no doubt will need some convincing for the advertising outlay, but I think we might be able to talk him into it."

"Toni, this is exciting!" Georgine said. "I'm sorry I'm not going to be around. You'll keep me posted, won't you?"

"I'm keeping my fingers crossed that you'll be living in Portland by the time I have my first wedding, and will take pictures for me again," Toni responded.

Georgine laughed. "Who knows? Stranger things have happened, I'm sure."

"So what do I need to do first, Clark?" Toni asked. "Figure out those 'numbers' you were talking about?"

"You got it!" He pulled a gold pen from his shirt pocket and grabbed a napkin. "Number one," he said as he wrote. "What will your per-wedding expenses be? Based on that, number two: What do you need to charge your clients in order to make a profit for Jack and pay yourself a fair fee? Is that price competitive with other similar businesses? Number three: How many weddings can you expect to do in a year?" He stopped writing and looked up, concerned. "When do people get married other than in June?"

Toni and Georgine both laughed. "People get married every month of the year, silly," Toni told him. "The business would be seasonal, though. Spring and early summer, mostly. And Christmas."

She clapped her hands in sudden delight. "Wouldn't that be beautiful? A December wedding on the *Snow Swan,* decorated for the holidays, with the Christmas Boat Parade sailing by all lit up in the night?"

Toni looked positively enraptured by her vision. Clark couldn't take his eyes off her.

"Anything else?" he heard her ask from far away.

He shook himself and dropped his eyes to the napkin to remind himself what he'd been doing. "Number four," he said, his voice cracking. He felt as if he were in a fog. Clearing his throat, he tried again. "Number four: What are your options for marketing? How much would each option cost?"

He didn't remember anything else about the evening except for Toni's good-night kiss. *That* he would remember for a very long time.

❧ 21 ❧

The call came just as Clark was crawling into bed, not long before one in the morning. He reached languidly for the phone on the nightstand. Maybe it was Toni, he thought, wanting to tell him good night one last time...

"I'm trying to reach Clark McConaughey."

The unfamiliar woman's voice sounded urgent. Clark sat up, his heart picking up speed.

"This is he..."

"It's Peggy Flynn."

Will's girlfriend. A sudden feeling of dread wiped out the contented glow with which he'd finished the evening. "What's happened to Will?"

"He's been in a car accident. I'm calling from the hospital."

"Oh, no! How serious is it?"

Her voice was shaky. "Mostly cuts and bruises, but he hit his head hard. Gashed it open. They say he'll be all right, but they want to keep him overnight." She started to cry. "He's talking crazy, Clark. That he *killed* someone! Nobody died. The accident wasn't even his fault. I'm so scared. Please—can you come?"

Clark was already pulling on a pair of slacks. "I'll be there in ten minutes."

Peggy was waiting for him in the emergency-room waiting area. He'd met her a couple of times, maybe two years before. She was a fragile, waiflike woman with long brown hair and large blue eyes that looked ready to overflow with tears.

Before he could even say hello, she was speaking in a desperate, rapid-fire manner: "I moved out yesterday. I can't be with him anymore, do you see? He drinks too much and he pulls me down and I can't be around him. I've got to take care of myself. And *this* happens! I can't keep taking care of him. Do you see?"

He saw. The one person who'd been there for Will in the last few years wasn't going to be there for him anymore. And shouldn't be. Clark didn't know how she'd managed to stick with him as long as she had.

"Go home, Peggy," he said gently. "Take care of yourself. I'll take care of Will."

"I feel so bad, like I'm dumping him because of the accident, but it's not like that, I'd already left." She started to cry again. "I love him, but I just can't live with him anymore, do you see? He won't get help for his drinking. I can't let him keep hurting me!"

Clark put his arms around her and let her cry on his shoulder for a moment. "I do see, Peggy. It's okay. You've made the right decision for yourself. Maybe it's the right decision for Will, too. Would you like me to keep you informed?"

"Oh, would you? Please, yes. If only he'd get some help for his drinking. It's not that I don't love him, do you see?" She pushed away from Clark and rummaged in her purse for a pen and a scrap of paper. "Here's my number. Thank you. Thank you." She folded the scrap once, then again and once again, nervously, not even aware she was doing it. "I'm worried about him…"

Clark took the scrap of paper with her phone number and slipped it in his pants pocket, then gently took her elbow and guided her toward the exit. "I'll call you, Peggy, if anything changes. Okay?"

An emergency-room nurse filled him in on the details. The driver of the other car had apparently misjudged Will's speed and pulled out in front of him from a side street. Clark breathed a sigh of relief to hear his half brother had been sober; he'd dreaded for years that Will was going to end up killing someone.

A sudden thought made him ask, "Peggy was right, wasn't she—no fatalities?"

"No fatalities," the nurse said. "The other driver and his eight-year-old daughter were both released with minor cuts and bruises. Your brother's injuries appear minor, too, but we're keeping him overnight for observation. He has a fever and seems delirious, symptoms not necessarily related to the accident. His alcoholism...you're aware of it?"

Clark nodded, feeling sick to his stomach. "I am. He's not."

"He will be before he leaves the hospital. We have him scheduled for a psychiatric exam tomorrow morning, too."

"Can I see him?"

She hesitated, then made a call upstairs. A few minutes later a floor nurse led him to the door of a private room. She knocked and entered without waiting for an answer, Clark following close behind. "Got someone here to hold your hand," she said cheerfully.

"Peggy? Don't leave me!" Will was partially reclined on the bed, a large bandage covering one side of his head. His eyes met Clark's in a wild stare.

"It's Clark, Will. Peggy's gone home to get some rest," he said quietly, pulling up a chair next to the bed. It was true, if not the whole truth.

"Clark! I killed her. It was me!"

Clark and the nurse exchanged glances. "We can't convince him no one died in the accident," she murmured. "The doctor gave him a sedative not long ago. It should start to take effect anytime." She pulled the blanket up around Will's shoulders.

"Thanks for letting me stay with him."

"I killed her," Will said again as the nurse left the room, his voice less wild but filled now with infinite sorrow.

Clark placed his hand on the other man's and felt his fingers gripped tightly. He looked down at the long, sensitive fingers wrapped around his own. His half brother should have played piano with those fingers. He shook his head. A lot of things Will should have done with his potential. Maybe he'd never believed it. Maybe no one had ever believed it for him...

"The little girl in the other car is fine, Will. They sent her home," he soothed. "Everything's okay. You're going to be okay."

"Not okay. Sunny's dead."

Clark jerked his eyes up to Will's, startled to hear Sunny's name. Tears were running down his half brother's face.

"Sunny died ten years ago, Will."

"My fault. I killed her."

"What!"

But the sedative finally took effect. Will's eyes closed, and his fingers relaxed around Clark's.

Clark stared at him, shocked. Will was seriously delusional. What could have made him say such a thing? Sunny had been killed by a drunk driver, a skinny little teenager with a blood alcohol level so high it was a wonder he wasn't dead. Will wasn't the only one who'd seen it; it was the middle of the day, plenty of traffic driving slowly through the school zone where Sunny skipped happily up the sidewalk toward Will, who was coming from the high school down the street to walk her home, as he did every day.

How horrible it must have been for him: close enough to see, but too far away to do anything as the car sped across an intersection, lost control, bounced up on the sidewalk and hit Sunny, throwing her a dozen yards before crashing through a fence and coming to a stop against the concrete foundation of a house. Witnesses said Will had raced to the little girl, screaming, had fallen to his knees, and tried to resuscitate her. He held her in his arms bawling when he'd realized there was nothing he could do. He'd tried to save her. How could his mind have twisted his heroism into murder?

He sat with Will all night, sleeping in fits, waking in starts, wanting his brother to wake up and tell him more, wanting to understand…

When Will did wake up, his fever was down, and he seemed coherent, if still emotional. "You been here all night?" he asked.

Clark nodded.

"Thanks. Peggy said she'd call you. She's left me, you know." Tears escaped the corners of his eyes. "I don't know why she stayed with me as long as she did."

"She loves you, Will. She said if only you'd get some help for your drinking…"

"I'm no good for her. I'm no good for anyone."

Clark hesitated, unsure if it was the time to bring up Will's baffling reference to Sunny's death. He decided to ask. "Last night before you went to sleep you said something I didn't understand."

"I don't remember much about last night. What did I say?"

"You said—you said you were the one who killed Sunny."

Will was silent for a long moment. Clark waited.

"What's the use of trying to hide it anymore?" Will started to cry in earnest. "I did it. I thought you'd always known. I thought that's why you hated me."

Clark winced. "I don't hate you, Will. And there were all kinds of witnesses to the accident. You didn't kill Sunny."

"Might as well have." He looked at Clark straight on, his eyes filled with honest pain. A more honest expression than Clark had seen in Will's eyes for years. Whatever he was thinking, it was clear he believed it.

Dropping his gaze to his hands, Will said, "I was Ludlow's supply line."

"You were—" Clark stopped. Jeremy Ludlow was the boy who'd hit Sunny. "What d'you mean?"

"The booze. Ludlow was drunk on what I'd stolen from Willis's liquor cabinet. I knew from the minute I saw whose car it was that Sunny died because of me."

Toni had planned to invite Clark to join them for lunch after church, but to her disappointment, he hadn't shown up for the service. *Probably a good thing,* she thought as she dropped Wynona off at her home later. Both she and the girl concentrated better without him around. She smiled as she thought about Wyn looking around the congregation as if in search of someone, then whispering to Toni, "Doesn't Clark come to church here?" No surprise, really, that the teenager had ulterior motives for coming to church. Wyn was no different than Toni had been at fourteen.

"Usually," she'd whispered back. "Something must have come up."

"Know where I'd like to go after lunch?" Georgine interrupted Toni's musings as she backed out of Wynona's driveway.

"No, where?"

"Felice told me about this place off Sandy in Northeast called the Grotto." Felice was the clothing designer for the Child's Play line.

"I've heard it's a neat place," Toni responded. "There should be a lot of flowers in bloom now, too. Did you want to take some pictures?"

"Actually, I want to take my journal and write some thoughts about Chappie's sermon today. Felice says the Grotto is serene and peaceful, and it's where she always goes when she needs to think."

"You don't have to be Catholic to go there?" Toni asked. The Grotto was home to a Catholic church and a monastery as well as grounds that were purported to be among the loveliest in the city.

"I wondered that, too, but Felice says no."

"If you're going to be writing, maybe I could take my sketchbook," Toni said as she turned the corner onto Dearborn Street. "I haven't done any drawing since I finished that art class last fall." She glanced in the rearview mirror. "Pop—would you mind watching Danny this afternoon for a couple of hours so George and I can spend a little more time together?"

"I wanna go, too," Danny pouted.

"You'd have more fun with your grandpa," Toni said, opening her door and sliding out.

"I was thinkin' about takin' us for a Sunday drive up the Gorge, Danny Boy," Doc said. "An' then I'd like t' take you an' Brannigan to that park with the Ramona statue. The one your mama was fixin' t' take you to when Brannigan got loose in the store."

Whether it was the reminder of the trouble he'd gotten into or the promise of an afternoon adventure, Toni didn't know, but Danny seemed satisfied with the arrangement. He was out the back door and running around the apple tree with his dog almost before the adults were in the front door.

"It's so weird how Chappie's sermons always seem to be directed specifically to *me*," Toni told Georgine as they made lunch together.

223

"Really? Today's message seemed made-to-order for *me!*" Georgine answered.

In the third of his sermon series, Chappie had addressed the second beatitude: "Blessed are those who mourn, for they will be comforted..."

When Chappie had opened by defining true mourning as a divine sadness humans can share with God, Toni had furrowed her brow, puzzled. Given the choice, who would want to feel sadness, divine or otherwise?

"God is heartbroken by the condition of the world," the minister had explained. "Hunger and poverty and the abuse of power aren't part of God's plan. Sickness and death and the destructive forces of nature weren't set up as God's *modus operandi*. He doesn't desire that we suffer the pain of disease or addiction or broken relationships. He grieves over those things."

Toni spread cream cheese on three slices of bread and spooned cranberry sauce on another three. "God must be heartbroken at the way I've lived my life, Georgine."

"I think he's heartbroken at the way you had to grow up, Toni," her friend answered, slicing carrots for a salad. "Not getting what you needed because your mother couldn't give it to you."

"Then he has to be heartbroken at how Danny's had to grow up, too."

"Yes. But remember Chappie said God doesn't want us to wallow in guilt and regret for the bad choices we've made. The part that really got to me is what he said about God wanting us to feel heartbroken instead of *guilty*. Heartbroken the same way he is, about living in a fallen world where people make selfish choices as a matter of course. Choices that hurt other people. It made me want to *do* something about all the pain in the world." She scooped the carrots up and tossed them in the salad bowl, then moved to the sink to rinse a handful of mushrooms.

"Being heartbroken with God motivates us to action," Chappie had said in his sermon. "It makes us want to do something about drug babies and battered women and gang wars. About cancer and mental illness and homelessness. About loneliness and disappointment and unrealized dreams..."

Toni placed slices of roasted turkey on the sandwiches. "It made you want to help even though Chappie says you have to go through the pain yourself to be able to?" she asked.

Georgine stepped back to the chopping block. "Not at first," she admitted. "I mean, who wants to feel pain? Voluntarily? But then I realized how long I didn't let myself heal after my divorce because I avoided feeling the pain. For *years*. Being a workaholic may have been good for building my business, but it sure didn't help me deal with other parts of my life. Maybe it works the same way for bigger issues."

Toni nodded. "What Chappie said about denying the pain being a way we unconsciously keep it alive sounded like stuff I learned in rehab. And I loved what he said about the grieving process. What was it, exactly?" She wiped her hand on a towel and pulled her sermon notes from her Bible on the counter.

"'By mourning our losses and feeling our pain, we open ourselves to comfort,'" she read. "'We open ourselves and the world to healing.' Isn't that beautiful?"

She thought about what Chappie had said next: "To act as healers to the world, we must first be healed. To be healed, we must learn to say with God, when we see the results of our bad choices, 'That's really sad. I'm really sorry,' instead of 'I'm a horrible person. I don't deserve to be happy. I don't even deserve to live.' We must transform our regret into mourning."

It was a powerful message for Toni. She knew she hadn't stopped struggling with guilt and regret.

"Feeling guilty about our selfish actions isn't the same as mourning the results of those actions," Chappie had continued. "Yes, we may have made choices that had irrevocable, destructive consequences. But when we live with regret, when we invite guilt to make itself comfortable in our souls at the expense of our own well-being, we are locking ourselves into the past. We constantly relive our bad choice, constantly feel fresh guilt about it, and begin to think, 'I'm a bad person,' instead of, 'I made a bad choice.' Our attachment to the past blocks our ability to live in the present and look with hope to the future.

"Feeling guilty focuses on the impossible—trying to change the past. Feeling divinely sad focuses on the possible—healing the present. Shame and guilt that chain us to the past are never from God," he said. "God's gifts are love and joy and peace."

Toni arranged the sandwiches on plates and carried them two at a time to the dining-room table. *Heal my shame, God,* she silently prayed. *I want to know your love. I want to know your joy. I want to know your peace.*

～ 22 ～

fter lunch, Toni dug out her sketchbook and a range of
graphite pencils while Georgine found her journal, and
they set out for the Grotto. Twenty minutes later they stood
in awed silence, gazing out the windows of the cliff-side chapel
at treetop level. The glass wall curved across the front of the
building, stretching from floor to high ceiling. Beyond the tree-
tops, the flat top of Mount Saint Helens in southwest Washington
stood as a backdrop to freeway interchanges and airport run-
ways crawling with cars and buses and planes, like exotic
insects. The Columbia River, shining in the sun, reached from
one end of the view to the other, disappearing in the distance in
either direction.

A group of teenagers, laughing and speaking rapidly in
some Asian tongue unknown to Toni, entered the chapel. A
couple standing near her sent disapproving frowns their way,
but Toni smiled at their energy and good humor. She liked the
balance: the quiet and the noise, the serenity and the vitality.

Georgine took out her journal and sat down in one of the
leather chairs facing the window. Toni followed, finding a chair
next to a pretty girl about Danny's age with long black hair, as

thick and straight as Toni had ever seen, sitting on the edge of the cushion and swinging her feet. Toni smiled at her, and she smiled shyly back.

"Mourning means becoming aware of the empty places in our lives, *feeling* the empty places, so that we can accept the inflow of love and joy and peace that are God's gifts to us," Chappie had said near the end of his sermon. Toni knew about George's empty places, about the desire for children that seemed as if it would never be filled. Yet George knew how to find joy even in her mourning...

"We can find joy in our mourning because God is with us in it, giving us comfort," Chappie had concluded. "God is not remote from our suffering. He feels our pain. His hand gets burned along with our hand. We are not alone. It is the comfort of his presence that gives us the will and the courage to go on."

Toni sat very still, watching a red-tailed hawk riding the wind below her, its dark wings outstretched and tipped up at the ends, its rust-colored tail spread wide. She sat still enough that she thought she heard God speaking to her heart.

Behold, I am with you always, he seemed to say.

I was with you in the loneliness of your childhood. I was with you when over and over again your trust was betrayed.

I was with you in the haze of your addiction—in the unfelt feelings from which you ran, and in your running, too.

I was with you on the floor of the hotel room where Georgine found you. I was with you at Red Rock Ranch, and I am with you every day of your recovery.

I am with you in your pain over Danny, your worry about Doc, your attraction to Clark.

I am with you in your anger at Mina.

I have never abandoned you. I never will.

"It's beautiful, isn't it?" Georgine said.

Toni jumped, startled from her reverie. George had closed

the journal on her lap and was once more gazing out the window.

"The hawk," her friend prompted.

"Oh! Yes, it is. And so free..." Toni's eyes followed the bird's graceful flight for a moment. "George...," she said.

"What is it?"

Toni turned her eyes to Georgine, her expression intent. "I want to go back home and look through the Chinese chest. I want to read Mina's letter. Will you be with me?"

Georgine reached across the space between them and grasped Toni's hand, squeezing it. "I will be with you."

They sat on the dusty floor of the attic together, the carved lid of the oriental chest propped open as Toni lifted the items out one by one, studying each with growing bewilderment. She wasn't quite sure what she'd expected her mother would think valuable enough to pass on to her only daughter when she died. Certainly not what she found.

Mina had never owned much of monetary worth, and when she had—when some boyfriend or another had turned out to be a generous drunk instead of a stingy one—the item was always eventually pawned. Toni knew what it was like. Sometimes a bottle of cheap whiskey seemed infinitely more valuable than a camera or a watch or a pair of diamond earrings. She was surprised that the chest itself, probably worth more than anything Mina had owned, had survived her mother's addiction.

The flat cardboard box Toni lifted from the top of the chest held memories long forgotten. Old class pictures, for one thing, one for every year from kindergarten through eighth grade, the earlier ones innocent and smiling, the later ones ranging from sulky to swaggering.

"I can see why Wyn reminded you of yourself," Georgine

said, looking over her shoulder. "You look downright scary in a couple of those photos!"

"I *was* scary," Toni said, shivering. "Please, God," she added, looking heavenward, "don't ever let Danny hate life as much as I did!"

She shuffled through a stack of small manila envelopes. "Look—I think these are report cards." Pulling one out, she gazed in astonishment at her first-grade marks: S+ all the way down the list. "I don't remember ever getting grades like this!" She pulled out another. Sixth grade. Mostly Cs, a couple of Ds. By eighth grade she was failing almost every subject. She passed the report card over to Georgine. "*That* I remember," she said.

The box also contained some early schoolwork: math papers, creative writing, drawings, each paper marked with a gold star or a happy face or a large red A+. There was nothing after fourth grade except the report cards.

"So maybe Mina paid more attention than you thought," Georgine said thoughtfully. "Maybe she was proud of you."

"Right." Toni's voice was sarcastic. "I'd be proud of those junior high report cards, wouldn't you?"

She reached into the chest for a large spiral sketch pad of heavy drawing paper. "More artwork?" Georgine asked curiously.

Toni frowned as she lifted the cover. "Not mine..."

Through the thin art tissue covering the page, the image was blurred, but when she lifted the tissue, the charcoal drawing fairly jumped off the page.

"Whoa!" Toni said, taken aback by the bold black image. It was a crude but powerful rendering of a child's face, eyes wide and staring, mouth twisted in an expression of terror. In the bottom right-hand corner was written in capital letters, "SELF-PORTRAIT, AGE SEVEN," and then in smaller script, "Hermina Tlustos, 1963."

"Hermina Tlustos...," George mused, looking over Toni's shoulder. "Oh! That's Mina!" She stared at the drawing. "She drew that at age *seven*?"

Toni shook her head. "No...in 1963 she would have been..." She stopped to calculate. "Fifteen. She must have been remembering." Staring at the picture, she added, "Remembering something horrible."

"You don't know what?"

"She never, ever talked about her childhood."

George studied the drawing a moment longer. "Fifteen." Her voice held awe.

Toni leafed slowly through the pages. The charcoal drawings expressed a variety of subjects, but all were equally dark in tone.

She felt increasingly bewildered. "I never even knew my mother could draw."

"I wonder how much *anybody* ever really knew about her..."

"I'm not ready to feel sorry for her, George." But her voice wasn't as brittle as it might have been. The pictures gave her insights into her mother's life that she'd probably never have gotten any other way. "Let's see what else is in here."

The chest held only one more item, hidden beneath a layer of brown paper. Toni lifted the quilt carefully and spread it across her lap, her brow furrowed once more in a puzzled frown. Pieced together in a traditional pattern of blue, yellow, and white starburst blocks, the hand-stitched quilt was exquisitely crafted. It looked as if it had never been used.

Had her mother made her a quilt in the last months of her life? Why?

"I don't get it, George."

"How about reading the letter?"

Toni hesitated, then reached for the manila envelope with

Sister Mary Alice's note and her mother's sealed letter inside.

The letter was brief and was written in a hand so shaky Toni hardly recognized it as her mother's. Hard to believe the bold black lines of the charcoal sketches in the artist's pad were drawn by the same hand. What had happened to her mother?

She scanned the single sheet of paper, then looked up, her eyes meeting Georgine's. "It doesn't say anything."

George looked puzzled. "What d'you mean?"

Toni handed the letter to her friend.

"'Dear Antonia,'" Georgine read aloud. "'At the end of my life, these are the things that mean most to me. Your school papers. My sketches. The quilt my mother made. I want you to have them. Mina.'"

Toni lifted her hands in a helpless gesture. "It explains where the quilt came from, but that's it."

"What were you expecting from her, Toni?" Georgine gently asked.

"I don't know. Groveling. Shame. An apology I wouldn't have accepted. Something to be angry about."

"You're not angry that she *didn't* apologize?"

Toni shook her head, completely mystified both at the contents of the trunk and letter and at her reaction to them. "She seems so—*pathetic*. If I'm feeling anything, it's..." She paused as if to figure it out. "Sad," she said. "Just very sad. Maybe I *am* ready to feel sorry for her."

Doc and Danny were home from the park by the time Toni and Georgine descended from the attic, Doc sitting on the back stoop reading the Sunday paper while Danny played in his tree house.

"Thought I'd let you be for a bit when I re'lized you was in the attic," Doc said, eyeing his daughter with speculation.

"Thanks, Pop. Maybe we can talk about it sometime, okay?"

He nodded. "Georgine, when's your plane fly out?" he asked.

She looked at her watch. "It's getting close. I need to be at the airport in an hour."

Doc nodded. "Thought we might all go t' see you off, then. Danny loves t' watch the planes takin' off an' landin'."

Georgine's smile lit her face. "That would be lovely, Doc. I haven't gotten to spend much time with you and Danny this trip. Let me go finish packing, and we can leave anytime."

"Oh, Toni—" Doc called as she started to follow Georgine into the house. "Clark called while you was upstairs. Said he has big news an' t' give 'im a call when you can."

"Big news!" she said. "I wonder what that could be about."

"Go ahead, Toni," Georgine told her. "I'll need a good ten minutes to get packed."

The phone rang five or six times before Clark answered. He sounded out of breath. "Hi, Toni!"

"Hi. Missed you in church this morning. I ordered a tape of Chappie's sermon if you want to borrow it."

"Whoooh!" He let out his breath in a long gust. "That would be great."

"What are you *doing* over there? And what's this about big news you've got to tell me?"

"I've been moving furniture around in my study. It's going to be Will's bedroom for the night."

"Will's bedroom!"

"Toni, you will *not* believe what's happened. It's a miracle. Will's promised to check himself into rehab tomorrow morning! He filled out the paperwork in the hospital after his psych exam this morn—"

"Hospital! Psych exam!"

Clark laughed, a sound of almost giddy excitement. "Maybe

I should start at the beginning…"

He told her about Peggy's late-night call, his hurried trip to the hospital, and finally Will's emotional confession about his self-perceived involvement in Sunny's death.

"Clark! What did you tell him?"

"I told him I was proud of him for facing up to the consequences of his actions but that he couldn't hold himself responsible for Jeremy Ludlow's choices. I told him I was so sorry he's carried around that burden of guilt all these years." He took a deep breath. "And I told him I was sorry I haven't tried to understand him more."

"Don't you blame him at all?"

"I have some feelings to work out," he admitted. "I told Will that, too. But mostly I feel incredibly sad for him. He's created his own hell these last ten years."

"Yes," Toni said. She knew all about creating one's own hell. "No wonder he started drinking like a fish after Sunny died," she mused. "All that guilt, and he couldn't talk to the people who could have most helped him—you and Ruth and Jack. He must have thought you'd hate him."

"You know, it's funny, but for the first time in my life I feel as if there's a possibility I might actually end up understanding Will."

"Clark, this is the weirdest thing, but I think I might actually end up understanding my *mother*." Toni told him about going through Mina's chest with George. "Those few things and those few words told me more about my mother than I've ever known. I think she wanted to love me, but there were reasons she couldn't. I might never know what they were, but there were reasons."

"Then you're ready to forgive her?"

"No way! But I'm more sad than angry right now. That's a change." She heard a rustling in the background. "What're you doing?"

234

"Flipping through my calendar. Trying to figure out when I can see you again," he answered. "Maybe—no, that won't work…Hmm…I've got a busy week ahead if I'm going to get away on Wednesday for the camping trip." He paused, and she could almost hear his brain humming. "Okay, then. Let's figure out some way to drive out to Rock Creek Reservoir together—just the two of us. We've got so much to talk about."

"We do?"

"Toni, I miss you."

A fine warmth spread through her. "Pop's truck is the official food-and-tent transporter," she said. "Want to ride with me?"

"Perfect! If we break down in the middle of nowhere, we'll have shelter, and we won't starve to death," he teased.

"You've seen Pop's truck," she said dryly. It was old and clunky and didn't look at all reliable. Totally deceiving. Doc took such good care of the old pickup that Toni declared it would still be around when Danny was old enough to drive it.

"I'm *counting* on it breaking down in the middle of nowhere," Clark returned. "More time to spend with you."

She laughed. "Be careful what you ask for."

"Toni?" Georgine poked her head into the kitchen. "Do you know what I did with my shampoo?"

"Gotta go, Clark! Good luck with Will. See you Wednesday."

"Good luck with Will?" Georgine asked curiously.

❧ 23 ❧

Toni wasn't sure how Ruth had managed it, but the store was going to get along without either of them for Wednesday and Thursday so they could both attend the Growth Group campout. Ruth and Jack were driving their own car so they could return to the city late Thursday night; Ruth needed to cover shifts on Friday and Saturday, and Jack had to be home for his weekend sightseeing cruises aboard the *Snow Swan*. The rest of the group would spend a second and third night camping and return to Portland on Saturday after a late breakfast.

Chappie owned a large van for his large family, and Keith Castle had borrowed a church van for the three-hour trip to Rock Creek Reservoir on the east side of Mount Hood. Wyn pouted when it became clear she wasn't going to get to ride with Clark.

When Toni scrutinized the mix of ages and personalities, she wondered if it had been a good idea to invite Wyn along on the camping trip. Chappie and Mary's twelve-year-old twins, Eddie and Alex, were the closest to Wyn's age, but much younger than Wyn's worldly-wise fourteen. Owen's girlfriend, Julie, was seventeen, but a sweet, sheltered seventeen that probably made her younger than Wyn, too, in effect.

Toni breathed a sigh of relief when she saw Wyn's expression change at the appearance of Beau and Emily Bradley with Elizabeth, who'd just turned a year and a half. The teenager was enthralled with the little girl and happily climbed into the van with Keith and Katie, Beau and Emily and Elizabeth, Danny, and seven-year-old Izzy Lewis, who would be good company for Danny. Doc joined Mary, Eddie, Alex, Owen, and Julie in Chappie's van. Eleven grown-ups, three teens, four kids, and a baby. It was certainly not like any camping trip Toni had ever been on.

The caravan was off by noon, sack lunches close at hand to eat on the trip. At the end of the line of vehicles, Clark drove Doc's truck as Toni pulled out sandwiches, chips, and chocolate-chip cookies and set up a picnic on the seat between them.

"Partial payment for that business proposal you're going to help me write," Toni told him.

"You gotten any of those numbers together for me yet?" Clark asked.

"Some. I called the yellow pages, *Willamette Week*, and the *Oregonian* for quotes on display ads, and I got a number to call for the Bridal Fair at the convention center. Jack could set up a booth there every January."

"Good. How about costs for color brochures—copywriting, photography, layout, printing?"

"Hmm. Something tells me I should be taking notes."

He continued to ask thoughtful questions, listen to her ideas, and stimulate new ideas as they drove. It was clear he knew his business. Toni felt increasingly encouraged to have his confidence.

"All right, enough about business," she finally said. "Tell me what's going on with Will."

She was happy to hear that Clark had taken her advice and attended an Al-Anon meeting earlier in the week. "What surprised me most," he said, "is how pertinent the concepts are to *anybody's* life, not just people dealing with an alcoholic friend or family member. A lot of what people there talked about reminded me of Chappie's sermon on the first beatitude."

Toni nodded. "I should have guessed sooner that Chappie knew something about twelve-step recovery work. I always find something practical to take home with me when he speaks. Wish you could have been there Sunday. The more you talk about Will, the more it sounds like the message would have helped you understand him better."

"And understand you better?" he asked gently.

"Yes." She looked across the seat at him. "I do want you to understand me, Clark. Sometimes I'm afraid you never could."

"Sometimes I'm afraid, too."

They were both silent for a moment.

"Toni…," Clark broke the silence

"What?"

"I've never asked you why you started drinking."

She hesitated. She *did* want Clark to understand her… But did she trust him enough to start sharing her secrets? "Are you asking me now?" she hedged.

"Yes. Please."

"All right," she said, deciding that if she couldn't begin to trust him now, she wouldn't ever give herself a chance to learn. "At the beginning…well, it was normal behavior at my house. I saw my mother drinking all the time, and her boyfriends, and alcohol was always around."

"The same way it was for Will," Clark interjected.

"Yeah. You'll find similarities in every story about growing up with an alcoholic parent. I liked the way drinking made me feel, too. Sort of…*happy*, I thought, at least compared to how I usually felt when Mina was yelling at me or criticizing me or just ignoring me."

"Will certainly got all that from his father."

239

Toni nodded. "Common. Alcohol didn't really make me feel happy, of course. It made me numb. It made me not care. When you're lonely and miserable most of the time, feeling numb can feel like happiness."

"When did you start drinking?"

"About the same time you said Will did. Sixth grade. Not a whole lot, but every once in a while."

Clark shook his head. "That just totally blows me away."

I must seem so alien to him, Toni thought. How could anyone who hadn't been through it understand?

"Listen…do you mind me asking all these questions, Toni? I don't want to bring up things that might upset you."

She cracked a wry grin. "That's what recovery's about, Clark. Looking at the things that upset me instead of acting like they don't exist. Go ahead."

"When did your drinking become a regular habit? I mean, when could you not *not* drink anymore?"

She took a deep breath. "Something happened when I was fourteen that made me see my mother so clearly I couldn't pretend anymore. I couldn't make believe she really loved me. She didn't. She couldn't have loved me and hurt me the way she did." Toni tried to keep her tone neutral, but she knew bitterness had crept into her voice. She might come to understand Mina, but how could she ever forgive her?

"You sure you want to talk about this?" Clark asked gently.

"Afraid you won't be able to handle it?" she asked, unable to keep the sarcasm out of her voice.

He was silent for a long moment, and when he did speak, Toni knew she'd hurt him. "I was thinking of you, Toni. That's all."

She squeezed her eyes shut. "Clark, I'm sorry." She rolled her head back and opened her eyes to look at the ceiling. "Sometimes it's still—unexpected. Confusing. When someone thinks of my needs."

Clark reached over and took her hand. "I do, Toni. Now, do you want to tell me the rest of the story or not? I want to hear it, but not until you're ready."

"It's okay. I'm as ready as I'll probably ever be." She removed her hand from Clark's and crossed her arms over her chest.

"I told you in one of our earlier conversations that Mina pretty much ignored me until I got to an age where she thought I was trying to steal her boyfriends. Well, I wasn't trying to steal Raymond—he was trying to steal *me*." She looked at Clark. "You understand?"

He nodded, his expression pained. "Did you tell your mother?"

"Once. She screamed at me, told me it was my fault, that I'd been flirting with him."

"Oh, Toni!"

"I fought him off for months. One night—he was very drunk—he came into my bedroom, and my nightgown ripped as I was trying to get away from him. I ran shrieking into Mina's room with him after me. I remember screaming, 'Mama, Mama, help me!' And she *watched* him without saying a *word* while he beat me up. I don't mean a slap or two. I mean he *beat* me. And after he'd gone—I'm lying on the floor, sobbing—Mina said, 'You didn't get anything you didn't deserve.'"

Without warning, the truck screeched to a halt at the side of the road. Clark got out, slamming the door behind him, and lifted his head in a bellow of pain that should have rocked Toni to her core. When he climbed back into the truck, tears were streaming down his face.

He pulled her into his arms, almost roughly, but his touch gentled as he held her against his chest and stroked her hair.

She felt nothing. She couldn't even cry.

~~~~~

The caravan stopped in Tygh Valley for gas and ice. Keith ambled back to the pickup as the pump ran for the church van. He knocked twice on the hood as Clark rolled down his window.

"The beast running okay?" Keith asked. "Looked in my rearview mirror a ways back, and you'd disappeared. I pulled over, was ready to turn around and hunt you down, when you showed up over that rise."

Clark nodded. "Thanks for watching out for us. Just needed to stretch my legs."

Keith grinned and punched him playfully on the arm. "Hey, old man—should have figured!"

"Watch it, young whippersnapper!" He glanced at Toni as Keith walked back to pay for his gas. "Old man!" he grumbled. *"Old man!"*

"Youngsters just have no respect for their elders these days," Toni said, deadpan.

Clark wrinkled his brow in mock distress. *"Et tu, Brute?"*

Toni frowned in confusion. "What?"

"You know, from *Julius Caesar...*" Clark looked suddenly embarrassed. "I'm sorry, why would you know? It's one of Shakespeare's most famous lines," he explained as he moved the truck forward to the gas pump. "Caesar is being stabbed to death and suddenly recognizes his friend Brutus among the assassins. With his dying breath he utters, 'Even you, Brutus?'"

"Even me, Julius," Toni answered lightly. *One of Shakespeare's most famous lines,* she thought. Any educated person would have recognized it, but they hadn't taught Shakespeare in remedial English. What had ever made her think she and Clark had enough in common to have a relationship?

They arrived at Rock Creek Reservoir in the Mount Hood

National Forest twenty minutes later. Their two adjoining campsites were right on the lake. When Toni stepped out of the truck, she was glad she'd followed Katie's advice to dress in layers. She pulled on her jacket and zipped it up.

The top of Mount Hood peeked above a bank of clouds through the trees. Whitecaps frothed across the deep blue-green water of the reservoir, and the high branches of the ponderosa pines rustled and whispered overhead. The leaves of the brushy plants growing at the water's edge silvered as the wind played through them, revealing their dusty undersides. The chill east wind had also cleared the sky overhead of clouds except for one feathery strip of cirrus too high for it to reach.

"Going to be a cold one tonight," Clark said, coming up behind her and placing his arms around her waist. He laid his cheek against her hair, and for just an instant Toni relaxed against him before pulling away. She wished she hadn't told him about Mina. She didn't want him feeling sorry for her.

As she lifted Clark's hands and moved out of his embrace, Toni saw Wyn stepping out of the church van, glaring in their direction. *Oh, great,* she thought—*Wyn at her most sullen is just what I need.* Another reason to keep her distance from Clark.

Everyone pitched in to set up the large two-room tents, one for the men and boys, the other for the women and girls. "Far enough away from each other," Mary Lewis said with satisfaction, "that Chappie's snoring won't keep us awake all night."

Keith bounced the heel of his hand off his forehead. "And I didn't bring my earplugs because I knew Katie would be in the other tent."

"Keith!" Katie said in an aggrieved tone. "D'you have to give away all my secrets?"

"Won't be a secret after tonight anyway," he answered, grinning crookedly. "I thought it was only fair to warn your tent-mates."

Katie put her hands on her hips and gave her husband a look that said clearly, "Just wait till we get home, Buster!" Then she tossed her head and said, "I'm going to pick wildflowers for a bouquet for the table. Anyone else want to come?"

Toni began to relax as she roamed the campground with Katie, Emily, Mary, and Chappie, concentrating on the beauty around her and slowly letting go of the unexpected tension her conversation with Clark had created. If she'd known how he'd react, she'd never have told him the story from her past. It was frightening, his empathy. It was frightening having him express pain she didn't feel herself.

When she'd first confronted the memory of her mother's betrayal during her rehabilitation program, she'd cried and raged enough that she'd gotten most of her anger out of her system. Or so she'd thought. She could tell the story now with only a trace of resentment in her voice, the way she'd told Clark.

But if it was out of her system, why had it taken so long to lift the latch to her mother's Chinese chest? Why had it taken so long to open her mother's letter? What was it she'd been afraid to find?

I can't forgive her, God.

Then you're still angry.

I can't forgive her.

If you don't forgive her, you will never forgive yourself.

She thought of her last visit with Chappie, earlier in the week. She'd talked a lot about her mother, told him about the letter and the items in the chest.

"What are you thinking about your mother, Toni?" he'd asked.

"I think she was the sorriest excuse for a mother anyone could have." Her voice had expressed no emotion.

"And how are you *feeling* about her?"

She'd shrugged. "Mina was what she was. The pictures she

drew as a teenager showed me someone in pain. Like I told George, there were reasons she couldn't love me."

"So you're not angry?"

She had shrugged again. "What good would it do, at this point? She's dead."

"You have a right to be angry. How will you forgive her if you don't ever feel your anger?"

She'd looked at him strangely. "Forgive her? I don't know that I ever want to forgive her. I don't know that I ever could. Besides, isn't it a little late for that?"

"Forgiving Mina wouldn't be for her, Toni," he'd told her gently. "Forgiving Mina would be for you. For your own healing."

Suddenly she realized what Chappie had been trying to get her to see. Her ability to forgive Mina and her ability to forgive herself were all tangled up together. Her judgments about her mother were the same judgments she made about herself: *I'm the sorriest excuse for a mother anyone could have...*

She hadn't gotten to the point of betrayal with Danny that her mother had reached on the night Mina had stood by and watched her being beaten. But she'd betrayed her son in other ways.

Until Providence had intervened.

"Forgiveness doesn't mean saying that what happened was okay," Chappie had told her. "You might see that Mina's treatment of you was a continuing cycle from her own childhood she didn't know how to break. But what your mother did to you and what she didn't do for you were wrong, no matter what her reasons. You have a right to be angry.

"What forgiveness means is acknowledging your anger and your pain, and then letting go of it. Letting go of your 'right' to punish someone for it." He'd stopped and looked at her with great compassion. "I wonder if you understand that right now the only one you're punishing is yourself."

"Toni?"

She started.

Katie was looking at her curiously. "You all right?"

Toni looked at the redheaded woman standing next to her in the tall grass as if she couldn't remember who she was. "Oh! Katie! I'm…" She shook her head, smiling sheepishly. "Nothing's wrong. I was a million miles away."

"I was just saying I thought we had enough flowers. The others have already headed back to camp."

"They're beautiful, aren't they?" Toni held out the flowers she'd been gathering and fanned them out with her other hand: yarrow, wild roses ranging in color from pale to deep pink, white and yellow daisies, shiny buttercups, purple clover. "So fragile…" There was a note of sadness in her voice.

"Yet they survive the harshest winters to bloom again in the spring," Katie said. She hesitated. "That's how I see you, Toni. Beautiful and fragile, but strong at the core. Tough. Resilient."

Toni shook her head. "'When I am weak, then I am strong,'" she quoted.

"Admitting you're weak takes guts. More than most people have. Don't sell yourself short, Toni. You're an incredible woman. I have so much respect for you."

"Well!" Toni said, feeling her face flush at the compliment. "We'd better get back to camp and find some water for these blooms before they wither."

Keith and Clark had set up the cooking center while they were gone. A campfire blazed, and several camp chairs were grouped upwind from the smoke. A pan of water boiled on the grill, and an enamel coffeepot steamed next to it.

"Is that what I think it is?" Toni asked, eyeing the coffeepot.

"Hot, black, and boiled," Clark answered. "Can you handle it?"

"No problem!"

246

"Pour you a cup?"

"Thanks, I'll get it in a minute," Toni said without looking at him. She carefully laid her flowers on the table next to the others, then walked over to rummage in the pickup for the box she'd brought with tomorrow morning's breakfast ingredients and an assortment of utensils.

By the time she located her large plastic commuter mug, the back of the truck was organized and set up as a pantry for snacks, drinks, and dry goods. Several ice chests sat nearby on the ground.

"Like to come over and organize my kitchen?" Emily, sitting at the picnic table with Elizabeth in her lap, teased.

"Just as soon as I do mine," Toni answered, smiling at the petite blonde and holding a finger out for the baby to hold on to.

"You won't get your finger back all afternoon," Emily warned.

"No? I could think of worse fates. Can I give you a break for a little while?"

"Absolutely! I'd love to round up my husband and go for a walk before dinner." She lifted the little girl as Toni bent to pick her up. "Anybody seen Beau?"

"He's hunting for abandoned firewood," Clark called. He pointed. "Thataway."

There were several camp chairs available. Toni chose the one next to Katie instead of the one by Clark, but she smiled at him across Elizabeth's head and raised her mug. "You could get me that coffee now."

Keith was helping Danny and Izzy whittle down marshmallow sticks for later in the evening. Wynona hovered over the fire, complaining about the cold, the taste of the hot chocolate, and especially the lack of lavatory facilities.

"Come help me entertain the baby, Wyn," Toni said to distract her.

She sat down next to Toni, but grudgingly. In only a few minutes, however, she was engaging with Elizabeth, who couldn't take her eyes off the diamond in the teenager's nose. Wyn's hair was still the pretty auburn it had been for her mother's wedding, and she was sticking with the softer eye makeup George had showed her how to apply. Toni wondered if she'd brought her makeup on the camping trip. The outhouse didn't have running water, let alone mirrors.

As evening approached, Jack lit the propane stoves and Ruth pulled out salmon dip and crackers for hors d'oeuvres while dinner cooked: pork chops on the grill, rice, and Caesar salad, plus a pan of macaroni and cheese for picky kids.

"Pretty gourmet for a campout," Toni said in admiration.

"Especially the macaroni and cheese," Ruth said, laughing.

The wind was still blustery after dinner; Toni added a couple of layers of clothing and made sure Danny was dressed warmly enough before she sent him off with Izzy and the twins to feed the ducks at the edge of the lake below their campsite.

Twilight was incredible; the water paled to a silvery blue, reflecting the glow of the evening sky. Behind Mount Hood the clouds were golden; another dark train of clouds chugged across the mountain's peak. The hills across the lake were smoky blue, the trees black against them. Several stark spurs jutted into the pale blue-and-gold sky.

"Awesome!" Owen said, the tone of his voice expressing as much as the word. He and Julie had been off somewhere alone most of the afternoon, but they had joined the adults around the fire after dinner.

Toni silently agreed. As a child growing up in southern California, she'd rarely been out of the city; had known nothing about this kind of awe-inspiring peace and serenity. The beautiful, shadowy edge of evening took her back in her mind to the mountains of southwestern Montana. She was convinced that being in the midst of God's creation, where the sun set over mountains and trees instead of over houses and skyscrapers, had been a significant part of her rehabilitation.

How could anyone be in a place like this and not believe in God? she asked herself. *How could anyone not acknowledge his love and power?*

Night fell. The kids returned from their twilight adventure and distributed roasting sticks while Clark got out the marsh-mallows, graham crackers, and chocolate squares for s'mores.

When it started to get noisy at the campfire later on, Doc had everyone stop and "listen to the quiet." After several min-utes, they went around the circle naming things they'd heard in the silence: frogs, crickets, the wind in the trees, an owl, the buzz of mosquitoes, the waves lapping, creek water running.

And though she didn't say it, Toni thought she heard a still, small voice: *I am a forgiving God.*

Teach me, she answered silently.

～ 24 ～

Somehow the position of "camp nurse" had fallen to Toni. As always when there were kids around, the minor injuries started early and promised to continue throughout the campout. Already, by mid-afternoon on Thursday, she'd made impromptu ice packs out of plastic bags for a twisted ankle and for an eye accidentally poked with a marshmallow stick, and had dug out the antibiotic cream and a bandage for a scratch, aloe for a couple of cases of mild sunburn, and hydrocortisone for a host of bug bites.

"You're quite the nurse," Clark teased as she applied cream to a cut on Danny's leg.

"Danny has me trained," she said, giving her son an affectionate rub on the head before he pulled away.

Clark wanted to be alone with her, Toni could tell. Part of her wanted to be with him as well, but another part needed some distance. Their mutual attraction was too strong and too frightening for her to deal with right now. She knew how easily she could be swept away, how good it would feel to use a romance with Clark to escape the feelings she needed to deal with if she would ever be able to love him. Or anyone, for that matter. She needed time.

Before he had a chance to ask, she called across the campsite, "Hey, Pop! Ready for that walk?" At her father's answering wave, she glanced at Clark again. "Promised I'd spend some time with Pop. Catch you later, huh?"

"Later. Yeah." Clark's voice was flat, disappointed.

She reached across the space between them and squeezed his hand. "We'll have dinner together, okay?" *Along with everyone else on the campout,* she added to herself. *Safe enough.*

"Twins found a path 'round t'other side o' th' lake," Doc said as she joined him. "Want t' try it out?"

"Sure. We can go anywhere. Mostly I just want to talk, Pop."

"About Mina?"

"Yeah." She bent to pick up a long, sturdy branch. "Walking stick?" she offered, stalling.

"Don't mind if I do."

She found another branch for herself before they'd gone much farther, and she busied herself with stripping it down as they walked along the road leading to the far shore of the lake. Now that she'd made the decision to talk to her father about Mina, she didn't know where to start. Pop wasn't helping.

"Did you look in Mina's chest?" she finally asked as they left the road to follow a narrow path around the lake, Toni leading the way.

"You said I was welcome."

"Oh, you were—you are. I just…" She turned her head to look at him over her shoulder. "Well, what did you think? Did it make any sense to you?"

"As much sense as Mina ever made to anybody, includin' herself," he answered.

"What about the pictures? The self-portrait?"

Doc was silent for a moment. "Never saw the self-portrait," he finally said. "She showed me th' others, and it was part what bound me to 'er. I didn't figger it till after she was gone, a long time after, but I was more a papa to 'er than a husband. She never liked 'er papa, an' she ended up not likin' me."

They'd come to a clearing along the trail that opened onto the lake. "Let's find a place to sit, Pop," Toni said. "I'm thinking I want to be sitting down."

Settled on a fallen log overlooking the water and hidden from the trail, Doc continued. "Mina was half a woman an' half a child when we married," he said. "All growed up in some ways, the most beautiful woman I ever seen, but still a little girl at the heart of 'er, hurt an' scared, needin' more than I could give 'er. *Thought* I could give 'er what she needed. Thought I could be 'er savior.

"I was forty already, never married, couldn't b'lieve I talked 'er into bein' my wife. Only twenty, and a vision, Mina was, like a angel." Doc paused, his expression dreamy, as if he were seeing the vision of Mina that had captured his imagination all those years ago.

"I still remember the last time I saw 'er," he said slowly, "standin' across the room starin' out the window as I said goodbye t' you that day in the judge's chambers, not knowin' she'd already packed your clothes t' run away." He shook his head then, as if to shake the mental image away.

It was the last time he'd seen Toni, too, for more than a dozen years while Mina moved from city to city and job to job and man to man. Until she started seeing Toni as her rival.

"There was hurtin' in 'er home," Doc went on. "Her papa, mostly, but 'er mama didn't do much t' keep 'er safe, neither. Just as scared as Mina was—I'd wager on it, was I a wagerin' man."

Toni's mind whirled. Pop's description of her mother's life could have been a description of her own. No, worse—it was Mina's own father who'd hurt her instead of strangers. Having been through that herself, having felt the pain expressed in those sketches in the oriental chest, how could Mina have treated Toni the way she had? Bitterness began to well up inside Toni.

"The quilt 'er mama made for our marriage bed was her way of sayin' sorry, far's I can tell. Mina wanted t' b'lieve she loved 'er, but never could quite bring 'erself to it. Kept th' quilt but never used it, least while she was with me."

Toni shook her head. "I don't think she ever did. It looks new."

"Anyways, I figgered years ago your mama married to get away from home. Came clear t' me, later on. Made me promise we'd move far away, and I'd a done anything for Mina. Ended up in Oregon not long after. But marriage didn't feel no diff'rent to 'er than home had. She was like a wild animal tryin' t' get out of a cage. Took a long time to know there was nothin' I coulda done to make up for it. There was a big ol' empty place inside 'er I couldn't fill, is all."

Toni nodded. Her mother had tried to fill that empty place with alcohol and men. The same way Toni had tried to fill hers.

"She didn't know how to be a mother," Toni said slowly.

"No. She didn't."

It wasn't a new conclusion; Toni had worked this through in therapy during her rehabilitation. But somehow she understood it now at a level she hadn't let herself feel before. Mina hadn't set out to hurt her. She'd just been so consumed by her own emptiness she couldn't focus on anything else—any*one* else.

God, how can I ever thank you enough for pulling me out of that cycle? she asked silently. *My life began the way my mother's did. But for your grace, it could end the way hers did. Sad, alone, with no one there to care...* The bitterness inside her began to subside.

"D'you think the sketches were Mina's way of saying she was sorry?"

"I do," Doc answered.

Toni hesitated. The scene with Raymond that she'd described to Clark the day before played across her mind like a silent movie. It wasn't long after that incident that Mina had sent her away. For the first time, she wondered if her mother might have shipped her back to Doc out of love instead of jealousy. Could she have been trying to protect her?

"D'you think she loved me?" she finally asked.

"As much as she could." Doc reached his arm around Toni's shoulder and gently pulled her toward him. "As much as ever she could."

It wasn't that Clark wasn't having a good time. After the wind had died down, sometime during the night Wednesday, the temperature had warmed to shorts and T-shirt weather on Thursday, more what he'd expected for late June. He was enjoying getting to know the other men on the trip better, Doc and Beau especially.

He loved the outdoors, and Danny, Izzy, and the twins had been willing learners—and Wynona DeJong an ardent one—as he pointed out the wildlife around the campground: small brown killdeer and showy redwing blackbirds flitting in and out of the brush near the water, an osprey gliding overhead, hummingbirds whirring through the wildflowers, large yellow-and-black swallowtail butterflies dancing over the tall grasses.

Soon they'd made it a game to see how many different creatures they could spot: ducks and geese on the water, fish jumping out of it; lizards on the rocks at water's edge and one pencil-thin black-and-yellow striped garter snake swimming near the shore; tree squirrels, ground squirrels, chipmunks with their tails flicking; skinny wasps and fat bumblebees, iridescent dragonflies, and mosquitoes "big enough t' suck the blood from an elephant," Doc said. Within an hour of arrival everyone had slathered themselves with mosquito repellent.

Clark wondered if he'd accidentally doused himself in "Toni repellent" as well. By mid-afternoon on Thursday, he hadn't spent a moment alone with her. She was always busy with something or somebody.

He'd planned to take her out on the lake in the rubber raft this afternoon, but before he'd even had a chance to invite her, she was off on a walk with her father. When she got back, looking somewhat pensive, Clark thought, she and Wynona helped wash each other's hair at the edge of camp: boiling water on the propane stove, mixing it with cold water, pouring it over each other's heads to lather and rinse. At least Clark had had a chance to get away from Wyn for a little while.

It almost seemed that Toni was purposely avoiding him. The way that idea made him feel—anxious, lonely, a little afraid—told him as much about his feelings for Toni as anything had. Like it or not, he was growing increasingly attached to her. Being around her seemed necessary to his well-being. And he was increasingly aware that he wanted to be necessary to hers.

He finally caught up with her at dinner, barbecued chicken and foil-wrapped corn on the cob cooked on the grill—Keith and Katie's contribution.

"Toni," he said, sliding onto the bench next to her at the picnic table, "we haven't had a minute together since we got here. How about a walk later on, when the moon comes up?"

"In the dark?" she asked doubtfully.

"It won't be dark. The moon's full tonight," he coaxed. "And the kids and I discovered a great walk along the creek earlier today. Rushing cascades sparkling in the moonlight..." He waggled his eyebrows. "Very romantic."

She hesitated, and he wondered if he'd said the wrong thing. "All right," she answered, without much enthusiasm.

"Maybe Keith and Katie would like to go with us..."

"Umm," he murmured noncommittally. If that's what it would take. He didn't think Keith would mind if they "lost" each other at some point.

After dinner he took Emily aside and entreated her to keep Wynona occupied with Elizabeth long enough to let him and Toni slip away without the teenager inviting herself along.

Emily grinned. "Good thing we brought the baby on this trip or that girl would *never* leave you alone!"

"Then I'm not imagining things?"

"Hardly. Now get on with you. Romance Toni with all you've got."

He flushed in the dark. His feelings for Toni must be as obvious as Wyn's crush on him. A bit disconcerting, though he wasn't sure why. They were, after all, grown-ups, and falling in love was something that grown-ups did. Except that he never had before...

"Thanks, Emily. I owe you one."

The moon was a huge, pale medallion through the trees, so bright it cast shadows on the rough creekside path. When Toni stumbled over a rut, Clark took her hand to help guide the way. How could she object when he was only being solicitous?

Keith and Katie had fallen behind on the trail, purposely, it seemed to Toni. Keith's design, or Clark's?

No matter. Katie and Keith deserved a stroll in the moon-light, just the two of them. Married a year was still newly wed. Theirs was the first wedding Toni had helped coordinate. A beautiful wedding, and the beginning of many more she'd helped with at Tomahawk Community Church.

Then there'd been Suzanne DeJong's wedding.

And now she was ready to take on the bigger challenge of

planning and managing weddings for the *Snow Swan*. She'd be so pleased if she could make her idea reality. *Please, God, let Jack think it's a good idea,* she breathed.

She heard an owl in the woods close by: *"Whoo! Whoo! Whoo!"*

"Me! Me! Me!" she answered in sonorous tones.

Clark laughed and pulled her toward him. Toni deftly spun under his arm and away from him again, not wanting to get too close. She started to sing, "By the Light of the Silvery Moon," not caring she was out of tune.

Clark gamely joined in, his voice blending with hers. He caught her in his arms again, loosely, letting her whirl away and come back to him as they sang.

Toni felt exhilarated by the cool air and the night sounds and the ghostly glow of the woods around her. She launched into her entertaining best, dancing and singing and regaling Clark with stories, partly in response to her high spirits and partly, she was aware at some level, to keep things light between them. She wasn't ready for what Clark wanted. Or maybe she was *too* ready, in ways that weren't healthy for her right now. There were things she needed to settle in her heart before her heart would be ready to settle down with his.

Finally Clark whisked her around and grabbed both her hands. He laughed, out of breath. "Stop, crazy woman! You're wearing this old man out!"

"Old man," she scoffed. "As if you couldn't keep up with me!"

"Maybe I don't want to keep up with you," he murmured, drawing her close. "Maybe I want you to slow down with me." He placed his right hand loosely at her waist and grabbed her right hand with his left. "Dance with me."

"Got no rhythm without music," she protested.

"Music I'll give you," he said. "Come closer."

He leaned his head against hers and started to sing softly, "Beautiful dreamer, wake unto me..."

She closed her eyes and listened to the rumble of his voice as they danced, feeling the vibration against her ear, losing herself in the magic of the night.

Clark finished the song, holding out the last note dramatically. Then he tilted her chin and kissed her softly.

She couldn't help but kiss him back, but only for a moment. Turning her head away from the kiss, she placed a hand on his chest to push him away.

"I'm sorry, Clark. This just isn't going to work."

"Why not, Toni?" He sounded hurt.

"I—I don't know how to *be* with a man yet," she said quietly. "Except...when I'm drinking. Except when I'm with a man who wants...who wants..." She stopped, embarrassed, then laughed shakily. "Maybe that's all I need to say—except with a man who *wants*. I'm not sure how to be with a man who doesn't want something from me."

"But I *do* want something from you, Toni." Clark took her hand, twining her fingers with his, and started walking again. "I want to *see* you. I want to *know* you. Not the person you think I want you to be, or the person you think you *ought* to be. Who you really are. With all your bumps and bruises."

Toni shook her head. "Can you accept that who I really am isn't ready for you, Clark? I have to have other priorities right now. Danny. Pop. Making a decent living so I can take care of them." She paused. "And other stuff. My recovery process." She looked at him in the moonlight. "I just don't know if you're ready for all my bumps and bruises."

"I wish you'd let me be the judge of that."

"I'm not ready for a romance, Clark," she said firmly.

He didn't argue further and was silent the next hundred yards down the path. "Will you still let me help you with your business plans?" he finally asked.

"You don't have to do that."

"I know I don't. I want to."

"I'll pay you back some day. I promise."

"I know you will," he said and let it go.

~ 25 ~

They returned to an uproar at camp. Wynona had apparently stowed a bottle of whiskey in her duffel bag, then sneaked off with Eddie and Alex in the dark to introduce them to the joys of imbibing. The twins hadn't found the occasion especially joyous, however. Owen and Julie had stumbled across them retching in the tall grass outside of camp. It was clearly a deed they wouldn't soon be repeating. Wyn, for her part, was swaying back and forth on the rock where she sat, humming tunelessly.

It was a shock for Toni to see Wyn drunk. *This is what I was like,* she told herself. *For years. Completely checked out.*

She still had to fight the feelings of shame that the realization brought up. *I'm not a drunk,* she told herself. *What's past is past. I'm making different choices...*

Mary Lewis was taking care of her children, but no one seemed to know what to do with Wyn. She certainly wasn't in any condition to have someone sit down and talk to her. Toni took charge of her, cleaning her up and putting her to bed, sitting next to her on her sleeping bag in the tent and holding her hand until she fell asleep.

Toni joined the other adults around the fire when the kids were all in bed. "I'm so sorry—," she started to apologize. But her words were quickly stopped by a barrage of demurrals.

"—couldn't have known—"

"—not your fault—"

"—troubled kid—"

Chappie got up to poke the fire with a long stick, then sat back down in the chair next to Toni. "I'm glad you're here, Toni. If anyone knows what Wynona needs from us, it would be you. How can we help her?"

Toni ran her fingers through her hair, feeling suddenly old and tired. "I got drunk when I was Wyn's age because I was hurt and lonely and I didn't really think anybody cared, anyway. What I needed most was just believing someone cared."

"But doesn't the alcohol use need to be addressed?" Emily asked.

Toni nodded. "I'll talk to Wyn in the morning. Would it be the truth to tell her you're all more concerned about her than angry?"

She looked around the circle, her eyes tearing at the unanimous nods. If someone had cared about her as a young teen the way this group was willing to care about Wynona DeJong, maybe things would have been different.

Maybe things could still be different for Wyn...

In the morning before breakfast, Toni took Wyn for a walk along Gate Creek Ditch, where she and Clark had walked the night before. The girl was sullen and resistant when Toni gently asked about her drinking. "You wouldn't understand!" the teenager angrily told her.

"I do understand. More than you know," Toni returned quietly. When they came to a waterfall along the creek, she stopped and sat on the bank overlooking it and began to tell Wyn her story. "Your mother is a lot like mine was," she said. "I know how hard it is."

Wyn didn't say anything, but she sat down on the bank as well, looking everywhere but at Toni.

"I used to feel so lonely and so ashamed of how we lived," Toni said. "It seemed like the only way to make those feelings go away was to drink a lot and fool around with boys. But the problem was, that only worked for a little while. Deep inside, I kept getting lonelier and lonelier and more and more ashamed."

Wyn started to cry.

Toni thought of the way Georgine had comforted her. *Help me know what to say, God,* she prayed. She scooted closer to the girl and put her arms around her. "It's okay to cry, Wyn. Crying helps heal us when we hurt."

She told Wyn about Georgine finding her almost dead on the floor of a hotel room, about her rehab program, about the swans at Red Rock Ranch, about what she'd learned in the last two years. "Everybody on this camping trip has been there for me in my recovery," she added. "They want to help you, too, if you'll let them. If you'll stop running away."

Wyn was quiet but thoughtful on the way back to camp. Toni knew she hadn't convinced her in one sitting that there was a better way to live than the way she'd chosen.

But it was a start.

When Toni awoke the following morning, she knew in her heart what she needed to do. She'd tried it before, but she hadn't been ready. Sometimes healing happened in an instant, she reflected, and sometimes it took time. Either way, it was a miracle.

The campsite was quiet and the sun just peering over the trees as she gathered a notebook, a pen, and a book of matches and trekked around to the opposite side of the reservoir. *I'm ready, God*, she prayed as she walked. *I'm ready to face the music, and I'm ready for a miracle.*

She found a private spot by the lake, away from the path. There she wrote a letter to her mother, pouring out her hurt and anger, listing in as much detail as she could all the wrongs Mina had committed against her.

Then she wrote another letter, this one to herself, so similar in detail it might have been the same letter. Except this time she was listing all the wrongs she could think of that *she'd* committed against her son and her father and other people in her life.

And then the wrongs she'd committed against herself.

She didn't spare her feelings.

When she was finished, Toni dropped the notebook on the ground next to the rock where she sat, wrapped her arms around her knees, laid her head on her arms, and wept.

She wept for Mina's childhood. She wept for the shattered hopes and the unrealized dreams her father had endured; she wept for his courage and his faith and his unfailing love in the face of his losses. She wept for Danny's childhood. She wept for her own.

Her sobs eventually subsided, but the tears kept coming as she picked up the notebook and read through the letters one last time, aloud. Then she ripped the pages from the book and lit them with a match, holding them out at arm's length and watching the flames curl the edges, lick at the black ink, consume the words she'd written as if, finally, consuming the pain and anger she'd secretly held on to all these years.

I'm ready to let go, God. Do with my heart what needs to be done.

She tossed the last burning corner into the air and watched as the blackened fragments caught the wind and drifted out over the lake. She felt suddenly as light and free as the ashes dancing against the deep blue sky.

~ ~ ~ ~ ~

Clark fixed bacon and eggs for their last camp breakfast, standing at the propane grill for probably an hour frying eggs to order as the campers straggled into the clearing in twos and threes. Toni never showed up.

At first he thought she must be sleeping in, but Katie said she'd heard her get up early and steal out of the tent. "She must have gone for a walk and lost track of the time," the redhead said. "If she's not back when the tents need to come down, I'll get her gear together and roll up her sleeping bag."

He was dismantling the camp stove when he saw her walking through the woods toward the campsite, carrying her jacket and a notebook in one hand, a red sweatshirt tied around her waist. There was a lightness about her, a spring to her step he hadn't seen in the last few days. His heartbeat quickened as she caught sight of him and raised her hand.

"Toni! Are you okay?"

"I'm great!" she called, swinging her arms as she approached.

He squinted at her against the late morning sun. She didn't *look* great. In fact, she looked as if she'd been crying her eyes out.

"What's wrong?" he asked in alarm, instinctively hurrying toward her.

She stopped, her expression startled. "Nothing..."

"You've been crying," he said, his voice concerned.

"Oh!" She lifted a hand to her cheek. "I must look a sight. I *have* been crying."

"What's wrong?" Clark asked again.

The brilliance of her smile canceled out her puffy eyes and blotchy skin. She was gorgeous. "I'll tell you everything on the way home, okay?" She linked her arm through his as they walked back to the clearing. "In the meantime, I'm starving!

Any chance there's something left from breakfast?"

"I saved you a couple of pieces of bacon, but I'm afraid the grill's out of commission. I could maybe rustle you up a BLT."

"Perfect! Go ahead with whatever you're doing, though. I'll fix it."

Clark shook his head. "Wash your face so you don't scare everybody else the way you scared me! I'll have your sandwich ready when you're done."

"Oh, so I'm scary-looking now, am I?" she teased. "Not one of the most beautiful women you've ever known?"

His eyes met hers. Energy sparked between them. "The two are not necessarily mutually exclusive," he said. *In your case, definitely not,* he added silently.

On the trip back home Toni told him about her morning. He listened as he drove, skeptical at first but with growing respect for the experience she described. Clearly it had been profoundly spiritual.

"I know it's a cliché," she said, "but I feel as if a huge weight's been lifted off my shoulders." She hesitated. "I told God I was ready for a miracle. It feels like one."

"Maybe it was," he responded. He took his eyes off the road for a moment to look at her. "I'm afraid it's going to take another miracle for *me* to forgive your mother."

"She didn't hurt *you*."

"It feels like she did. Because it feels like you're part of me."

Toni looked distressed. "Clark, don't."

"I'm sorry. I know you don't want to hear it." He was silent for a moment. "Will you do one thing for me, Toni?"

"What?"

"When you're ready, will you let me know? Will you give me a chance with you?"

It was Toni's turn for silence. Finally she said, "I'll let you know."

It wasn't much, but it was something. It would have to do.

The next several weeks flew by for Clark as he threw his considerable energy into expanding his business in Portland, helping Toni with her business plans, connecting with Will at the clinic, and making time to do his own research on addiction and recovery. The latter task was proving eye-opening, valuable not only to his understanding of his half brother, but as Toni had predicted, to his understanding of her as well.

The Al-Anon meetings he began attending on a regular basis surprised him by also helping him understand himself. He found himself questioning his assumptions, exploring his own unhealthy patterns, contemplating the ways he still had to grow.

The more he understood, the more right he felt about loving Toni, and the more he knew he wanted her to be a permanent part of his life. He couldn't imagine ever growing tired of her; her endless energy and curiosity and eagerness to learn fed his own sense of the possible. Knowing her enriched his life in countless ways.

He also knew she wasn't ready for his love. Patience had never been one of Clark's virtues, but as Ruth had once told him, love was a grand teacher. He waited. He prayed.

By the end of the second week, Toni had finished the research he'd suggested she do for the *Snow Swan* wedding business proposal. Once again he was impressed with the quality and thoroughness of her work. He helped her come up with a solid marketing strategy over the first days of July, meeting with her for several evenings and printing out the finished business plan from his computer just before the fireworks started on the Fourth.

Toni set up her appointment with Jack the following week. Clark coached her on her presentation the night before: "Talk value—what's in it for Jack?" he prompted. He reminded her of the persuasive arguments they'd come up with for the business proposal: guaranteed bookings six months to a year in advance; a larger cut from the weddings than he was getting for the private parties he was booking now; a higher profile for the *Snow Swan* in the riverboat market. "You need to convince Jack he'll get his initial outlay of money back in spades," he said.

It was a good plan. Nonetheless, when Toni presented it to Jack, the captain said no. Clark had to thrust his hands in his pockets to keep from taking her in his arms to comfort her after the meeting. Her lovely face drooped with disappointment, and her dusky eyes brimmed with tears as she told him Jack had thought it was a "nice idea, *but...*"

But he'd just spent a small fortune having the boat repainted and refurbished. *But* he was maxed out at the bank. *But* weddings were so much more involved than the parties he was doing now; he could do without the hassle. Besides, he had said, business was picking up; he was getting enough bookings without having to make the cash outlay she said he'd need to start a wedding business for the boat.

"How would you feel if I offered Jack a no-interest loan to start up the wedding service?" Clark asked, knowing before he did what the answer would be.

"I'd be *furious!* Don't you see, Clark? I don't want to be rescued. I need to know I can do this on my own."

"But I'd be helping Jack out, too..."

"*No.*"

Clark hardly slept that night, thinking about it, and by morning he'd come up with a plan.

Toni was a hard sell; it took some smooth talking to persuade her, but after all, smooth talking was Clark's trade. He told her she could do better for herself running her own business than working for Jack, and she would be smart to locate a number of wedding sites so the boat didn't limit the size or location of the weddings she could take on.

She looked at him strangely. "I don't know where you got the impression I'd have twenty thousand dollars lying around to start my own business, Clark."

"Ever heard of venture capital? I want to be your business partner, Toni. A silent partner. I invest the capital; you do the work and make me a lot of money. What d'you say?"

She looked at him obliquely. "And how is this different than loaning Jack money?"

"Are you kidding! No return on the loan versus a chance to make my fortune?" he teased. Then he sobered. "I admit I was being patronizing, Toni. I know you don't want any favors. The fact is, you don't need any favors. Frankly, going into business with you would be a good investment. You've got a good plan. You're smart, energetic, creative, persistent."

He shrugged, as if it weren't important whether she said yes or no. "Based on the work and energy you've put into the project so far," he said, "I think you've got what it takes to be successful. I think I'll get a good return on my money."

"So I'd be sharing my profits with you?" she asked, her expression still skeptical.

"We share the risks and the rewards."

"Are you expecting—" She stopped. "Are there strings attached?"

He knew she was asking about their relationship. "Strictly business, Toni." He'd been careful to keep their meetings impersonal and businesslike, though he'd have liked nothing better than to end each evening with his arms around her, his lips tasting her sweetness.

"Well..."

"I can write up an agreement for you to look over this week. If you get started on your marketing plan, you may be able to book a few of those Christmas weddings you got so dreamy-eyed about that night you told George and me about your idea."

She shook her head. "December weddings are already planned. Except for the Suzanne DeJongs of the world, of course. I might get something, but I think I'd better shoot for spring." She pulled a small notebook out of her purse. "Let's see... I'll want to book space at the January Bridal Fair pretty soon..."

He knew he had her. Smiling, he held out his hand. "Shake, partner."

~ 26 ~

Toni had never been so busy in her life. It was a good busy—an exciting, energizing, moving-forward kind of busy. Every morning before and every evening after her job at Paper Chase, every day off, she was making phone calls or meeting with graphic artists, printers, suppliers, service providers. A dozen things a day came up that she needed to ask Clark about, and with his pager and a cellular phone he was always available to answer questions, give advice, offer encouragement.

Pop offered to take over the grocery shopping and cooking—chores she'd taken over from him when she'd first moved back home—to give her more time for her business-start-up tasks. And Danny seemed to be fine with her hectic schedule, maybe because he always got to pick the activities for the twice-a-week "dates" she always made time to take with him.

Before long, Antonia's Weddings had been born: *From design to delivery, everything to make your dream wedding come true,* the prototype for the marketing literature read.

The phone rang one morning before the first pot of coffee had even stopped dripping. Toni grabbed the receiver from the wall in the kitchen where she was already scanning the yellow pages for "Halls and Auditoriums."

"Hello!" she answered cheerfully.

"Happy recovery birthday to you…" a sweet voice sang.

Toni laughed in delight. "Georgine! It's so good to hear from you!"

"You're in good spirits," her friend said when she'd finished her song. "Got some good plans for the day?"

"I do. Exploring potential wedding sites."

"Wedding sites! So you and Clark—"

"Not for me, Georgine! For the business." She'd kept her friend fairly up-to-date on her life since Suzanne's wedding, but she launched into a description of her activities since they'd last talked.

"Sounds great, Toni. I'm so excited for you. But you *are* going to celebrate your recovery birthday tonight, aren't you? With Clark, maybe?"

"George! You've got Clark on the brain. He'll be here, of course. The Growth Group is getting together at my house tonight. Ruth and Pop have planned the whole thing. It's all hush-hush, of course; I have no idea what's going on. Wish you could be here."

"Me, too. I will be, pretty soon. I'm taking the job with Child's Play."

"George!" Toni said again. After she'd settled down from that bit of good news, Georgine brought up Clark yet again.

"So—what's going on with you and 'the man of the hour'?"

"Nothing. I mean, we talk every day, but it's about the business. George…do you think he could ever really love me?"

"He'd be a fool not to. The question is, could *you* love *him*?"

"Oh, yes! I mean—George, what am I saying!"

"I think you're smitten. And vice versa."

"But I'm not ready!" Toni protested.

"Are you *crazy*, girl? What else needs to happen?"

272

Toni asked herself the same question, silently and then aloud, as she hung up the phone: "What else needs to happen?"

She tilted her head, thinking hard, then felt the corners of her mouth creeping up into a smile. "Nothing," she said to the kitchen walls. She laughed aloud and spun around. "Absolutely nothing!"

Even when nothing was going on there, Clark mused, walking into the house on Dearborn Street was like walking into a party in full swing. The place pulsated with life and energy. The jewel-bright colors, the jungle of house plants, the profusion of pictures on the walls and pillows on the sofas and chairs all added to the effect. With a dog and a boy loose inside, the amperage increased, and when Toni walked in—well, you might as well forget everything but having a good time.

"Hi, Clark!" Toni grabbed his hand and pulled him through the house toward the back door, Danny and Brannigan galloping in front of them. She was wearing a sundress of white cotton eyelet. How could anyone look so cool in this heat?

She laced her fingers through his and smiled up at him. "I thought you'd *never* get here."

"Mmm." He smiled back at her and squeezed her hand. "This feels nice. It's been a long time since you've let me hold your hand."

"Silly me."

Clark jerked his head in surprise, but Toni was already off in another direction as she led him into the backyard. "Did you know Keith and Katie grew up next door to Pop, one on either side? It must feel like old home week when they come over. You've got to see Pop's garden. What a year for tomatoes! I can't believe Danny let Izzy Lewis up in the tree house—he told *me* no girls allowed."

She continued to jump from subject to subject with such caprice, Clark felt dizzy. Or was it the feel of her long fingers twined together with his? Or the subtle smell of her perfume?

Doc and Chappie, wearing aprons and tall chef's hats, stood watch over a pair of smoking barbecue grills with long-handled spatulas. Kids seemed to be everywhere—climbing the trees, poking heads out of the tree house, hiding in the lilac bushes. Beau, Keith, and Owen were tossing a football as Brannigan leaped between them, barking wildly. Wynona and Julie played with little Elizabeth in a shady corner of the yard. Jack and Ruth were investigating Doc's garden, and Mary, Katie, and Emily sat in the shade of the house in folding chairs.

Toni stayed with Clark, keeping her hand in his in almost a proprietary way as he greeted the friends who'd gathered to celebrate her sobriety. He felt a little lost in her attention. Had he missed something?

"Have I said congratulations yet?" he asked her as they strolled around the large yard.

She raised her eyebrows. "You most certainly haven't."

"A horrible oversight on my part. Congratulations! Two years clean and sober!" He smiled at her. "You deserve to celebrate, Toni."

"Thanks, Clark. Thanks for being here." She leaned in close to his side for a moment, then pulled away. "How's Will doing in his rehab program?"

He tried to concentrate. Toni wasn't making it easy. "Good. He'll be out in a couple of weeks. I wish he was in a long-term program, though, like yours was. There aren't too many of those around."

"No. I was lucky."

Clark had heard the story: Georgine had gotten Toni into an experimental drug-and-alcohol program designed specifically for women. Most of her expenses had been paid out of a federal grant that George's aunt, a therapist, had received the very week George discovered Toni on a hotel floor, nearly dead from the drugs in her bloodstream.

God's grace at work in Toni's life before she'd even acknowledged his existence, Clark had thought with awe.

He walked her out to the garden and kneeled to examine Doc's neat rows of salad vegetables, letting go of Toni's hand. "*My* rehabilitation's going pretty nicely, too," he said.

"*Your* rehabilitation?"

He laughed as he stood and took her hand again. "That's what it feels like. Since I've started looking at my own life more closely in the context of addiction and recovery, everything's changing. My relationship with Will. My understanding of myself." He paused to consider how to express his thoughts.

"Thinking about addiction as a search for power and love instead of a weakness—however misguided that search might be—has sort of leveled the playing field for me," he said. "Made me aware of my own addictive tendencies." He shook his head. "I can't believe I'm saying this! I mean, I never realized before how obsessed I am with perfection or how much I need to be in control." He looked at Toni, his blue eyes direct and sincere. "I'm sorry I ever judged you harshly, Toni. I didn't have the right."

"Apology accepted," she said lightly. And then in another lightning change of topic, she said, "Want to see if Pop and Chappie have any burgers cooked to medium rare?"

The food was good and plentiful, as usual when this group got together: potato salad, pasta salad, fruit salad, green salad made entirely from Doc's garden, and burgers with all the fixings.

After dinner, Doc placed Toni in a chair in the middle of the lawn, and Ruth brought out a cardboard party hat with an elastic band and placed it on her head. "I'M TWO!" the pointed hat proclaimed in hot pink letters on a turquoise background.

"Danny? You got the present?" Doc asked his grandson.

Danny scrambled up the rope ladder to the tree house and disappeared inside, reappearing a moment later with a large package wrapped in shiny red foil. He tossed it down to Izzy, waiting below. She staggered backward as she caught it and promptly fell on her bottom, but she managed to keep the package from hitting the ground. By that time, Danny had clambered down the ladder. He grabbed the package from Izzy and presented it to his mother amid applause and laughter.

"You sure you should have entrusted a crystal punch bowl to a couple of hyperactive kids?" Keith quipped.

"Keith! Don't give it away!" Katie reprimanded him.

It wasn't really a crystal punch bowl, of course. The package contained a very nice soft-sided leather briefcase that everyone had pitched in to buy.

"For my new business!" Toni cried in delight. "It's perfect. Thank you, thank you, thank you."

Emily came out the back door carrying a sheet cake with two candles in the center. "Chocolate with mocha frosting," she told Toni. "I heard it was your favorite." A white swan decorated one corner of the cake, and written across the top in pale blue lettering were the words, *Congratulations! You deserve all the best.*

"All right, I need volunteers," Ruth said. "Beau, Keith, Clark, and Chappie."

"I like the way you recruit volunteers," Chappie teased. "Care to help me find Sunday school teachers for the fall term?"

Ruth handed them each a kazoo. "You're the Happy Birthday Boys," she told them. "As soon as Toni blows out the candles on her cake, you can do your thing."

"Make a wish, Mom!" Danny cried as Toni puckered up to blow the candles out. He and Izzy were doing an impromptu dance around her chair, Emily was holding the cake in front of her, the two candles lit, and Katie was busy snapping pictures.

Toni closed her eyes for a moment, then opened them again and blew out the candles. "Out in one blow. Guess my wish is going to come true," she said.

She was looking at Clark with a coquettish smile. Or was he imagining things?

The Happy Birthday Boys were so pleased with their rousing barbershop-quartet rendition of "Happy Birthday," they entertained the crowd with several other songs as Emily cut the cake, Mary added a scoop of ice cream, and the Lewis twins passed the bowls around.

When everybody had a serving, Ruth raised her voice above the chatter. "Okay, time for admirations and appreciations," she said. They all knew what she meant; celebrations were never complete in the Growth Group without "admirations and appreciations" of the honored guest.

Toni took a deep breath, as if she were bracing herself.

"Relax, Toni," Ruth teased. "You look like you're about to face a firing squad!"

Toni laughed shakily. "Why is it compliments are so much harder to take than criticisms?" she said.

"Depends on what you're used to," Clark answered. *If you'd let me, I'd get you plenty used to compliments,* he tried to telegraph her.

Doc started out: "I 'preciate the life, love, an' color Toni's brought t' my old house. You're the best thing ever t' happen to me, Toni."

Toni sat in the folding chair like a queen on a throne, Clark thought, regal and gracious. The party hat made an odd sort of crown, but it didn't take away in the slightest from her beauty.

"Thanks, Pop," she said, smiling at her father.

"I 'preciate Mom's cooking," Danny said. "'Specially grilled cheese sandwiches with tomato soup and celery sticks with peanut butter."

Laughs all around. "Your reputation as a gourmet cook just went down the tubes, Toni," Clark said.

"Thanks, Danny," Toni said to her son, opening her arms for a hug. He allowed a quick squeeze before bounding away to wrestle with Brannigan.

After the first few minutes of listening to her friends describe their experience of her, Toni was too choked up to do anything but nod her thanks.

Ruth: "Dependable."

Emily: "Creative."

Eddie and Alex: "Fun!"

Chappie: "Courageous."

Mary: "Caring."

Clark looked directly at her when it was his turn. "One thing I appreciate about you is your self-honesty," he said. "It's made me more honest with myself, Toni. Not that I'm always happy about that! But because of you, I'm learning to listen more and judge less. And I hope I'm becoming less arrogant and more compassionate."

When everyone in the circle had had their say, Ruth pulled an envelope from her purse. "One more," she said. "Georgine Nichols sent this from San Diego and asked me to read it to you, Toni." She opened the envelope and began.

"'My dear friend Toni: Congratulations on two years of sobriety! I'm so proud of you! You're saying yes to so many good things in your life because you've had the courage to say no to your addictions. I can't tell you how much I admire your courage.

"'In the last few months, I've watched you look into the past as if it were a mirror, and find only an ugly duckling staring back. But do you know what I see when I look at you? A beautiful swan.

"'My prayer for you is that you will be able to shatter the mirror of the past and let the people who love you be your mirror instead. When we look at you, we see what is the best in you. We see what God sees—a beautiful woman, inside and out.'

"'Take our word for it. Take God's.

"'I love you. Georgine.'"

Tears were running down Toni's cheeks by the time Ruth finished reading. She tried to say something but couldn't get any words out. It took every ounce of Clark's willpower not to rush to her and take her in his arms.

As Ruth handed her a Kleenex, Danny announced to no one in particular, "George always makes my mom cry. Sometimes people cry when they're happy." He looked at Toni anxiously. "Right, Mom?"

Her laugh sounded more like a hiccup. "Right, Danny. I'm feeling *very* happy. And very lucky."

The group broke up not long afterward. When Toni asked Clark if he'd mind staying to help clean up, he agreed before she'd even completed the question. Any excuse to be with her for just a little longer...

He was standing at the kitchen sink with his hands in soapy water when she came up behind him, circling his stomach loosely with her slender arms and laying her head against his neck. His heartbeat quickened.

"Clark?"

"I'm here."

"Remember when I told you I wasn't ready for you?"

The plate he'd been washing slipped out of his grasp in the water. He stood very still. "Yes..."

"I'm ready."

Slowly lifting his hands from the water, he looked at his reflection in the darkened window over the sink, hardly daring to believe...

Toni loosened her arms and stepped back. "Clark?" she asked hesitantly.

When he turned, she was looking up into his face, her dusk-colored eyes shadowed with doubt.

Toni, he thought, *that is an expression I hope never to see in your eyes again.*

She must have been able to read his mind. Or maybe it was the look in his own eyes. Or the fact that his arms were reaching to hold her, his head was lowering to kiss her lips.

Whatever it was, the shadows cleared from Toni's blue violet eyes, and it seemed to Clark as if the moon had risen in them.

Epilogue

O ne more—hold it—right there—good! Perfect!"

The viewfinder on Georgine's camera framed Danny, dressed in a pint-sized tuxedo, with his arm around the neck of Izzy Lewis in a red velvet dress, both mugging for the camera.

Click.

Danny and Izzy raced off to some other corner of the stern-wheeler. It was just as well; she'd already used up half a roll of film on them.

There was something about taking pictures of children that George found nearly irresistible. It was a way to have them in her life, she supposed. A way of holding on to them…

She kept her eye to the camera and focused on the magnificent swan ice sculpture that graced the reception table. *A fitting centerpiece for the occasion,* she thought.

Click. Another angle. *Click.*

The table was laden with beautifully presented food: hot honey-baked ham ready for carving, turkey breast with cranberry condiments, fresh fruits and vegetables, a smoked-salmon mousse, a sun-dried-tomato torte.

Click. Click. Click.

In the forward section of the lower deck, George discovered where Danny and Izzy had gone. They sat on either side of Wynona DeJong, who was reading to them on a bench next to the guest-book table, where she would greet the guests as they entered the boat. Her long auburn hair looked lovely against the emerald velvet of her dress. She smiled at Georgine. What a pretty girl!

Click. Click.

"God rest ye, merry gentlemen, let nothing you dismay..."

Through the window, Georgine saw the quartet gathered on the dock outside the boat, costumed in English Victorian finery. Katie Castle and associates, warming up their vocal cords, would entertain arriving guests with carols while they waited to board. She stepped outside, pulling her silk blazer close against the chill December air.

Click. Click. Click.

Georgine was rapidly changing her mind about wedding photography. She'd never had so much fun on a photo shoot in her life. Of course, Toni had given her full rein to do whatever she wanted to do.

"I want to remember this day forever, George—every beautiful detail," Toni had told her. "That's all I'm going to tell you."

Rarely did she have an opportunity to express the whole range of her interests in one project, from commercial to photojournalistic to art shots: candids, portraits, family lineups, fashion, still life... In short, everything *except* traditional, staged, clichéd wedding photography.

"Georgine?" Wynona poked her head out the door. "Toni says to tell you they're ready for the wedding-party pictures if you are."

"Tell her I'll be right up." When they'd first boarded the boat, George had gotten some marvelous fashion shots of Toni

on the sundeck as the sun was going down, in front of the latticework archway where the ceremony would take place. The
purple sky and the latticework arch, adorned with evergreen
boughs and white gardenias and twined with white lights that
looked like fireflies twinkling in the dusk, had been a lovely
backdrop.

Toni was as stunning in the elegant floor-length cloak that
Georgine's friend Felice had designed as any model she'd ever
photographed. Made of white silk brocade with a fur-trimmed
hood, the cloak was perfect over her wedding dress on a winter
evening. A white-fur muff completed the look. And Toni's
face—the porcelain skin and delicate bone structure and mysterious, blue violet eyes and wisps of raven hair—was exquisite
surrounded by white fur.

George climbed the narrow stairs to the upper salon. The
windows were framed with lavish swags of pine, holly, and
cedar, decorated with large gold bows, gold-glazed nuts,
pinecones, pomegranates, and white gardenias. Beribboned
mistletoe hung in several places over the dance floor and from
every doorway. On a table to one side, sugary gardenias and
swirling white-chocolate ribbons cascaded down the tiers of the
elegant wedding cake. Doc stood next to it, fidgeting like a boy
in line for Santa.

"Relax, Doc!" George told him. "It'll be over in no time. And
remember, you're not losing a daughter—you're gaining a son."

"It ain't the weddin' got me in a dither, George, it's this dag-
nabbed monkey suit Toni talked me into." Doc reached a finger
beneath the collar of his tuxedo shirt and pulled at it.

Perfect candid! George lifted her camera and squinted
through the viewfinder. "You're beautiful, Doc."

Click.

Doc waved his hand in a dismissive gesture. "Off with you,
girl!" he said. But he was smiling.

Georgine rotated around, the camera still to her eye. Two men and a heavily bejeweled woman probably about Ruth's age stood in a corner of the salon engaged in conversation: Clark's father—a tall, slightly balding man with a commanding presence—and his mother, showing off her new husband, who wasn't much older than Clark. Royce seemed unperturbed by his ex-wife's obvious posturing.

Click. Click.

Will and Peggy joined the group a moment later. They were starting to date again, Toni had told George, now that Will was working at his recovery. It was taking some doing on Will's part to regain Peggy's trust, but things looked promising.

Click. Click. Click.

George rotated again. Toni was lining up the wedding party along the stair railing. The photographer grinned. *Toni in charge, as usual,* she thought. She caught Clark's eye and waved as she lifted the camera. "Clark, you're looking as elegant as a penguin."

Click.

"Thank you *so* much, George," Clark answered dryly.

"And Ruth and Jack—" She shook her head as she walked toward them. "Pretty stiff competition for the bride and groom tonight."

"Right," Ruth and Jack said in unison, with equal dryness. Jack was dressed in a white captain's uniform for his best-man duties, and Ruth, the matron or honor, wore a slim-fitting gown with a black velvet bodice and a lustrous taffeta skirt that shimmered between black and royal purple. They truly did look stylish and debonair.

But no one could compete with Toni.

The bride had removed her cloak for the indoor shots with the wedding party. Her floor-length gown, of unadorned winter white panne velvet, was simple but spectacular, with a dropped waist, long, narrow sleeves, and a fitted, off-the-shoulder bodice that showed off her graceful neck and slender figure. A single strand of pearls and pearl-drop earrings added to the effect of elegant simplicity. The fluid motion of the softly gathered skirt made her seem almost to float as she moved into position for the group portraits.

Click. Click. Click. Click.

More shots, just Clark and Toni together. Then the four of them on the sundeck again, the bride with her brocade cloak pulled around her and the matron of honor with a black velvet cocoon cape to keep her warm against the evening air. Another half a roll of the bride and groom alone. A slight breeze ruffled the hair around Toni's face and added color to her cheeks.

Click. Click. Click.

It wasn't just that she was beautiful, George reflected, in the way every model she'd ever photographed was beautiful. Toni possessed an inner beauty that was expressing itself now in ways George hadn't seen when they'd first met. Lovely as she'd been then, there was a different kind of energy to her beauty now: a sense of self-assurance in the way she held herself, a glow of happiness that seemed to radiate from her skin and play at the corners of her mouth and glow in her dusk-colored eyes.

"Hi, Auntie George!" Danny stuck his head out the salon door. "Mom? Is it okay if I have some hot cider now?" Another nice touch for a December wedding—hot chocolate, spiced cider, and warm eggnog for arriving guests.

There wasn't any question that Toni's wedding business was going to be a huge success. After Suzanne DeJong's wedding last June, word of mouth alone had gotten her half a dozen inquiries. The work she'd done for her own dream wedding confirmed in Georgine's mind Toni's creativity and capability. She was downright inspiring.

Toni held out an arm to her son. "Five minutes for some pictures with me and Clark first, okay? And Pop." She gestured through the window, and Doc joined them.

Georgine framed the picture in her viewfinder: the handsome, clean-cut groom; the beautiful, radiant bride; the small boy, his grin cheerful and mischievous. A happier little boy than George had ever seen him. Doc, looking pleased in spite of his "monkey suit."

Click. Click.

She zoomed in on their faces and refocused the lens. A mom, a dad, a child, a grandfather.

Click. Click. Click.

A family, Georgine thought as she finished the roll of film. Living proof that God's grace was at work in the world.

Dear Reader,

I wondered, as I did my research for *Snow Swan,* how I could write the story of a character so different from me as Toni Ferrier is. Yet once again, as I have often found, the writing itself became an exercise in self-discovery. What I realized as I finished the manuscript was that Toni and I aren't so different after all.

As Clark McConaughey comes to understand on these pages, there is something at the core of our humanity that unites every human being, something that levels the playing field for all of us in the sight of God. The choice for each of us, no matter what our circumstances, is the same every day—to open ourselves to God's free-flowing love and power, or to close ourselves off.

Toni discovers on her journey of faith, as I have discovered on my own, that resentment, fear, and shame are the enemies of spiritual health and well-being. She also learns, again as I have, that forgiveness is the key to healing—forgiving not only those who've hurt us, but forgiving ourselves, the two so closely intertwined it's impossible to know, afterward, which came first.

My prayer for you as you walk these miles in Toni's shoes is that you will begin to see yourself as Toni begins to see herself on these pages, through the eyes of a loving God: no longer an ugly duckling, but a beautiful, pure, snow-white swan.

Barbara Jean Hicks

Write to Barbara Jean Hicks c/o Questar Publishers, Inc.
P.O. Box 1720, Sisters, Oregon 97759

PALISADES...PURE ROMANCE

～ PALISADES ～

Reunion, Karen Ball

Refuge, Lisa Tawn Bergren

Torchlight, Lisa Tawn Bergren

Treasure, Lisa Tawn Bergren

Chosen, Lisa Tawn Bergren

Firestorm, Lisa Tawn Bergren

Wise Man's House, Melody Carlson

Arabian Winds, Linda Chaikin (Premier)

Cherish, Constance Colson

Chase the Dream, Constance Colson (Premier)

Angel Valley, Peggy Darty

Sundance, Peggy Darty

Love Song, Sharon Gillenwater

Antiques, Sharon Gillenwater

Song of the Highlands, Sharon Gillenwater (Premier)

Secrets, Robin Jones Gunn

Whispers, Robin Jones Gunn

Echoes, Robin Jones Gunn

Sunsets, Robin Jones Gunn

Coming Home, Barbara Jean Hicks

Snow Swan, Barbara Jean Hicks

Irish Eyes, Annie Jones

Glory, Marilyn Kok

Sierra, Shari MacDonald

Forget-Me-Not, Shari MacDonald

Diamonds, Shari MacDonald

Westward, Amanda MacLean

Stonehaven, Amanda MacLean

Everlasting, Amanda MacLean

THE PALISADES LINE

*Ask for them at your local bookstore. If the title you seek is not in stock,
the store may order you a copy using the ISBN listed.*

Wise Man's House, Melody Carlson
ISBN 1-57673-070-0
Kestra McKenzie, a young widow trying to make a new life for herself, thinks she
has found the solidity she longs for when she purchases her childhood dream
house—a stone mansion on the Oregon Coast. Just as renovations begin, a mysterious stranger moves into her caretaker's cottage—and into her heart.

Sunsets, Robin Jones Gunn
ISBN 1-57673-103-0
Alissa Benson loves her job as a travel agent. But when the agency has computer
problems, they call in expert Brad Phillips. Alissa can't wait for Brad to fix the
computers and leave—he's too blunt for her comfort. So she's more than a little
upset when she moves into a duplex and finds out he's her neighbor!

Snow Swan, Barbara Jean Hicks
ISBN 1-57673-107-3
Life hasn't been easy for Toni Ferrier. As an unwed mother and a recovering alco-
holic, she doesn't feel worthy of anyone's love. Then she meets Clark
McConaughey, who helps her launch her business aboard the sternwheeler *Snow
Swan.* Sparks fly between them, but if Clark finds out the truth about Toni's past,
will he still love her?

Irish Eyes, Annie Jones
ISBN 1-57673-108-1
When Julia Reed finds a young boy, who claims to be a leprechaun, camped out
under a billboard, she gets drawn into a century-old crime involving a real pot of
gold. Interpol agent Cameron O'Dea is trying to solve the crime. In the process,
he takes over the homeless shelter that Julia runs, camps out in her neighbor's RV,
and generally turns her life upside down!

Kingdom Come, Amanda MacLean
ISBN 1-57673-120-0
In 1902, feisty Ivy Rose Clayborne, M.D., returns to her hometown of Kingdom
Come to fight the coal mining company that is ravaging the land. She meets an
unexpected ally, a man who claims to be a drifter but in reality is Harrison
MacKenzie, grandson of the coal mining baron. Together they face the aftermath
of betrayal, the fight for justice…and the price of love.

A Mother's Love, Bergren, Colson, MacLean
ISBN 1-57673-106-5
Three popular Palisades authors bring you heartwarming stories about the joys and challenges of romance in the midst of motherhood.
By Lisa Bergren: A widower and his young daughter go to Southern California for vacation, and return with much more than they expected.
By Constance Colson: Cassie Jenson wants her old sweetheart to stay in her memories. But when he moves back to town, they find out that they could never forget each other.
By Amanda MacLean: A couple is expecting their first baby, and they hardly have enough time for each other. With the help of an old journal and a last-minute getaway, they work to rekindle their love.

Also look for our new line:

PALISADES PREMIER
More Story. More Romance.

Arabian Winds, Linda Chaikin
ISBN 1-57673-105-7
In the first book of the Lions of the Desert trilogy, World War I is breaking upon the deserts of Arabia in 1914. Young nurse Allison Wescott is on holiday with an archaeological club, but a murder interrupts her plans, and a mysterious officer keeps turning up wherever she goes!
Watch for more books in Linda Chaikin's Egypt series!

Song of the Highlands, Sharon Gillenwater
ISBN 0-88070-946-4
During the Napoleonic Wars, Kiernan is a piper, but he comes back to find out he's inherited a title. At his run-down estate, he meets the beautiful Mariah. During a trip to London, they face a kidnapping…and discover their love for each other.
Watch for more books in Sharon Gillenwater's Scottish series!